THE THEATRE OF CHRISTOPHER DURANG

Miriam M. Chirico is Professor of English at Eastern Connecticut State University. She has authored numerous articles on twentieth-century playwrights and comedy. She is a board member of the Comparative Drama Conference. Along with Kelly Younger, she is editor of *How to Teach a Play: Essential Exercises for Popular Plays* (2020), also by Methuen Drama. This is her first book.

Also available in the Critical Companions series from Methuen Drama:

BRITISH MUSICAL THEATRE SINCE 1950
Robert Gordon, Olaf Jubin and Millie Taylor

BRITISH THEATRE AND PERFORMANCE 1900–1950
Rebecca D'Monté

A CRITICAL COMPANION TO THE AMERICAN STAGE MUSICAL
Elizabeth L. Wollman

DISABILITY THEATRE AND MODERN DRAMA: RECASTING MODERNISM
Kirsty Johnston

MODERN ASIAN THEATRE AND PERFORMANCE 1900–2000
Kevin J. Wetmore, Siyuan Liu and Erin B. Mee

THE PLAYS OF SAMUEL BECKETT
Katherine Weiss

THE THEATRE OF ANTHONY NEILSON
Trish Reid

THE THEATRE OF EUGENE O'NEILL: AMERICAN MODERNISM ON THE WORLD STAGE
Kurt Eisen

THE THEATRE OF TOM MURPHY: PLAYWRIGHT ADVENTURER
Nicholas Grene

THE THEATRE OF TENNESSEE WILLIAMS
Brenda Murphy

VERSE DRAMA IN ENGLAND, 1900–2015: ART, MODERNITY AND THE NATIONAL STAGE
Irene Morra

For a full listing, please visit www.bloomsbury.com/series/critical-companions/

THE THEATRE OF CHRISTOPHER DURANG

Miriam M. Chirico

LONDON • NEW YORK • OXFORD • NEW DELHI • SYDNEY

METHUEN DRAMA
Bloomsbury Publishing Plc
50 Bedford Square, London, WC1B 3DP, UK
1385 Broadway, New York, NY 10018, USA
29 Earlsfort Terrace, Dublin 2, Ireland

BLOOMSBURY, METHUEN DRAMA and the Methuen Drama logo are trademarks of Bloomsbury Publishing Plc

First published in Great Britain 2020
This paperback edition published in 2021

Copyright © Miriam M. Chirico and contributors, 2020

Miriam M. Chirico has asserted her right under the Copyright, Designs and Patents Act, 1988, to be identified as the author of this work.

For legal purposes the Acknowledgments on p. ix constitute an extension of this copyright page.

Cover design: Louise Dugdale
Cover image: *Vanya and Sonia and Masha and Spike*, Lincoln Center Theater, New York, starring Kristine Nielsen, David Hyde Pierce and Sigourney Weaver.
© T. Charles Erikson.

All rights reserved. No part of this publication may be reproduced or transmitted in any form or by any means, electronic or mechanical, including photocopying, recording, or any information storage or retrieval system, without prior permission in writing from the publishers.

Bloomsbury Publishing Plc does not have any control over, or responsibility for, any third-party websites referred to or in this book. All internet addresses given in this book were correct at the time of going to press. The author and publisher regret any inconvenience caused if addresses have changed or sites have ceased to exist, but can accept no responsibility for any such changes.

A catalogue record for this book is available from the British Library.

A catalog record for this book is available from the Library of Congress.

ISBN: HB: 978-1-4742-8892-7
PB: 978-1-3502-4664-5
ePDF: 978-1-4742-8891-0
eBook: 978-1-4742-8893-4

Series: Critical Companions

Typeset by Deanta Global Publishing Services, Chennai, India

To find out more about our authors and books visit www.bloomsbury.com and sign up for our newsletters.

Dedicated to three funny men in my life:
Frank, Nicolas, and Arthur

CONTENTS

Acknowledgments	ix
Foreword: Christopher Durang Explains It All for Me	
David Lindsay-Abaire	x

Introduction: Christopher Durang's Dark Comedy   1

1   Perverting the Classics   21
    The Idiots Karamazov   23
    Vietnamization of New Jersey: A American Tragedy   32
    A History of the American Film   38
    Mrs. Bob Cratchit's Wild Christmas Binge   49
    Adrift in Macao   56

2   Seeking Is Believing   59
    The Nature and Purpose of the Universe   61
    Sister Mary Ignatius Explains It All for You   68
    Laughing Wild   74
    Sex and Longing   79
    Miss Witherspoon   86

3   One-Act Plays   93

4   Family Dysfunction   115
    Titanic   117
    Death Comes to Us All, Mary Agnes   121
    'dentity Crisis   125
    Baby with the Bathwater   131
    The Marriage of Bette and Boo   138

Contents

5	**American Anomie**	**149**
	Beyond Therapy	150
	Media Amok	155
	Betty's Summer Vacation	162
	Why Torture Is Wrong, and the People Who Love Them	168
	Vanya and Sonia and Masha and Spike	177
6	**Critical Perspectives**	**189**
	We Laugh Track People: Christopher Durang's Drama of Audience Participation *Robert Combs*	189
	The Marriage of Parody and Satire: The All-American Comedy of Christopher Durang *Jay Malarcher*	202

Conclusion   **213**

Notes   217
Works Cited   221
List of Contributors   230
Index   231

ACKNOWLEDGMENTS

I am grateful to Dr. Kevin Wetmore, Loyola Marymount University, for giving me the opportunity to write this book, as well as Eastern Connecticut State University, for providing the sabbatical leave that made this book possible. Among my colleagues at Eastern Connecticut, I would like to thank Dean Carmen Cid for providing financial support for research travel; Miranda Lau, Administrative Assistant, for professional support; Mia D'Amico, in the Writing Center, for high-caliber editing; David Vrooman and Kellie O'Donnell-Bobadilla, Research Librarians, for assistance locating material; and Anik Vasington and Michael Palumbo in the Center for Instructional Technology for technical expertise. Additional thanks go to The New York Public Library, Billy Rose Theatre Collection, for access to its collected videos and material on Durang, as well as to the Yale University Arts Library and the Harvard Theatre Collection, at Houghton Library, for access to manuscripts and prompt books related to Durang's work.

FOREWORD
CHRISTOPHER DURANG EXPLAINS IT ALL FOR ME

When I was fourteen, my experience of theatre was mostly limited to whatever we had been assigned in English class—some Shakespeare, a little Ibsen, and (oof!) *The Oresteia*. Plus, my mother had dragged me to a local production of *A View from the Bridge* in which my middle-aged portly uncle was inexplicably cast as Rodolpho the young Italian love interest. I remember he wore a blonde toupee for the role. I don't think anyone was fooled.

It's no wonder that I was under the impression that most plays were like vegetables—good for you but sometimes hard to swallow. It was admittedly a very narrow and inaccurate assessment of an art form that I would grow to love and eventually make a life in, but I was young and I still had a lot to learn. Luckily Christopher Durang came along just in time to teach me what I needed to know.

I first encountered Christopher Durang's work when I was cast in my ninth grade production of his *A History of the American Film*, a wild musical comedy that barrels through several decades and at least a dozen Hollywood genres—from gangster epic to screwball comedy and from a Busby Berkeley backstage musical to a natural disaster epic. There's a lot of parody in the show, and social satire, a love story, some mayhem, and, of course, songs! It was unlike anything I had ever encountered, and I loved every second of it.

Soon after closing night of that show, a classmate said to me, "That was amazing! We should all do a TENTH grade play next year! Only this time YOU should write it, because you're the funny one!" I had never written a play. Never even considered it. But we had all just had the time of our lives, and my eyes had been opened to a theatrical landscape that I hadn't known existed before, so I was all in. "Sure, I'll write a tenth grade play," and that's how I became a playwright. It was Christopher Durang's fault.

I spent the rest of high school writing plays and reading whatever scripts I could get my hands—John Guare, Marsha Norman, August Wilson, Edward Albee, Tina Howe—but mostly Durang—*Beyond Therapy*, *Baby with the Bathwater*, "The Actor's Nightmare." I went on to Sarah Lawrence College, continued to study theatre and write plays, and the more Durang I read the deeper my appreciation for his work grew. Sure, I knew that plays were important and worthy of study, but Chris showed me that they could also be ridiculous, violent, sweet, political, heart-breakingly sad, and hilariously inappropriate—often at the same time.

Needless to say, the plays that I was writing were heavily influenced by the plays that I was reading and seeing. I can't look at any of my earliest scripts without noticing the fingerprints of my theatrical idols on them. The most obvious and indelible fingerprints on my plays belonged to Chris Durang. I see those same fingerprints on the work of my peers, especially the ones writing comedies, all of whom admit to the influence that Chris's plays had on their writing.

After graduating Sarah Lawrence, I considered grad school, but knew there was no possible way I could afford it. But then I heard about the Juilliard playwriting program, which was free and flexible enough that I could attend and still hold down a full-time job (which I had to do). Also, the program was run by two of my heroes—Marsha Norman and . . . yup, Chris Durang. I had to apply.

When I got into Juilliard it was of course the thrill of my life, but also totally surreal to be sitting in the room with Christopher Durang. The man who I had always thought of as my spiritual playwriting teacher was now my *actual* playwriting teacher. This guy (unbeknownst to him) had changed my life when I was fourteen, and I still only knew him through his work. I remember thinking, "Will he be like his plays? As loopy as that crackpot woman in *Laughing Wild*? As mean as Sister Mary Ignatius? As unhinged as pretty much everyone in *Beyond Therapy*?"

As it turned out, Chris was (and is) wonderfully warm, funny, mild-mannered, sly, and one of the kindest, most thoughtful people you could ever meet. And so, in that way, he *is* very much like his plays. Because no matter how over the top or disturbing Chris's writing might be, there is always a huge and generous heart underneath it all. Yes, the plays can be outlandish and sometimes angry and hyperbolic, but they're also emotional, personal, and above all else, deeply human. That's why his plays stick with me and resonate the way they do.

My time at Juilliard proved invaluable. Not just because we were learning how to craft plays, but because we were also learning how to live the life of a playwright. Chris and Marsha were always sharing their theatrical war stories and advising us in ways to maneuver situations that might come

Foreword

up with collaborators, agents, producers, or critics. When I first started at Juilliard, Chris was just opening *Sex and Longing* on Broadway, which proved to be a difficult experience for him. He was so open with us about rehearsals and the audiences, and the not-so-great critical reception the show was getting, and how hard all of that was. I remember thinking, "Oh, right, this is also what happens if you're lucky enough to have a career in the theater—sometimes things don't go your way," which was so important for us to understand as young writers. And just as important was seeing Chris dust himself off afterward and charge ahead again with the brilliantly funny *Betty's Summer Vacation* just a couple years later.

In the years since graduating Juilliard, I've also grown to recognize more fully the range of Chris's work and how he's refused to be boxed in. When considering whether I should venture away from my earlier absurdist plays to write something more naturalistic, I only had to, once again, look to Chris Durang for the guidance and courage I needed. He is, after all, someone who's as adept at writing a straight-up parody like *For Whom the Southern Belle Tolls* as he is at writing a moving, deeply personal (and scathingly funny) family remembrance like *The Marriage of Bette and Boo*. He can write a political satire like *Why Torture Is Wrong, and the People Who Love Them* or a fun beach house farce like *Betty's Summer Vacation*. He can write a furious takedown of Catholic doctrine in *Sister Mary Ignatius Explains It All for You* that has people picketing the theatre, but he can also write a sad, bighearted comedy like *Vanya and Sonia and Masha and Spike* that has audiences lining up on Broadway and earns him a Tony. If Chris can do all of that, I thought, then I can try something different too, and so I started writing what would eventually become my play *Rabbit Hole*. I was, yet again, indebted to Chris Durang.

It's hard to overstate the importance of Christopher Durang and his work. Not just to me but to several generations of theatre-makers. He was and will always be our teacher.

David Lindsay-Abaire
July 2019

INTRODUCTION
CHRISTOPHER DURANG'S DARK COMEDY

During the summer of 2012, after having successfully written for the theatre world for forty years, Christopher Durang finished writing his first well-made play. He submitted *Vanya and Sonia and Masha and Spike* to the McCarter Theatre Center, a play that would later earn him his first Tony Award when it transferred to Broadway. With this work, Durang had given audiences what they wanted to see: the requisite first-act exposition, rising conflict between siblings, a climatic expurgation of long-held animosities, and a denouement that provided hope—a rare note in a Durangian drama. Gone from this play are the preposterous scenarios, the anarchic spirit, and the violent underpinnings. After years of writing scenarios in which quirky characters are stymied in bizarre predicaments, Durang turned to another master of tragicomedy and challenged the premise behind this playwright's work. Anton Chekhov, whose characters originated out of his belief that people were incapable of transformation, frequently posed the question: "What really can you change?" With this new play, Durang seems to have found a sanguine response: "Actually, you can change—a bit."

Edith Oliver, theatre critic for the *New Yorker*, once praised Durang as being "one of the funniest men in the world" (1987, 135). Durang has had one of the longest and most sustained playwriting careers of the American stage, and he has consistently experimented with varied writing styles. Comedic playwrights rarely develop a reputation; in the American repertory, only Neil Simon and Wendy Wasserstein have made names for themselves, producing witty and realistic character-driven comedies, where characters use humor to surmount pain or bond with others through challenging trials. In contrast to their comedic style, Durang's plays are mordant and provocative. His predominant style is black or dark comedy, a form of comedy that approaches painful or morbid topics from a humorous perspective and results in discomfiting laughter. Whereas Durang's grotesque, absurd, and zany comedic style is unique within the American theatre, he has shaped much of the comedic potential for the stage. The erudite whimsy of David Ives or the dark farce of Nicky Silver, the surreal visions of Sarah Ruhl, or the grotesque violence of Tracy Letts are due, in part, to Durang paving the way in the early 1970s. Furthermore, his work as codirector along with Marsha Norman of The Lila Acheson Wallace American Playwrights Program at the Julliard School, starting in 1994, has had a significant impact; the program produced notable playwrights such as Pulitzer-Prize winning playwright David Lindsay-Abaire, as well as Noah Haidle and Joshua Harmon. When he stepped down from the position in 2016, he handed over the reins to his protégé, Lindsay-Abaire. As Ben Brantley, a lifelong reviewer of Durang's works, noted, Durang is "an essential and affecting presence in the American theater" (2005).

Christopher Durang's unconventional comedic style was forged in the crucible of his youth and adolescence; one could say that his humor never grew up. Born in 1949, Durang had a childhood that paralleled the commodification of television in American households. Television was first introduced on a wide-scale basis in 1947, with a scant 185,000 homes owning a receiver. Four years later, the number of TV sets had risen to 15 million, and the percentage of homes with televisions increased from 0.4 percent to 34 percent (Boddy 1990, 47, 51). Television was as important an influence on the American population as the automobile forty years earlier; while the automobile gave people greater geographical access, TV programs shaped the national psyche. Durang loved comedic actors. He and his mother would watch Mike Nichols and Elaine May on *Tonight Starring Jack Paar*, and his favorite show was *I Love Lucy*. It is fair to say Lucille Ball influenced many of his ideas about comedic writing (Hodgins 1996). He wrote his first play when he was eight years old, a two-page spoof based on an episode of *I Love Lucy* where Lucy and Dezi have a baby and their well-rehearsed plans fall apart when she goes into labor. To the young Durang, the slapdash frenzy that occurred when the carefully scripted plan of adults went awry appeared amusing and subversive, and it planted the seeds for Durang's later predilection for chaotic scenarios of adult waywardness and inefficacy. Many of Durang's pieces resemble situation comedies of the 1950s, an aspect that Robert Combs will address in his chapter "The Laugh Track People." These TV shows reveal a fabricated image of middle-class America as wholesome and secure with cozy breakfast nooks and welcoming firesides—and a conservative ideology that is embedded in this picture of materialism. Durang manipulates this wholesome depiction of familial domesticity in many of his set designs, poking at the acrimony that lies just beneath the surface, such as the contrast between the homey kitchen interior and the hidden armament room in *Why Torture Is Wrong, and the People Who Love Them*.

Introduction

The tense familial relationships Durang experienced growing up create the family background for many of his plays as well as the origins for this dark sense of humor. He states, "The reason I got into dark comedy seems psychological. There was a lot of unhappiness in my family background . . . so in an odd way, humor was my reaction to it. It was probably a distancing thing" (Lawson 1981). Durang was born in Montclair, New Jersey, and was raised in an affluent family in Berkeley Heights. His family lore actively encouraged a life in the theatre. Although his father, Francis Ferdinand (Ferd) Durang, Jr., was the fourth generation in his family to work as an architect, further back in the family's lineage was an early American stage actor, John Durang, who had also raised his children for life on the boards. Ferdinand Durang went into business for himself when Durang was twelve, creating some of the financial worries in the family due to his inconsistent salary; moreover, he became an alcoholic which created most of the family turmoil, as he and his wife fought about his alcoholism. Additionally, Durang felt a large emotional void as a child due to his mother's own depression over her inability to have a large family as she had dreamed. After Christopher's birth, his mother had three stillborn babies, due to an Rh blood factor incompatibility with her husband; the first stillbirth occurred when Christopher was three. Her frustration and sadness made her withdraw emotionally from Durang, to the point that for about a year, as she admitted years later, she did not even remember he was alive (Smith 2005). Durang sensed that his father did not want more children, but his mother insisted, as she possessed a strong faith in God and in miracles, and her willfulness contributed to the couple's demise. When he was thirteen, in the eighth grade, his parents finally separated; freed from the disputes with her husband, his mother turned all of her attention toward him, at times being overbearing with her drive and ambitions for his future, at times being caring, sweet, and funny. When he was nineteen, his parents' divorce was finalized, but not before he came to court to testify against his father regarding how his drinking problems affected the marriage, a heavy burden for the young Durang while he was away from home in college. This scene of a son testifying against his father figures predominantly in the play Durang wrote about his family, *The Marriage of Bette and Boo*.

Durang's parents and extended family were Catholic and he was raised in the Catholic faith. His parents sent him to Catholic schools from kindergarten through high school. He attended Our Lady of Peace School in New Providence, he went to mass with his parents every Sunday, and, by the time he went to Delbarton School for his junior high and high school years, he sang in the choir and would even, on occasion, lead the congregation in singing during church services. Among Christian religions, Catholicism is one of the more hierarchical, creating a chain of command with respect to power, authority, and values, and subordinating certain positions on the chain to others. The nature of this firmly entrenched institution may have had something to do in encouraging the young Durang's anarchic spirit when it came time for him to rebel. He recalls internalizing this hierarchical awareness from relatives in his family: "In my grandmother's generation, obedience was of very high value. And in the Catholic Church, if you were a priest or a nun, you took a vow of obedience and you were supposed to obey the Pope and obey your superior, no matter what, even if you were in disagreement," he remarks, referring to the doctrine of papal infallibility (Durang and Wasserstein 1996). Catholicism, and its theological teachings, created within him an unquestioning faith in authority and from an early age, Durang witnessed others practicing this absolute obedience, even when the theology or doctrine seemed illogical, such as going to hell for eating meat on Fridays; as he points out, "That way, Hitler would be in hell alongside someone who ate meat on Friday. I thought there was no justice there" (Smith 2005). In Durang's comedies, arrogant, authoritarian figures prevail frequently over others' lives, often wreaking havoc and causing irreparable harm.

From a young age Durang understood theatre's potential. His parents often took him to see shows in New York City; his mother in particular loved theatre and musicals, and Durang remembers her inviting friends over to the house to read Noël Coward's play *Hay Fever* aloud. His family and teachers encouraged his early interest in writing; his second-grade class at Our Lady of Peace performed the two-page spoof he wrote. His mother's two sisters were both music teachers and introduced the young Chris to their favorite pupil, Kevin Farrell. When the two of them were only thirteen years old, they wrote the musical *Banned in Boston*, with Durang writing the book and Kevin Farrell composing the music. In *Banned in Boston* siblings Clara and Edmund live with two conservative maiden aunts who work to shut down a local play they found offensive, a scenario that seemed to prophesize Durang's future predicaments with censorship. By staging the local show within the larger piece, the young Durang allowed the actors to depict the scene that offended the aunts, thereby illustrating the thin line between prurient imagination and the reality. With a maneuver borrowed from the Sondheim-Styne musical *Gypsy*, a young woman sings the song

"I Love Money" and allows her shoulder strap to drop. The subversive comedy rights itself at the end when the musical ends with four marriages. This musical was performed at their all-boys Roman Catholic high school, Delbarton School, in Morristown, with girls from a Catholic school invited to assist in the production. For the young Durang, who was only in eighth grade, to watch junior and senior high school students perform his piece was encouraging and planted the seed of playwriting in his soul. It was also his first experience with audience criticism: the nuns from the nearby school expressed concern over the allusion to strip tease and prevented any further co-curricular theatrical participation. *Businessman's Holiday* was the second musical, written when the two boys were fifteen and Durang was in the tenth grade. With its setting in the world of business, this second piece was reminiscent of the musical *How to Succeed in Business without Really Trying*, which Durang had seen on Broadway starring Robert Morse in the original 1961 production. But Durang's version had a twist: the heroine sees the leading man for the pretentious upstart he is and turns down his marriage proposal. The musical *How to Succeed in Business*, along with *Carnival!*, intrigued the thirteen-year-old Durang: *How to Succeed* because of its arch, amusingly exaggerated vision of the business world, and *Carnival!* because of the bitterness of the characters and the existential dilemmas they encounter. Durang attributes his comedic style to 1950s musical comedies, with their extravagant stereotypes and animated positivity, but he also recognized in some of the darker ones their potential to pop the bubble of jejune hopes and dreams with their introspective lyrics (Durang 2009b).

Due to a strange turn of fate, his parents' divorce led to his going to Harvard in 1967. First, he had to transfer to a less-expensive Catholic school when his parents separated. This new school was inferior in educational quality, which frustrated Durang. Delbarton, recognizing the young man's aptitude, offered him a scholarship to return to their school, provided he maintained good grades. The challenge to excel prompted Durang to work diligently and drew the attention of his teacher and guidance counselor, who suggested he apply to a number of high-caliber schools, including Harvard University. Second, due to the urging of his mother's divorce attorney, an alum of Harvard, Durang sent in the application, and he was accepted. However, the academically challenging atmosphere at Harvard initiated a two-year period of depression for Durang, from the end of his freshman year to his junior year. He found that he lacked motivation to go to classes and could not write, and took no joy in the scholarship he had relished so much in high school. He withdrew from social activities and friendships; he stayed in his room, he stopped attending his morning classes, and he frequently went to the movies by himself at night. Professors were lenient enough to allow him to hand in papers late. While undoubtedly his campus work-study job of cleaning bathrooms inevitably lowered his spirits, more likely it was the competitive pressure he placed upon himself which prompted the social withdrawal, as is the case with many students who enter such a high-caliber collegiate environment such as Harvard (Lawson 1981). Underlying these reasons, more significantly, was a delayed reaction to the emotional conflicts of his home life. Away from home for the first time and released from his role as family peacemaker, Durang experienced a kind of post-traumatic paralysis—the psychic burden of having been unable to resolve his parents' situation for the better hit him full force. As he admitted, "As a peacemaker, I failed as a child, and it was depressing. Being the peacemaker when you're young, you become a little adult, and I think that the anarchic part of me and the angry part of me has filtered into my play more than my life" (Hayes 2000). Attending therapy sessions at Harvard's psychological counseling center helped him out of his depression by showing him how his family's behavior had created his pain. The psychologist pointed out to him that he laughed at inappropriate moments, a comment Durang found perspicacious (Durang 2012b, 52). His essay about a seventeenth-century devotional poem by George Herbert, written from the confused perspective of a nun, is certainly evidence of his "inappropriate laughter," but it also cheered him up (Rawson 2002). Finally, the therapy helped to contextualize his depression as the type of plight many smart, motivated students underwent and reassured him that his need for assistance was normal.

Durang had many formative experiences at Harvard that focused his interest in writing for the stage. He studied Contemporary American and British Theatre with Professor William Alfred, a professor, scholar, and playwright who had the remarkable gift of providing oral interpretations of the characters during his lectures (Durang 2012a). Alfred accepted Durang into his selective playwriting seminar during Durang's senior year and gave him valuable advice when he pointed out that his comedic pieces were more interesting than his dramatic ones. Durang also wrote a musical comedy, *The Greatest Musical Ever Sung*, that depicted stories from the Gospels in entertaining fashion, and the students at Dunster House decided to perform it, after hearing Durang share a few of the songs at dinner with them. A student designed a poster for the show with an image of a pregnant Virgin Mary and a dove winking in the foreground. Also, Al Franken, a classmate at the time who would go on to be a comedian as well as a US senator, played a part. Although the musical received a positive review in the Harvard student newspaper, the *Harvard Crimson*, with songs like "Everything's Coming Up Moses," "You Can't Get a Man with a Prayer" sung by Mary Magdalene, and "The Dove that Done Me Wrong," this musical led to Durang's first taste in controversy. Letters to the Editor appeared in the *Harvard Crimson* complaining that the play was offensive to Catholics. An English professor wrote a rebuttal, reminding the students of the tradition of satire, while, in turn, a Jesuit priest serving as a teaching fellow wrote a scathing letter, arguing that Harvard should not permit students to poke fun of religion and calling Durang and the *Crimson* theatre reviewer "pigs trampling in the sanctuary." Not to be undone by this criticism, Durang turned lemons into lemonade; in his application to the Yale School of Drama, he used the vivid phrase "pigs trampling in the sanctuary" to promote the value of his work and it worked—he was invited to study at Yale.

It was at the Yale School of Drama where his dramatic career was truly launched. While a student, Durang found excellent guidance under Howard Stein, Richard Gilman, and Jules Feiffer, who would give young playwrights very specific feedback about their writing. Although he studied for a year under the Polish novelist Jerzy Kosiński, who was hired to teach playwriting and dramaturgy, he found his classes frustrating (Durang 2017b, 73). Fortunately, he received attention and encouragement from two figures in particular, Stein and Robert Brustein, who were at the time the associate dean and the dean of the drama school. Upon accepting Durang into the prestigious playwriting program, Stein cannily announced to Brustein: "We took in a kid from Harvard who is about twenty-one or twenty-two and who already has a subject: A scream for help in a world he knows provides none, so he keeps on screaming and laughs at it" (Stein 1995). In addition to being in a nurturing environment, the drama school was the ideal place for the young playwright because first-year actors and first-year directing students would be assigned to the playwrights' workshops; Durang found that, more than the comments of his fellow writers, he benefited from hearing the actors read his plays aloud or ask him clarifying questions about his scripts. Robert Brustein, while directing the drama school, saw a need for the young actors, playwrights, and artists to free themselves from the serious, professional environment of the Yale School of Drama and consequently created the Yale Cabaret in order to provide such an outlet. Durang participated actively in all aspects of the cabaret and enjoyed both writing skits and performing. The Yale Cabaret was a smorgasbord of eclectic fare, from tragedy to farce, from one-person stand-up comedy to a full-ensemble musical revue; and as Brustein intended, the Cabaret deliberately encouraged playful experimentation as a way to prevent a new group of practitioners from mindlessly repeating the techniques of a previous generation. The spirit of the Cabaret, satiric and rebellious, permeated the drama school as well as Durang's creative sensibility. Moreover, because of the Cabaret, he was able to develop his playwriting craft from the inside out, to understand from a pragmatic and technical perspective how a scene could play out or a character be acted. He also had close interactions with actors, befriending several up-and-coming acting classmates, such as Meryl Streep and Sigourney Weaver, an actress with whom he is still friends today; Weaver would star in several of his plays, including *Vanya and Sonia a Masha and Spike*. He drew support from other gifted writers and actors, such as John Rothman, William Hauptman, Robert Auletta, Stephen Rowe, Lizbeth MacKay, Charles H. Levin, Kate McGregor-Stewart, Christine Estabrook, and Lewis Black (Brustein 2012, 21).

His collaborative work with fellow writers Wendy Wasserstein and Albert Innaurato grew out of friendships with the two; he befriended Wasserstein when he was a third-year student and she was beginning the program, while he and Innaurato affiliated with each other early on due to their Catholic backgrounds and wicked sense of humor. The two horrified the Ladies' Committee at the Yale Art Gallery with their performance of two priests, chanting a mock mass to the tune of "Cabaret," and almost got expelled. They coauthored pieces for the Yale Cabaret, including *I Don't Generally Like Poetry but Have You Read "Trees"* (1972) and *The Life Story of Mitzi Gaynor; or Gyp* (1973). His close friendship with Wasserstein lasted until her untimely death from lymphoma in 2006, and they collaborated frequently over the years, together writing *When Dinah Shore Ruled the Earth* (1975) for the Cabaret. It was she who convinced him to move from New Haven to New York City and helped him to get an apartment for himself—a daunting task for those unfamiliar with the city. Durang was at Yale for three years, with a fourth year in residence on a CBS grant. After graduating in the spring of 1974, he took three part-time jobs: a stint teaching acting at Southern Connecticut State College (now University); a position helping a doctor at the Yale Medical School index his book on

Introduction

schizophrenia; and a secretarial job at the Yale Medical School, typing letters to people whose bodies could no longer be used as donations to Yale and informing them of alternative plans for the disposal of their bodies upon their demise. The peculiarity of the last two jobs is remarkably in line with the bizarre attitude found in his plays toward death, psychiatric disorders, and inopportune communication.

Closer to home, Durang's sensitivity toward death was more likely colored by his mother's premature passing. His mother, Patricia Durang, died from cancer in March of 1979 at the age of fifty-six, having battled the disease off and on for eight years. She lived to see her son's work nominated for a Tony Award for Best Book of a Musical, although *A History of the American Film* did not receive the prize that year. Prior to her passing, Durang was very involved in her care, visiting her three to four times a week over a period of several years. She was in great pain and the fragility of her body was such that the mere act of turning over in bed caused a bone to break. The last year of watching her suffer was so horrific he found that he could not write; once while visiting her, his mother awoke briefly from a coma only to experience a panic attack, which deeply distressed him. He marveled at how one of Patricia's sisters found solace and strength in her Catholic faith during this time and how her ability to reconcile herself to her sister's suffering stood in sharp contrast to his own grief and anger. He simply could find no meaning in prayer in the face of witnessing his mother suffer from such a debilitating disease. After she died, he went through an intense period of contemplation from which emerged the play *Sister Mary Ignatius Explains It All for You*, a play that reflects the anger and disillusionment he felt from his Catholic faith (Keating 1988). He credits his agent at the time, Helen Merrill, with encouraging him to push through his writer's block and complete *Sister Mary*; despite it not being a full-length play, she was able to place it with the Ensemble Studio Theater (Durang 2017b, 81). The period following his mother's death also brought about a resurgence of emotions created by the dysfunctional familial dynamics; "I was indeed in a very dark mood during that whole period [following her death]," he expressed, but his despondency "wasn't just about her death. I was feeling very ensnared in a destructive family situation" (McGill 1982). His father also relied upon him more after his mother's death and would himself die ten years later in 1988 from stroke-related complications.

During this same time period, Durang became the off-kilter darling of the downtown New York theatre scene because of his outlandish scenarios and off-the-wall characters. He was a rising star during the late 1970s, bursting onto Broadway with the musical *A History of the American Film*, which later became a hit in the nation's capital. Merrill, who liked edgy, quirky plays and would often go to late-night productions of Durang's comedies at small Manhattan theatres, was instrumental at enlisting three regional productions to offer sequential productions of the musical, which helped to move it to Broadway (Gussow 1997). He received a lot of notoriety with the controversial play *Sister Mary Ignatius Explains It All for You*, leading to guest appearances on *Entertainment Tonight* and *The Phil Donahue Show*. The 1970s was a time of highly charged political fervor which the theatre reflected by attacking traditional dramaturgy, as illustrated most readily by such experimental artist collectives as The Living Theater or the Wooster Group. Durang emerged on the theatrical scene along with a group of iconoclastic playwrights and performance artists. In an essay written for the *New York Times* in 1977, Mel Gussow wrote a profile piece wherein he grouped together four contemporary writers as having "daring vision": Durang, twenty-eight at the time; David Mamet, who, at the age of twenty-nine, was Chicago's leading playwright with *Sexual Perversity in Chicago* and *The Duck Variations*; Albert Innaurato; and Michael Cristofer. "Each has an irrepressible comic impulse, a heightened social consciousness and a sense of moral dismay," Gussow wrote. "Even in their bleakest works—the plays by Mr. Innaurato—there is a plea for understanding and communication. These are not easy plays to watch. They challenge the mind and occasionally affront our sense of dignity. The playwrights are not afraid of offending, even alienating, an audience" (Gussow 1977a). While the cartoonish comic Durang and the neorealistic Mamet seem on opposite ends of the theatrical spectrum, they share similar origins of a theatrical moment in time when playwrights, critical of authority and society and desiring to shock audiences out of complacency, defied typical approaches to the theatre. Accordingly, Gussow also situates this group as part of a dramatic tradition initiated by Edward Albee and continued by Sam Shepard, whose theatrical legacy included a rupture from traditional theatre models through the use of rock 'n' roll music, modern folk myths, and the youth culture.

This period of time brought in other successes, too, with such plays as *Das Lusitania Songspiel*, *Titanic*, and *The Vietnamization of New Jersey*. But when Frank Rich, who had been a strong supporter of Durang earlier, panned *Beyond Therapy*, and Walter Kerr followed suit, the play flopped on Broadway despite the audience's obvious enjoyment. Durang's play *Baby with the Bathwater* premiered next, which Rich liked a lot, even though it troubled audiences, but with the arrival of *Bette and Boo*, Durang fully understood the "Butcher of Broadway's" power. Even though *Bette and Boo* garnered Obie Awards for the play and the cast and earned mostly good reviews, because Frank Rich panned it, the play did not move to Broadway. Years later, after Rich had retired from the *New York Times*, Durang ran into him at a public event. Durang revealed that he had wanted to contact Frank Rich and invite him to see the play a second time so that he might reconsider his opinion, and Rich replied that he wished Durang had done so (Durang 2016). However, the damage had been done to the playwright's creative spirit. In the face of such powerful critical opinion, where one or two theatre critics have the ability to affect whether a play transfers to Broadway or not, Durang felt a sense of powerlessness and stopped writing for the theatre. During this time, he wrote TV pilots and screenplays, some in collaboration with Wendy Wasserstein, although they were not ultimately produced. He maintained a theatrical presence with a satiric lounge act, *Christopher Durang and Dawne* (1989), as well as taking great pleasure performing with Julie Andrews and other magnificent performers in a Sondheim Revue, *Putting It Together* (1994). He acted in minor roles in movies such as *The Secret of My Success, Mr. North*, and *Penn & Teller Get Killed*; he met his long-term partner John Augustine while on the set of *The Secret of My Success*, drawn to his upbeat, optimistic nature. When a collection of his one-act plays *Durang Durang* was produced in 1994, Frank Rich had moved to the op-ed page of the *New York Times*; consequently, the new chief theatre critic, Vincent Canby, saw the collection and wrote a positive review. At last, the playwriting hiatus was over.

 The family dysfunction from which Durang emerged in early adulthood left a large imprint on his psyche and his plays. His father's alcoholism and his mother's grief ultimately led to their divorce, but not until Durang had witnessed the same fights, mistakes, and hurtful behavior occurring over and over at home. Nor was it only the argumentative dynamic between his parents that disturbed him; he found his mother's relationship with her mother and siblings to be equally toxic: "There was often no diplomacy," he explains, "it was 'You do what I want or you're one hundred times in the wrong'" (Durang 2017b, 71). Perceiving all of these harmful relationships at an early age, he developed a fatalistic belief system regarding human nature. He connects the dark, destructive spirit in his plays to his own feelings of entrapment in his family situation; the characters caught in a nihilistic loop reflected the learned helplessness he observed in the adults around him. He considers his own early plays, those written primarily in the 1970s, as "raw in their maniacal darkness," the dramatic outpouring of a young playwright both angry and wryly amused by his childhood pain, but a muted version of this acerbic attitude continued throughout his career. In a review written in 1994, Ben Brantley summarized key themes from Durang's plays written during the 1980s: (1) narcissism; (2) fear of engagement with a danger-filled world; (3) the strangulating nature of family ties; and (4) sexual disorientation and the tenuousness of individual identity (Brantley 1994), to which can be added (5) the abusive power of authority figures, more than likely originating from Durang's experience with the Catholic Church as well as the undue weight of Frank Rich's theatre reviews. The first play he wrote with a sunnier ending in 1982, *Beyond Therapy*, marked a change in perspective: "I used to believe that people couldn't change. I actually do believe now that people can change to some degree," he revealed during an interview regarding his play. He correlates his optimistic endings to his new view of positive behavioral change (McGill 1982). However, one man's optimism may be another man's grief, as no one would consider the next two plays Durang would write about family life as uplifting: *Baby with the Bathwater* (1983) and *The Marriage of Bette and Boo* (1985). Referred to by one critic as "the play about the dead babies," the play still showcased the satirically mordant side of Durang. Even his most positive play *Miss Witherspoon* (2005) has as its premise a woman who commits suicide multiple times. Over the years, as his plays grew lighter in mood, the anger at life and its needless suffering were still present, and resulted in the creation of his preposterous scenarios and inexplicable characters. While the origin of the anger in Durang's plays is clear, what still warrants explanation is his dark sense of humor.

Discussing the aesthetic behind black comedy is indispensable for understanding Durang's plays. When Durang discusses his own sense of humor, he speaks to a particular frame of mind that requires the viewer to distance himself from the horrific episode of human suffering and pain: "I exaggerate awful things further, and then I present it in a way that is funny," he explains, "and for those of us who find it funny, it has to do with a very clear suspension of disbelief. It is a play, after all, with acted characters; it allows us a distance we couldn't have in reality. To me this distance allows me to find some rather serious topics funny" (Durang 1999a). What Durang is suggesting here is that his form of humor requires a double consciousness, an ability to register scenes of cruelty or pain, and to simultaneously comprehend the artificiality of the events in order to find the humor. He credits Arthur Kopit's "tragicfarce" *Oh Dad, Poor Dad, Mom's Hung You in the Closet and I'm Feelin' So Sad* as an early influence on his creative vision, a black comedy in which a woman totes her dead husband's corpse on vacation with her (Durang 2012b, 51). While it might seem strange to offer human suffering for entertainment purposes, that is precisely what black comedy does. Humor is our way of resolving conflict and anxiety, and black comedy uses such dark laughter to relieve inner tension regarding subjects that are typically difficult to think about, such as death, family dysfunction, or torture.

While it might be easy to write off black comedy as a form of theatre for a peculiar sensibility, that would overlook the utility of the genre. One of the key functions that dark laughter serves is to acknowledge a fatalistic view of life, a perspective that sees human aspirations as futile. In the theatre, laughing at a cruel prank or at painful or humiliating circumstances underscores the cynical belief that people are the helpless victims of fate. For example, in *The Nature and Purpose of the Universe*, Durang encourages laughter at the character of Eleanor who, despite patiently waiting for God to save her from her misery, is abandoned at the end. The term is credited to André Breton who published an *Anthologie de l'humour noir* in 1940 which consisted of fictional pieces from several dozen writers who treated painful, morbid, or pornographic incidents in a comic way. Reviewing the many examples of "humor noir" in his anthology, Breton noted that this particular type of humor is preeminently "the mortal enemy of sentimentality" (Breton 1997, xix). In other words, black comedy as a technique warns us away from investing emotionally in the characters and their problems. In a more recent examination of black humor in film, Greg Tuck argues that the use of this technique allows for an examination of difficult or problematic subject matter without the investment of emotional empathy that would preclude thought. Much of the subject matter of today's movies or TV entertainment consists of the personal plights of other peoples' lives and encourages, as he calls it, a "sugar-rush of sentimentality" (Tuck 2009, 160) that is done at the expense of any rational critique of societal forces, such as prejudice or economic deprivation. Durang's use of black comedy does not allow an audience to indulge in this cathartic pleasure. Rather, it asks us to confront societal problems, such as child neglect, for example, without losing ourselves in the emotions of self-righteous anger or hopelessness.

The idea that we would laugh at such violent actions or cynical perspectives is discomfiting to the ideal of ourselves as humane creatures, who prefer to contemplate scenes of joyful humor. Yet Baudelaire speaks of diabolical laughter that derives from the dark realms of the human psyche, the Germans refer to the laughter at another's misfortunes as schadenfreude, and small children laugh at the violent puppetry between Punch and his wife Judy, or the calamities of the Looney Tune cartoons. The list of physical abuses in Durang's plays run a gamut of degeneracy: we find a man being tortured and having his ear removed (*Why Torture Is Wrong*); a patient shooting his therapist with a starter gun (*Beyond Therapy*); two vacationers cutting off the penis and head of a visitor (*Betty's Summer Vacation*); or a father who casually remarks he's tied his daughter to the piano leg after giving her a force-injected enema ("John and Mary Doe"). Comedy plays an important role in the Theater of Le Grand Guignol, a particular form of Parisian theatre specializing in scenes of fantastic depravity, such as a doctor performing open brain surgery, with the top peeled back for the audience's viewing, or a young woman whose eyes are gouged out by two inmates in an insane asylum, jealous of her beauty. These horrific one-act plays of the Grand Guignol Theater alternated with comedic farces, which allowed, as Felicia Ruff has argued, the audiences to accept more easily the horror unfolding before their eyes (Ruff 2008). In other words, the laughter permitted a release of social inhibitions and enabled audience members to endure horror by lowering—or laughing away—their tolerance thresholds for abnormal behavior.

In addition to the bodily grotesque, Durang trolls in areas of the psychological grotesque, most notably the neurotic behaviors in his characters: narcissism, schizophrenia, and borderline personality disorder. Psychological disorders in performance are highly dramatic, and Durang creates confrontations between more-or-less normal characters and those who possess psychotic disorders. The Woman in *Laughing Wild* has been institutionalized; a sibling in *'dentity Crisis* has multiple identity personality disorder; and in *Baby with the Bathwater*, the Nanny warns the child, "Don't depend on Mommy. . . . She's not all there." Durang's fascination with such "head cases" is exemplified by using a photograph of "Liv Ullmann having a nervous breakdown" as the official image on his website; one must "click" her face, frozen in Munch-like scream, in order to enter Durang's site.

The grotesque, as a formal art category itself, is an apt descriptor for Durang's *oeuvre* with its focus on the sadistic and obscene. The grotesque possesses elements that inspire laughter, not because objects that are grotesque are funny, but because they offer disturbing propositions in a humorous way, rendering the familiar world alien and unsettling. The crazy, wild, and unrestrained impulses found in Durang's earlier works, such as *The Idiots Karamazov* and *Titanic*, offer such unsettling worlds that encapsulate the material grossness of the body. Replete with such behavior as hauling around corpses, incestuous relationships, and small animals that reside inside a character's vagina, these plays elicit not only the disgust that is warranted but also shock mixed with laughter. The grotesque, as Wolfgang Kayser argues in *The Grotesque in Art and Literature* (1957, 1963), is a mode of reception; it is the subtle awareness that beneath a "playfully gay and carelessly fantastic" surface an ominous, sinister note is sounded. Durang's comedies have elicited this response as evidenced by such oxymoronic terminology expressed by reviewers of his plays: "Patented brand of venomous whimsy" (Lepidus 1999); "healthy anger encased in absurdist humor" (Isherwood 1999); "blithely demented" (Winer 1999); "anger-fueled comedy" (Isherwood 2005); and "outrageously upsetting" while also being "entertaining and provocative" (Kennerley 2008); "disturbing and hysterical" (Sheward 2008); "welding kindergarten-like form to dire content" (Feingold 2008). The tonal ambivalence and discomfiting feelings are best summed up by the concept of the grotesque.

The subversive energy behind a Durangian comedy is not merely anarchic, but pointedly directed at a target, making most of his plays satirical in nature. Satire often overlaps with the grotesque to make its critical point; the cruelty of its nature can be considered a type of witty sadism. The term comes from the word "satyr," a lascivious, mythical creature that was half man, half beast, and the Latin phrase *lanx satura*, the "mixed platter" of fruits and nuts served at Roman banquets. Both origins of the term correspond perfectly to the libidinous nature of Durang's characters, as well as the many kooks and nuts who inhabit his worlds. The hypermasculine, ex-military Uncle Larry who booby-traps the living room is one such eccentric figure in *The Vietnamization of New Jersey*, as is the exasperating dinner guest who never leaves in *Wanda's Visit*. But the crazy individuals Durang creates are more than mere fun. Like Jonathan Swift in *A Modest Proposal*, Durang's derisive laughter is polemical. As a keen observer of society and its ills, Durang's plays offer shocking inversions of conventional morality; his scenarios frequently encourage us to look at what Americans aspire to be, from our families to our relationships to our government, and to see how far we fall from those ideals. Gussow, reflecting upon Durang's plays over the years, notes how his works are "rife with some of the most devastating jibes at . . . society. With his chilled scalpel, he has committed surgical mayhem on Catholic education, sibling rivalry, sempiternal maternalism [sic], country club snobbery, the movie images that shaped our youth and the myth that, in Mr. Durang's eyes, masquerades as modern marriage" (Gussow 1985). To this list, we could add self-centered therapists, homegrown militias, government policies on same-sex couples, and the twenty-four-hour news cycles, and still these targets would not give a full sense of the damning indictments Durang heaps upon society. Moreover, a good satirist is genuinely amused by his subject matter. As Northrop Frye attests, "One cannot merely adopt satire to express a personal or moral feeling; one must be born with the sardonic vision" (Frye 1944, 77). Even as Durang indicts a political figure or social malfeasance, he hits the funny bone with his wacky invectives and unexpected scenarios.

Durang sets his sardonic sights mainly on authoritarianism, focusing on individuals who misuse their power and impose their rampaging will or cockamamie ideas on helpless individuals. Psychologists, teachers, parents, and ministers, individuals who are the most capable of abuse due to their positions of leadership and their responsibility over the lives of others, figure prominently in Durang's plays. Mrs. Willoughby, for example, the school principal in *Baby with the Bathwater*, refuses to see the emotional pain of the students entrusted in her care; rather than refer Daisy to a school therapist for the disturbing content of her essay, Mrs. Willoughby predicts she will be a literary genius, comparable to Virginia Woolf or Sylvia Plath: "Who cares if she's dead as long as she publishes?" (291). The Captain in Durang's version of the *Titanic* indulges in sexual peccadilloes with his passengers rather than lead his ship, while Mrs. Seizmagraff in *Betty's Summer Vacation* encourages a miscreant guest to sexually violate her daughter. Several of his characters grant themselves license to harm others based on their perception of God's injunctions: in *Sister Mary Ignatius Explains It All for You*, Sister Mary justifies murdering her former student in order to send him to heaven; she does this after learning he went to confession and was forgiven for his sins, including—she assumes—his homosexuality. Hilton Als points out how Durang criticizes those institutions that vividly wield their power, like the Catholic Church, noting that his satires offers "cogent dissections of power and illusion and our collective abuse of both" (Als 2008, 87).

Satire operates in Durang's literary lampoons of fellow playwrights, or more specifically, his parodies. Jay Malarcher explores the connection between the two genres more fully in his essay entitled "The Marriage of Parody and Satire: The All-American Comedy of Christopher Durang." Parody is typically understood as imitating the defining features of a literary, musical, or artistic work, and devaluing the original by applying the imitation to an inferior topic. The laughter generated from Durang's theatrical parodies comes from the incongruity between the familiar, original version and the malformation that he gives us—a factor that some critics seem to overlook when reviewing his plays. Although parodies can be considered a derivative form of literature, they can be instructive in revealing new understandings of the original works; for example, Durang has something to say about Russian literature (*The Idiots Karamazov*), American movies (*A History of the American Film* and *Adrift in Macao*), and famous plays ("For Whom the Southern Belle Tolls"), and even artfully mocks the stylistic mannerisms of his contemporaries, David Mamet and Sam Shepard. His parodies, teeming as they are with the punch lines, personages, or preoccupations that define America, also capture the zeitgeist of the time. As Robert Brustein describes it, "Christopher Durang's unwashed brain is an uneasy compound of Hollywood movies and sitcoms, Eugene Ionesco plays, and Monty Python skits" (Brustein 1997, vii).

Durang's plays are lighthearted and not sinister, as the form of black comedy would suggest; tonally, they are reminiscent of farce. As one critic fittingly phrased it, "His characters seem like graphic portraits drawn with Ben Day dots. They are simplified, two-dimensional, colorful" (Herman 1997). Comparing the atmosphere, tone, and settings of his plays to pop-art captures the artificial quality of his characters' emotions and the detached, humorous handling of their pain; Roy Lichtenstein's *Drowning Girl* (1963) does provide a perfect comparison. Durang dislikes the term "farce" applied to his plays (Durang 2016), because it suggests characters who behave in a mechanized fashion, yet this term captures the zany ambiance of his work. Moreover, he cites Joe Orton as an early influence on his plays, whose black comedies were no more than farce injected with cynicism; Durang, in fact, performed in Orton's play *Loot* while a senior at Harvard (Durang 2012b, 51). It is true that farce has been viewed historically as a lowbrow form of humor, the pin-ball movements of the characters and the slamming doors of bedroom farce were only meant to elicit laughter, not thoughtful reflection, from the audience. John Dryden, for one, disparaged farce for lacking the introspection that comedy could offer, commenting how "comedy presents us with the imperfections of human nature: [but] Farce entertains us with what is monstrous and chimerical" (Dryden 1956, 203). Dryden could not have provided a more apt descriptor of Durang's plays, in which the "monstrous and chimerical" is alive and well. Robert Brustein credited Durang, his former student, with inventing "painful farce" (Brustein 2019, x), which reflects the same overlap between the grotesque and farce seen in such literary forebears as Southern American writer Flannery O'Connor, whose use of the grotesque has been described as "violent slapstick" (DiRenzo 1993, 73).

What is particularly potent about farce as a comic form is its ability to illustrate the darker aspects of humanity without passing into tragedy. Leonard Pronko's study of Georges Feydeau, for example, gave more serious consideration to the conditions of the genre than had previously been expressed. Pronko revealed how a world in paroxysm lurked beneath the frenetically joyous surface, giving both depth and bite to these farces previously understood as lightweight (Pronko 1982, 483). The vision of the world that farce depicts is one of chaos and confusion, but also of the powerlessness of individuals in the face of authority, such as doctors or one's boss. Thus, farce becomes an ideal comic metaphor for framing the individual within a crazy and destructive environment, which Durang wished to show in multiple plays, ranging from *Identity Crisis*, where a young woman loses her identity because of her crazy family, to Vanya, Sonia, and Masha, in Durang's latest work, who discover new identities in a world that has changed. Farce, with its roots in vaudeville, resembles the spirit and gaiety of the cabaret, but the nightmarish world the characters inhabit with the limits placed upon them ultimately speaks to their fears and anxieties: fear of failure, fear of losing one's dignity, fear of being discovered as a fraud.

These comedic forms—the grotesque, satire, parody, and farce—are the puzzle pieces that make up the black humor of Durang. They attest to the dualistic, hybrid vision of his work, the joyful fatalism, the macabre hilarity. The following chapters will rely upon these descriptive terms to examine his plays. Rather than a strict chronological division, the book provides a thematic view of Durang's oeuvre, considering his various preoccupations across time. Chapter 1, "Perverting the Classics," focuses on Durang's use of parody, where the audience's knowledge of the original text feeds the comedy. Chapter 2, "Seeking Is Believing," considers the religious satire and spiritual longing of Durang's theatre, especially in light of his own lapsed Catholicism. Chapter 3 offers an examination of Durang's one-act plays, relevant because of Durang's particular ability to write sketch comedy. "Family Dysfunction" is the topic of Chapter 4 and explores Durang's focus on the family as the site of individual madness, including Durang's own personal experience with harmful family relationships. Chapter 5, "American Anomie," focuses on the damning effects society has on the individual who finds him or herself at odds with the status quo. Finally, essays authored by Robert Combs and Jay Malarcher in Chapter 6, "Critical Perspectives," will round out the discussion, attending to the interactive nature of Durang's theatre, as well as the playwright's use of parody and satire.

Ultimately, Durang's dark comedy reveals the fault lines in society. In our uncomfortable laughter, as we find ourselves both attracted to and repulsed by the ludicrous scenario at hand, he makes us more aware of the personal destruction caused by authority, hypocrisy, and intolerance. As he writes in the afterword to *Baby with the Bathwater*, "Taking Daisy's pain (and for that matter, his parents' pain) seriously at the same time that I expect the audience to find humor in it has become for me the definition of my style: Absurdist comedy married to real feelings" (306). In *Baby with the Bathwater*, the "absurdist" premise is how immature people are allowed to bring children into the world, despite their own carelessness and blatant ineptitude. The "real feelings" evoked beneath the humor of the play involve a child's pain of being ignored and the ache of loneliness. One tableau in particular comes to mind, an image forceful in its indictment of irresponsible parents and grotesque in its illustration of child abuse. It shows a child, depicted onstage by a toy doll, stuck head first into a pile of laundry, his feet sticking stolidly out, his neglectful mother nearby, folding laundry. This humorous image is all one needs to telescopically imagine the life of the real boy behind this tale, ignored and manipulated, thrust head first into a topsy-turvy world. As a cartoon character, he's funny and laughable. As the real-life suffering individual, he's in pain. Durang always encourages us to see both.

CHAPTER 1
PERVERTING THE CLASSICS

It is fitting that Christopher Durang's first major production should tackle head-on one of the world's greatest authors, Fyodor Doestoevsky. In finding his dramatic voice, Durang and his fellow classmate at Yale, Albert Innaurato, juggled, subverted, and dismantled *The Brothers Karamazov*, tossing in parodic allusions to Eugene O'Neill, James Joyce, and Charles Dickens for good measure. As every novice writer must clear an authorial space for himself, so Harold Bloom has argued, Durang took on his creative forebears in an imaginary wrestling match where he emerged triumphant. Borrowing Bloom's phrasing from *The Anxiety of Influence* (1973), one could say that Durang deliberately "misread" or "misinterpreted" his literary precursors—except even that descriptor would be too polite. Durang's misreading is an all-out war, a barbaric yawp in the stoic face of the classics. Durang's *mano a mano* approach to literary, cultural, theatrical, and film history resulted in a battlefield of maimed quotations, lampooned characters, and bastardized plots. Oh, and lest we forget, it's riotously funny.

Parody is a derogatory form of art, a piece that pokes fun at the content or the style or the conventions of another work. Max Beerbohm pronounced parody the specialty of youth rather than mature wisdom (Beerbohm 1970, 66), and Durang would be the first to admit his theatrical humor is absurd and juvenile. Taking the nuanced religious debates between Alyosha and his rationalist brother Ivan from *The Brothers Karamazov*, Durang reduces the two characters' positions to childishly repeating, "Yes, there is [a God]" and "No, there isn't" back and forth ten times. Durang's parody of the novel does not attack so much the work itself, but the overweening respect people have for literary masterpieces. The OED defines parody as a genre whereby "an author or class of authors are imitated in such a way as to make them appear ridiculous," but the true attack of *The Brothers Karamazov* is the institutionalized reverence surrounding highbrow culture, especially the Great Works. The unquestionable placement of the Great Works in the academy was a ripe target for dismantling during the antiauthoritarian 1970s, which Durang must have felt viscerally in the liberal but also rarefied atmosphere of Yale University. Much of Durang's work during this early decade took well-known literature or cultural stories for his parodic targets: the classics, the Bible, and American television and film. In fact, this parodic style would become Durang's signature in his satiric revisions, allusions, and appropriations for the rest of his career.

That said, it would be shortsighted of us to consider Durang's work only as mocking and satiric. In doing so, we would disregard the quality of homage paid to the original writer or text that is inherent in parody. In *A Theory of Parody: The Teachings of Twentieth-Century Art Forms*, Linda Hutcheon adjusts the commonly-held view of parody as disparaging ridicule and encourages a broader definition of parody as one that reverses the formal features of another piece, what she calls "ironic inversion." This type of parody is not necessarily a critique of the parodied text, but a thoughtful and playful response. By engaging with the original work, the artist (and by implication the audience) comes to terms with both the literary conventions of the piece and the past. Furthermore, parody requires the reader or the audience member to be "in the know," to be so familiar with the original text that audiences can perceive the similarities as well as the differences and be in on the joke, so to speak. She writes that "parody is repetition with critical distance" (2000, 4) and explains that

> a critical distance is implied between the background text being parodied and the new incorporating work, a distance usually signaled by irony. But this irony can be playful as well as belittling; it can be critically constructive as well as destructive. The pleasure of parody's irony comes not from humor in particular but from the degree of engagement of the reader in the intertextual "bouncing" (to use E. M. Forster's famous term) between complicity and distance. (32)

It is important to give this definition some thought because all the plays in this chapter can be considered parodies: they all ironically invert a background text or "bounce" between texts; they are as "critically constructive" as they are joyfully destructive. Durang requires his audience to know the original text in order to enjoy his rambunctious routing. Consequently, the plays in this chapter can be understood as playful *and* critical, as responses to or assessments of the cultural weight each piece holds in society. Only a work that has artistic significance and substantial meaning can withstand the onslaught of parodic play; each of his plays exposes much of what

American society considers worthwhile as it tears it to bits. To read Durang's plays is to take a journey within the archives of literary and film history as he appropriates and parodies the work of major novelists, playwrights, and directors, while respectfully attesting to the original's sustained hold over the public imagination.

The Idiots Karamazov

If, according to Bloom, "a poem is a poet's melancholy at his lack of priority" (Bloom 1997, 96), then a play could certainly represent this, too. *The Idiots Karamazov*, a chaotic dismantling of *The Brothers Karamazov* (1880), was cowritten by Durang and Albert Innaurato.[1] However, the operating mood behind their parody is not so much melancholia as a joyful bloodletting. Durang and Innaurato provide Doestoevsky no filial respect, but rather diminish the serious moral quandaries and patricidal obsession in his novel through their wicked wit. Furthermore, their lampoon includes a large swath of literary history, comically referencing Chekhov's *Uncle Vanya*, Beckett's *Endgame*, O'Neill's *Long Day's Journey into Night*, and Charles Dickens's *Great Expectations*. Meanwhile, modernist authors Anaïs Nin, Djuna Barnes, and Ernest Hemingway are ridiculed for their pretentiousness and literary style. The masterpieces seem to weigh heavily on the young playwrights' psyches, if only evidenced by their nonsensical inversions of famous lines. When the young monk Alyosha tells Mrs. Karamazov, who doubles as Mary Tyrone from *Long Day's Journey into Night*, in a despairing tone of voice, "Mama, I'm going to be a pop star," Mrs. Karamazov slaps him and yells, "Edmund, stop saying that! It's just a summer cold" (Durang 1997, 43), deflating the original Mary Tyrone's maternal obsession over her son's tuberculosis. "The history of fruitful poetic influence," Bloom writes, referring to Western literature, "is a history of anxiety and self-saving caricature of distortion, of perverse, willful revisionism without which modern poetry as such could not exist" (30). Durang's revision of *Long Day's Journey* could not be more distorted, willful, or perverse.

It is not only the stories we tell as a culture that shape our narratives but the values inherent in those stories that establish our morality and laws. The Greek definition of "hamartia," for example, meaning "mis-step," was translated erroneously by the early Christian Church Fathers as "fatal flaw." This mistranslation affected how Westerners saw themselves as imperfect beings, incriminated by their own or their predecessors' actions, doomed to suffer for "the sins of the fathers," as it is figuratively known. The concept of the fatal flaw and its concomitant morality is imbricated in the Western tragic motif and pervades all literary education. Durang's parody of *The Brothers Karamazov* takes examples of such arbitrarily assigned morality, ridicules it, and demotes its importance. For example, his character Dimitri, after being told that his mother was a "Venus Flytrap" who enticed men to their destruction, feels biologically compelled to eat flies; he is ultimately killed by a poisonous spray and his death solemnly labeled "insecticide." This joke refers back to the early Greek culture's concern with the taboos involving family liaisons and their linguistic categorization of family-member murders: patricide, infanticide, etc. "Insecticide," a poisonous substance used for pest control, has no place in this list of taboos, beyond a simple repetition of the root word "cida" (to kill). Labeling his death as such undercuts the neat classification system of family-member murders. The choice to parody *The Brothers Karamazov*, a novel whose Oedipal themes fascinated Freud himself, further drives home the point that the literary tradition of classical morality weighs paternalistically on young, up-and-coming authors. Several characters carry the bodies of their dead fathers around the stage with them, a literal embodiment of the poetic precursors' heavy weight, according to Bloom. The onstage narrator, Constance Garnett, becomes obsessed with Fyodor Karamazov's death, providing the definition of CHALIAPIN, "meaning to be murdered by one's own son with a pestle," and detailing its nonsensical conjugation with linguistic glee: "CHALIAPINE, CHALIAPINSKI, CHALIAPINSKIYA, CHALIAPINSKOI . . . CHALIAPINSKINSKI" (Durang 1997, 24). Durang may be taking potshots at Dostoevsky's novel, but in doing so he targets the overbearing residue of Western literature's ethics and aesthetics.

What Western literature has given us, through stories of individuals frustrated in their desires, is an understanding of the moral strictures that bind us together as a society. Freud argues in *Civilization and Its Discontents* (1929) that the paradoxical condition of civilization is that it represses the instinctual drives of people, mostly sexual satisfaction and aggression, in order for people to live together safely. We establish laws that proscribe against violence, incest, adultery, murder, rape—even the eating of one's own species—but the constant pressure of laws and their more minor applications ("Don't run a stop sign, don't take someone's property, don't hit your sibling") curb our sense of freedom and happiness. The literary canon stands as a creative exploration of the dreams and fears that resulted from civilization's socializing influences; it offers countless stories about the vast "thou shalt nots" that weighed heavily upon people and were manifested in the conflicts, themes, and tragedies that make the Great Works great. Toward the end of the play, Durang's entire cast of characters (including the dead ones), as if to acknowledge the heavy weight of such interdictions, rise and sing the song "Totem and Taboo, and Toto, too," repudiating all the signs, symbols, and archetypes inherent in literary history, while giving a nod to Freud's 1913 work *Totem and Taboo*. Anaïs Pnin, Durang's caricature of Anaïs Nin, a French-American modernist writer who lived her life in defiance of norms, leads the cast in dismissing the constraining rules of society in favor of pursuing their life's desires with her summary line: "Dump totem and screw taboo" (57).

The sensual journey of the main character, Alyosha Karamazov, from faithful monk to Palace Theater crooner forms the narrative backbone of the play, but it is the wild antics of his father and three brothers that set the farcical tone. Fyodor, the father, and Alyosha's eldest brother, Dimitri, the sensualist, romantically pursue the same women, Grushenka, the town Jezebel, as they do in the original. This time around, however, they physically saw Grushenka in half, egregiously misunderstanding the parable of Solomon as told to them by the town's spiritual elder, Zossima. The two halves of the woman become Grushenka I and II, who join the Russian Revolution as well as the women's rights movement—it is, after all, the 1970s. While the tone is high farce, the style is densely allusive. When Fyodor fires a gun, he makes an allusion to the inconsequential firing in *Uncle Vanya*; he lapses into Vanya's self-abnegating speech: "Oh my life is ruined, I have talent, courage, intelligence.... Mother, I'm in despair" (16). Another brother, Ivan, grabs the pistol and shoots a seagull from the sky in a nod to another Chekhov play, then recites Astrov's question of Nurse, "Do you think that the people who will live a hundred years from now will speak well of us and appreciate our suffering?" (18). The fourth brother, Smerdyakov, supposedly the illegitimate offspring of Fyodor, falls into epileptic fits on the floor, while Alyosha wanders about looking for a spoon to place under his tongue. Father Zossima, no longer the sage religious of Doestoevsky's tale but a flamboyant monk, attempts to seduce the young Alyosha only to lose him to Anaïs Pnin, when she appears accompanied by Djuna Barnes. The musical number "Everything's Permitted" closes the play by aptly summarizing the wild excesses Durang has taken with the classical plots and characters. As Mel Gussow summarily concludes, "The brothers are more Marx than Karamazov" (42).

Dostoevsky is not the only precursor with whom Durang does battle; he takes umbrage with the famous nineteenth-century English translator Constance Garnett. Garnett was the first person to translate such authors as Dostoevsky, Chekhov, and Tolstoy into English, translating over seventy works by the end of her career and holding a linguistic monopoly over the field of Russian literature in English for the first part of the twentieth century. Despite her pioneering work, she was later criticized for her tendency to flatten and standardize the Russian writers' style in order to make it more palatable; as the academic Peter France writes in *The Oxford Guide to Literature in English Translations*, "She shortens and simplifies, muting Dostoevsky's jarring contrasts, sacrificing his insistent rhythms and repetitions, toning down the Russian colouring, explaining and normalizing in all kinds of ways" (France 2000, 595–6). Durang capitalizes on this criticism to make Garnett a figure of fun; as the onstage narrator in a wheelchair, the character rolls herself in and out of the play, her interference denoting the subjective nature of the translator's work. She confuses authors, bowdlerizes indecent sections of text, and mistranslates phrases of which she was uncertain. She uses outdated language (e.g., *especial*, *vouchsafe*), and furthermore proves her incompetence by allowing her Victorian sensibility to affect her translations; she prudishly cannot translate the Russian word "whorehouse" correctly, so Grushenka must say the line "Oh how unhappy it is to be a hostess in a Russian warehouse" instead (29). Although perhaps unfair to disparage this translator who did ground-breaking work, the gesture is more than lampoon. Making Garnett serve as the play's mouthpiece shows that translation could be another one of Bloom's revisionary ratios, a subjective adjustment of the original text. "The Russian word for mulatto is Pushkin," she states, referring to a little-known fact of Alexander Pushkin's great-grandfather being African. Played by Meryl Streep in a wheelchair in the original production, she parades through a series of such irrelevant translations, switching between languages: "Dans le jardin Karamazovi steht der junge Alyosha and his brother Ivan" (14) and delineating our knowledge of Russian literature by categorical trivia: "The Russian word for overcoat is Gogol. The Russian word for epileptic is Dostoevsky. The Russian word for accident at the train station is Anna Karenina. The Russian word for bumble bee is Rimsky-Korsakov. The Russian word for an hysterical homosexual is Tchaikovsky!"

(53). Because the play is depicted from her narrative point of view, the characters' absurdities seem a direct result of the warped wonderland of her addled brain. Repeatedly she states that her objective as a translator is clarity, but her resultant flotsam and jetsam could not be further from that case. For example, when she inadvertently refers to the Karamazov brothers with the character names from Chekhov's play, *The Three Sisters*, the characters onstage are likewise confused. The three Karamazov brothers, who are mistakenly introduced to the audience as Olga, Masha, and Irena by the translator, have no choice but to sing the song "O We Gotta Get to Moscow," which is a musical number alluding to the Chekhovian sisters' plaintive refrain of deferred hopes, rather than anything the Karamazov brothers said: "We'll Moscow go, / We won't take no, We'll Chattanooga choo choo off to Buffalo" (13). Illogical and inconsistent as Garnett is, she acts as a thread holding together the chaotic plot details, as she weaves in and out of the scene and reacts viscerally to the unfolding action, at times even shooting the characters. The play closes with Garnett sliding into a stream-of-consciousness pastiche of famous first lines from great literary works, a disintegrating monument to Western literary scholarship.

The contradictory nature of parody lies in its tendency to be threatening while at the same time legitimizing; the same anarchic attitude that attacks the aesthetic quality of an artwork simultaneously warrants that work as worthy of critique by its high status and notoriety. As Hutcheon notes, "Even in mocking, parody reinforces: in formal terms, it inscribes the mocked conventions onto itself, thereby guaranteeing their continued existence" (75). Any student of drama knows that *Long Day's Journey* stands as the definitive play of painful American family relationships. By taking the character of Mary Tyrone and making her the matriarch of the Karamazov clan, Durang legitimizes *Long Day's Journey* even while turning it into a source of amusement. The impact of O'Neill's work comes from the family's inability to discuss Mary Tyrone's opium addiction openly or to confront her. Moreover, the father and sons wallow in self-recrimination for past mistakes that led to her addiction. The poisonous guilt they feel, coupled with keeping her problem behind closed doors, creates the play's tension. In *The Idiots Karamazov*, most of her speeches are quoted verbatim; it is the mismatched context that renders them humorous. Mary Tyrone slips on and offstage, talking about the fog, her son's cold, and her marriage; she remembers how she "fell in love with Fyodor Karamazov and was so happy for a time" (45)—the incongruity of the harsh-sounding Russian name in the middle of the dreamlike nostalgia creating laughter. The striking contrast of O'Neill's lines set against the Karamazov nonsense is an example of Hutcheon's description of "repetition with critical distance." When Ivan finds his mother's hypodermic needles and gently asks her, "Have you then resumed your . . . 'knitting'?" (29), his lines are in blatant disregard of the obvious. Moreover, the tragic impact of Mary Tyrone trying to hide her morphine addiction is undercut in Durang's version as she shoots up in front of the audience. Similarly, removing the contextual markers of Jamie and Edmund's love-hate relationship foregrounds how petty Jamie's jealousy and guilt are; the skeletal conversation shows the nuttiness of his cycle of pain and forgiveness: "I love your guts, kid, but I gotta warn you. I hate your guts, you goddam bastard. (*Hits Alyosha over the head with the pestle.*) Gee, kid, I'm sorry, I love your guts" (55). As sophomoric as the humor may be, Durang's parodic appropriation of the classical texts is a revolutionary gesture, not against the Great Works per se, but against an obsequious respect toward them.

Pretentiousness comes under attack in Durang's parody, whether it is the stuffiness of Father Zossima's religious discourses or the conceit of modern art. The serious exploration of spirituality, religion, and morality at the core of *The Brothers Karamazov* devolves into high camp. Father Zossima, revered as a sagacious man of the cloth in the original, becomes a joking nod to the repressed homosexuality of the priesthood; he is carried onstage rolled up in a carpet flanked by two blond altar boys and his first words, upon being unrolled, are a luxuriating "come lie with me, Alyosha." The spiritual grounding of the original character becomes little more than a mask, just like the costume of a wedding cake that Zossima wears to attend Anaïs's parties, the two accompanying altar boys this time dressed as candles. The mysticism of his lengthy homilies is undercut; instead Zossima gives a ridiculous disquisition about the meaning of the world void of any sense: "Everything in the world has a purpose and meaning, Alyosha. This ground we sit on has meaning. This crucifix around my neck has meaning. (*Points to Boy.*) This child on my right has meaning. (*Points to other Altar Boy.*) This child on my left has meaning. (*Picks up sandwich.*) This has meaning. (*Picks up another sandwich.*) This has meaning" (19). The speech devolves in a banal litany on how the most mundane of objects, a carrot or a hair on one's head, has meaning, although it is patently clear that no one knows what that meaning is. Ivan, in similar fashion, also has moments of philosophical questioning about the nature of empirical reality: "You see a garden, I see but ashes," he explains, investigating how perceptual awareness can be influenced by a character's spirituality, or lack thereof. But his demonstration of his perception of nihilism devolves quickly into empirical nonsense: "(*Picks up grapes*) Look at these grapes. (*Crushes them*) CRUSHED! Look at this plum. (*Squashes it*). SQUASHED!" (50). In divorcing the spiritual quest from any real substance, Durang turns philosophical questioning into no more than what Karl Marx considered it: wanking off.

Modernist art's onanistic quality is fodder for fun with the self-aggrandizing figure of Anaïs Pnin, whose life story upstages that of the Brothers. She documents exaggeratedly every detail of her life in her diaries, because she finds herself more fascinating than fictional characters; taking a picture of herself holding a picture of herself is one example of her solipsism, as is centering the party's entertainment on the moment she unbinds her feet (which adds to the running gag about foot fetishes). Djuna Barnes serves as Pnin's personal secretary and makes notes of every action, whether she sits or makes a joke. In a stylistically heightened gesture of performance art, Barnes appears stacking wood and draping a black cloth over the pile, and declaiming, "Niiiiiiiiiightwwwwwwwwooooooooooood" (31). Continuing the lampoon of modernism, the hyper-macho Ernest Hemingway makes an appearance, playing the butler and talking in clipped sentences about the Fitzgeralds, his macho sporting adventures, and his own elliptic prose style. But it is the real-life Anaïs Nin, as a strong feminist figure, who Durang targets. Nin triumphed in a male-dominated publishing industry with her frank talk of female eroticism and the publication of her diaries, filled with scandalous details about her affairs; Durang portrays her as a monstrous ego lacking in any artistic merit. He travesties her feminist philosophy, making her sound stupidly illogical as she angrily retorts to being called a woman: "It is typical of men in this oppressive society that just because I have two breasts and a vagina, he calls me a woman" (51). Because Nin's writing focused on erotica, Durang characterizes her as enacting sexual perversions; in scenes where Djuna is either bathing Anaïs Pnin or simulating drizzle noises while Pnin takes a shower, the humor lies in the sexualized language. "Hotter, Djuna," she instructs her, regarding the make-believe water, or moans, "Ah, yes, this is helping my writing. Wetter, Djuna" (42). When she asks Djuna to pull out her "plug," the double entendre suggests freeing her libido to pursue Aloysha.

The overt preoccupation with fetishizing and degrading the body is prevalent throughout *The Idiots Karamazov*, starting with sawing Grushenka in two. Constance Garnett represents prurience; as the decorous figure of repressed sexuality, she is fascinated with the sexual peccadilloes of her characters, yet has trouble expressing sexual matters regarding "the body": "Even that odoriferous word makes me shudder," she moans. "The body . . . oooooh! (*Shudders in her wheelchair.*) (24). The Priest Zossima flirts with Alyosha by eating peanuts out of Alyosha's hands and directing him to rub peanuts between the soles of their feet, excited by his fetish. A repulsed Aloysha's spiritual crisis comes down to this moment of questioning: "How can there be a God if there are feet?" (40). Toward the end of the play, as people starve and die during the Russian Revolution, a group of characters caught in a cold, wintry forest resort to cooking the dead Smerdyakov in a soup. Thus, the group resorts to cannibalism, once again confronting societal taboos, at which Zossima draws a line: "I used to warn the monks about these literal interpretations of the Eucharist" (55). Rather than bury their dead, several dead characters are carted around in body bags. Invoking yet another taboo, incest, Durang alludes to Anaïs Nin's sexual relationship with her own father, which she documented in *Incest*, published posthumously in 1992. Lying on her back with the body of her dead father on top of her, melding both incest with necrophilia, she asks Alyosha to join her in a "body sandwich" by lying on top of her father's dead body; Djuna spreads the mayonnaise over all of them, adding to the lubricity.

This emphasis on bodily fetishism and functions is a type of art form defined by Mikhail Bakhtin as the carnivalesque, whose humor—as subversive as it is celebratory of life—"degrades, brings down to earth, turns their subject into flesh." Associating this scatological laughter with the common people, "das folk," in defiance of the refined upper classes, he characterized this kind of humor with all "the forms of grotesque realism from immemorial times [and] was linked with the bodily lower stratum" (Bakhtin 1984, 20). The figures representing the masterpieces of the literary world who have been placed on pedestals now reveal themselves to have clay feet by their grotesque, unseemly behavior—and not just clay *feet*. Dimitri eats flies in Durang's play and Smerdyakov becomes a dog. Grushenka I and II are two parts of the same body and are later joined by a chorus of female legs, referred to as the Leather Girls. Fyodor is killed with a pestle and spends the rest of the play in a body bag, being carted around; later

Djuna dies and is placed in the same plastic bag. The injunction against desecrating corpses is trespassed with glee. In the original novel, the plot focuses on Father Zossima's dead body as an example of the hypocrisy behind religious indoctrination; the townspeople erroneously believe that the bodies of holy men do not decay, thus Zossima's putrescent body is proof that he is not divine. Durang subverts this story line by exaggerating the number of corpses on the stage: Alyosha brings the body of his dead father onto the stage at Anaïs Pnin's request. This play that involves bodies of fathers being carried around in bags—symbolic as it is of throwing off the weight of literary forbears—paradoxically has a celebratory quality. As Bakhtin argues, such humor is a reminder that death in itself is never the end, as the body is the material remainder that resists being simply disposed of. The vitality that is loaded into the grotesque nature of death in this play, as well as the sheer bestial physicality of much of the caricature acting (i.e., a dog, a Venus flytrap, an army of legs), is a form of carnivalesque humor. By the end, Durang's stage looks like a Hieronymous Bosch pandiabolist landscape, part nightmare, part rollicking fun.

The Idiots Karamazov premiered against the political backdrop of the women's rights movement, and Durang's production taps into a societal uneasiness regarding sexual liberation. After the men selfishly saw Grushenka in half, the two women, Grushenka I and II, although only halves, become ultra-feminists, espousing militant rhetoric to deplore the horrors of men and arming themselves. They are joined by a group of mannish Leather Girls, who are also only legs and sing a rallying cry that parodies Helen Reddy's liberation song "I Am Woman": "See our arm, see our fist / And we're feeling good and pissed, / . . . We're omnipotent, We're Woman, Nous Les Femmes!" (23). At the time, the newly formed National Organization for Women insisted on greater equality for women, and emerging groups of radical feminist organizations protested such misogynistic events as the Miss American Contest with attention-grabbing stunts, such as crowning a sheep and parading it through the crowd to represent the judgment of women contestants like animals at a fair. The Grushenkas' and Leather Girls' guerrilla behavior tactics as well as their transforming themselves into the Bolshevik army is ridiculous and seems to lampoon the strains of the women's movement through his caricatures of virile women—as well as hints at women's potential to create a revolution. Parody conveys Durang's dualistic message of criticism and celebration in the same breath.

Saul Bellow, in an essay he wrote on humor, defines nihilism as "seeing no reason why you should not do what you wish to do. No moral prohibition from the past has the power to prevent its being done, for your actions are meaningless by any standard of meaning. You have rejected all standards" (Bellow 2003, 239). In *The Idiots Karamazov*, Durang proves there is no reason he cannot do what he wants to do with Doestoevsky's masterpiece. Djuna Barnes performs as a stand-up comedian in the final cabaret scene at the Palace Theater and Alyosha becomes a sentimental crooner. In the closing musical number, "Everything's Permitted," the characters sing "Everything's allowed, / And God we have outwitted, . . . All things fall apart" (61). These lyrics allude to Ivan's famous line, summarizing his crisis of faith: "In a world without God, everything is permitted." Durang's world is truly godless. The Karamazov family members, including the dead Fyodor, reunite as a German-Swiss family yodeling group that sang on the radios and traveled about the United States in the 1930s and 1940s. As Smerdyakov barks, they ring bells and sing:

> Und when we are cranky, we frown,
> Und when we stand up, we sit down,
> Und when we are gloomy, we weep,
> Und when we are happy, we sleep!

Notably, their song also repeats the play's spiritual questioning of God's existence: "Und Gott is in himmel und taking a Napp" (47). While Doestoevsky's literary tome ends with a testament to Christian love, Durang's piece ends with a song of cheerful nihilism. In *The Idiots Karamazov*, Durang casts off the esoteric and ecclesiastical weight of his authorial precursors, as his characters nonsensically invent themselves anew.

Vietnamization of New Jersey: A American Tragedy

Durang's next play is a parody of a parody. David Rabe's anti-war play, *Sticks and Bones* (1971), part of a trilogy of plays responding to the war in Vietnam, is Durang's background text. A darkly twisted play that won numerous awards, including the Tony Award for Best Play when it was first produced, *Sticks and Bones* is about a family incapable of reconciling their comfortable middle-class lives with the moral indictment cast upon them by their son, a soldier returning from the Vietnam War. In order to make its point, Rabe's play uses the quintessential family TV drama *The Adventures of Ozzie and Harriet* as its parodic source text, incorporating the idealistic vision of family that appeared weekly in Americans' living rooms. In Rabe's play, David has been physically and mentally damaged by the war; he is blind, but enlightened to the atrocities perpetuated by American troops, and he attempts to share this knowledge with his family, but they ignore him, indulging instead in superficial, unreflective conversation. David is plagued by the ghost of a Vietnamese woman with whom he had a relationship, suggesting that he is deeply disturbed by experiences. His parents and younger brother refuse to accept this angry, war-traumatized member into their family, and instead they assist him to commit suicide at the play's end. When it was produced in 1972, Clive Barnes commented that the play was a "shattering indictment of that moral condition sometimes known as Middle America and its rising flood-tides of human conformity" (Barnes 1972, 23). In Durang's hands, however, Rabe's play becomes easy fodder for parodic playfulness, exaggerating both the darkly comic undertone and the American imperialist critique. Just like Rabe's play, Durang's *Vietnamization of New Jersey* offers an assault on American hypocrisy, but Durang goes further and questions the practice of using theatre as a propagandistic tool to awaken moral consciousness. In other words, he furthers Rabe's satire of American imperialism, but challenges the liberal self-righteousness implicit in such criticism.

The play's title derives from euphemistic term by Richard Nixon to describe the process of transferring power from American troops to the South Vietnamese. Nixon preferred the word "Vietnamization" to "de-Americanization" because of its focus on empowering the South Vietnamese, but the linguistic irony reveals the arrogance of giving a country back its own identity. Durang establishes an ironic tone from the start of his play. Opening with the wholesome image of the nuclear family gathered around the breakfast table, he signals an impending attack on the American family as the bedrock of societal values and stability. Following Rabe's decision to name his characters after the TV characters Ozzie and Harriet, Durang reverses the genders, calling the addle-brained mother Ozzie, the ineffectual father Harry, and their teenaged son Et. The tone is cartoon-light at first, with Ozzie making references to the *Jack Benny Show* when she quips, "I'm the worse housekeeper on the Eastern Seaboard. We'll have to pack our bags and move to Anaheim" (Durang 1997, 72). The morning routine is shaped by the debate between Harry and Ozzie, punctuated by the maid entering to ring a bell each time Ozzie scores a point. Hazel, the family's black maid, is an allusion to Thornton Wilder's savvy maid Sabina in the apocalyptic *The Skin of Our Teeth*, who manages the disorganized family. The younger brother proves a dark note, however; he is unlikeable in both versions. Rabe's original character, Rick, knocks his sibling unconscious with his guitar and encourages him to commit suicide. Et, the parodic counterpart, is an incorrigible pervert who pours cereal down his jeans and eats from unzipped pants. David, the returning hero, is blind, just as in Rabe's version. Rather than being haunted by an admonishing ghost, however, David brings home Liat, his Vietnamese fiancée, who is also blind. Et later has sexual relations with her, unbeknownst to the un-seeing David. In Rabe's play, the returning war vet disturbs the composure of his politically naive parents, yet withdraws from them, into his room and into himself. Durang's David, however, excoriates Ozzie and Harry about the horrors America has committed on the Vietnam people until they accept their complicity in the war. Deciding to inflict onto his family members the same pain and violence that Liat and other Vietnamese have suffered, David stages a reenactment of a village being bombed. The idea of not only determining but enacting a reparative equivalent for wartime atrocities is preposterous and points to Durang's larger message: liberal guilt-mongering in the wake of the Vietnam War is ineffectual. Hazel throws Minute Rice all over the floor to recreate a minefield, and Liat is given a gun that she fires without direction around the room, accidentally shooting David in the arm. Chaos ensues in the darkness; when the lights come back up, Et has his father's head in the fish tank, and Liat is riding Ozzie like a horse. David requires Ozzie and Harry to get on their hands and knees and kiss Liat's feet before they turn around so she can kick them both, a gesture of self-mortification that Durang reads into Rabe's play. Describing Durang as "a social satirist [and] a malicious caricaturist," Mel Gussow remarks how he "carries everyday scenes—a family around a breakfast table—to the most cataclysmic, even perverse, conclusion" (Gussow 1977b). The perverse conclusion in this case is Liat's revelation that she is neither blind nor Vietnamese but rather spent her childhood growing up in Schenectady, New York—an admission that undermines the burden of guilt that David carries. The heavy-handed fist of self-righteousness turns out to be an empty hand.

Act 2 begins with dispossession; the family loses both their home and their breadwinner during the economic downturn when Harry commits suicide after losing his job. The family's suburban lifestyle is proven to be a sham, and the stage is denuded of all appliances and decor, with various appliances, such as the refrigerator connected via long extension cords trailing offstage. Durang owes credit for this meta-theatrical device of a bare stage to Wilder's *The Skin of Our Teeth* (1942), where the absence of scenery in Act 3 highlights the destruction following a major war, but also points to the artificiality behind their values and practices. As the family is unable to pay for Harry's burial, his body is stuffed into a Hefty garbage bag to be picked up by the garbage truck, further pointing to the moral bankruptcy of their lives. The family's economic fortunes are transformed by the arrival of Uncle Larry, played by the same actor as Harry, a clever piece of dual acting commended by several critics. Commanding, violent, hypermasculine, the Sergeant Larry drops from the sky with a silver-sparkled parachute, drawing a connection between the military-industrial complex and divine intervention. Larry exemplifies masculine prowess and competency; he purchases back their house and furnishings and demeans David's Buddhist robes as looking like "Barbra Streisand" (Durang 1997, 98). As the moving men return the walls and furniture to the stage, Larry's presence transforms the earlier traumatized, yet familial space of the home to one of even greater violence. Et is drawn to his aggressive demeanor and tries to get his attention by performances of masculinity—standing up straight, swearing profusely, and physically beating on David despite his disability. At the breakfast table, the family eats with forced politeness, fearful of Uncle Larry's anger, especially when he sexually demeans Liat and commands that she go-go dance at the table for the men's enjoyment. David, refusing to be present, is forcibly dragged onstage by Uncle Larry, who compels him to eat breakfast and starts to strangle him when he will not comply. Seemingly oblivious to the hostility, Ozzie attempts to reconcile her brood with the image of the happy family, just as Rabe's maternal character offers to cook meals for her sons as a way of preserving normalcy. When Larry calls David a "little jerk-off," Ozzie calmly requests that he say "ejaculating, or something" (104). Later, when the house is loaded with bear traps and barbed wire, David has gone into hiding, and Larry and Et stalk through the house with guns and knives to hunt for him, she invites Father McGillicutty to the home with the naive belief that he can direct a session of family counseling. Their efforts of familial harmony are undermined by David's screams of pain from his foot stuck in a bear-trap, Et pointing out "Father's a queer," and Larry repeatedly yelling "shut up, asshole!" at David (108). Durang reinforces Rabe's point about the painful homecoming

Vietnam Veterans received in the face of an obdurate American populace, yet he also provides the absurdist view, turning the domestic space into an outlandish combat zone.

Wilder's play *The Skin of Our Teeth* (1942) echoes allusively throughout *The Vietnamization of New Jersey*. George Antrobus, the family's father in the earlier play, opens a book that has survived the war and prays to God for guidance to begin their lives anew: "We've come a long ways. We've learned. We're learning. And the steps of our journey are marked for us here," he says, opening a book (248). The family's pessimistic servant Sabina, lacking in George Antrobus's confidence, complained sardonically about humans: "That's all we do—always beginning again! Over and over again. Always beginning again." Wilder offered a tempered optimism in the human race's ability to redeem itself, but Durang provides no such cheery hope for the future. Durang's play moves backward in time to indict the postwar era for creating a cultural fiction of America's indomitable spirit and for naively presenting that no past wrong cannot be undone. At a pivotal point in the play, Ozzie fakes resiliency when the family life is crumbling around her: she earnestly sings "I Ain't Down Yet" from the musical *Unsinkable Molly Brown* (1960) while moving men arrive to repossess the household furniture and while Et and Liat have sexual intercourse next to David's catatonic form. Molly Brown, who built her fortunes from nothing and survived even the Titanic's catastrophe, represents gumption and pluck. Unfortunately for Ozzie, she cannot remember the lyrics to her anthem, and thus mumbles the lyrics as the furniture—and her family's morality—disappears around her. Ozzie changes the onstage calendar from 1967 to 1971 and then to 1974 in a stubborn attempt to recreate their lives, to pretend the atrocities and political failure of Vietnam didn't happen, to turn a new page and live "in the land of Beginning Again" (88). Ozzie insists that they can move on with their lives and forget about Vietnam, but her reasoning sounds addle-brained: "I believe America is resilient. . . . If we fought on the wrong side, or whatnot—well, I say, that's behind us, let's get on with the business at hand" (87). In Ozzie's blithe encouragement, the postwar optimism appears nonsensical, yet so embedded in America's cultural mythology that it is difficult to uproot.

Durang examines America's spirited indoctrination through the performance of its public narratives. In 1976, the United States celebrated its bicentennial with nationwide celebrations, such as televised programs, museum exhibits, sport events, and school parades. Short clips about American history, known as "Bicentennial Minutes," were recounted by a famous American, and televised by CBS during its prime time programming.

A nationwide self-congratulatory PR campaign, sponsored by Shell, these "Bicentennial Minutes" were meant to instill patriotism through mini-history lessons. These speeches appear throughout the play, when, at key moments, the action stops and the character of Hazel breaks the fourth wall and shares with the audience a "Bicentennial Minute" which she recites incorrectly, as if she were a school child who hasn't quite absorbed the lesson, nor fully believed it. The comic incongruity between the United States celebrating its growth as a nation while withdrawing from Vietnam and smarting over Watergate and Nixon's resignation couldn't be greater. As the play goes on, the Bicentennial Minutes become more and more distracted and their meaning disintegrates; Hazel delivers a lampoon of the Declaration of Independence: "When in the course of human events it becomes necessary for one Thomas Jefferson to dissolve the political bands Glenn Miller, Benny Goodman." She then provides a twisted set of principles: that "all men are created evil, that they are endowed by their Creator with certain unavoidable blights," and lists these blights as "the Nixon years, the Johnson years, Mr. Wipple commercials" (111), the last referring to toilet paper advertisements. Larry insists that the family play-act Et's new play written for his social studies class, dramatizing another moment of stultifying celebratory nationalism: "We're going to perform it right here in the living room among the barbed wire and the ruined breakfast, because we've got to learn again why we're proud to be Americans" (112).

Finally, the play ends with an image of flawed patriotism; David, the war veteran, having poured gasoline over himself, sets himself aflame. Et and Larry watch the fireworks outside the window and note the comparatively similar shades of "red and blue and orange and purple" that David is turning. The country's foundational holiday of freedom and nation-building contrasts horridly with a man's act of self-immolation. Yet Hazel's apocalyptic speech reminds us of theatre's ineffectuality at solving the current American crisis despite what *Stick and Bones* tried to accomplish. She addresses the audience, parodying Charles Dickens's opening from *A Tale of Two Cities*: "It was the worst of times, it was the worst of times."

> There were Puerto Rican traveling companies of *Hello, Dolly*, and they would go from town to town, mugging the audience sometimes during the "So Long, Dearie" number. There were all-black productions of *Fiddler on the Roof*, and there were all-Jewish landlord productions of *To Be Young, Gifted and Black*; and after these performances the blacks and the landlords would meet in empty parking lots and rumble. (106)

The reference to ethnic groups performing musical numbers for which they are ill-suited appears to be an inside jab at Broadway's attempt to handle racial tension with musicals like *West Side Story* (1956), with depictions of balletic urban gangs wielding knives. Once again, Durang takes a potshot at the moralizing nature of theatre. His satire acknowledges the moral quagmire of the Vietnam War, but challenges the Rabe's intention to use theatre as a moral referendum.

Hazel also has the final lines of the play, as she rocks Ozzie Ann in her arms, and bemoans, "Oh, oh, oh, six o'clock and the master not home yet. Pray God . . ." signaling the lack of leadership in their world. Hazel is the play's strongest character, both as a character and as a theatrical role. Played by a male actor in both the original production at Yale Repertory Theater in 1977 under Robert Brustein's direction and the 2007 revival at the Alchemy Theater, NYC, she is the true source of power in the family: "Boss of the house. . . . She slams doors, interrupts conversations, sweeps dishes off the table, and runs everyone's life" (Gussow 1977b). Hazel follows a long line of witty black maids in Hollywood films and television played by Hattie McDaniel, Butterfly McQueen, Louise Beavers, and Amanda Randolph. As much as she is the stereotype of the tough-minded black maid, she has the authority and good sense to direct the family; only she can keep the delinquent Et in line, pulling out a kitchen knife when he takes out a switchblade to fight. She encapsulates the truth of David's despair: "It's American history of the past two-hundred years that's upsetting him. Killing the Indians, Manifest Destiny, the Monroe Doctrine . . ." (95). By incorporating this iconographic servant figure from all of American literature and film, Durang underscores white America's underlying need to have a maternal African American figure, bearing no rancor, to clean up the country's mess. In fact, it is Durang's ability to see such stereotypical patterns in American movies that will lead to his next work, a wide-ranging epic that encompasses the development of American dreams and beliefs into our national mythology, *A History of the American Film*.

A History of the American Film

While *The Idiots Karamazov* was Durang's tribute to—or travesty of— Western classical literature, his *A History of the American Film* is his humorous homage to the golden age of American cinema. The play had a successful staged reading at the O'Neill Playwrights Conference and opened up at three different regional theatres, before moving to New York. This musical encapsulates approximately sixty years of American cinema; it follows the trials of a young orphan, Loretta, from the early 1930s to the end of the twentieth century through the various filmic genres, from silent movies, to Screwball Comedies, to disaster films. The setting, costumes, and stage props of Act 1 are in black and white to recreate the early film era—even the orange juice, grapefruit, and the bananas on Carmen Miranda's hat are all gray. The sudden shift to full color at the end of the act recreates the marvel seen with the invention of Technicolor film in 1930s, and the rest of the musical showcases the perpetual love affair Americans have with their movies. Mel Gussow describes Durang's musical as "a significant act of film criticism as well as wise social commentary" (Gussow 1977c). The difference between Act 1 and Act 2 is not just the change in color, but in tone; the cinematographic heritage turns a critical eye on postwar America. Jack Kroll, writing about Durang's effect of telescoping so many stories together, believed that the musical demonstrated "how silly we are by showing us how silly are the movies we loved," but the cumulative effect is more perspicacious than this. More than mere pastiche, Durang's ploy of weaving together various film classics reveals the values and beliefs that define America's national character. Parody, as we have seen, can be a thoughtful critical response, a means of uncovering an element or aspect of the original text through hyperbole or repetition that had heretofore gone unnoticed. Paying homage to the creativity and inventiveness of American filmmakers over the twentieth century, Durang's love for the movies becomes clear. This love notwithstanding, combining sixty years of American cinematic creativity within a single evening makes a pointed statement about America's childlike fascination with the celluloid reflection of itself.

America, perhaps more than any other country in the world, has created an identity largely through cinematic narrative, most likely because America evolved into a world leader around the time film technology was developed as a form of mass entertainment. Marshall McLuhan, perhaps the first to understand the impact of technology on Americans, wrote that the medium itself shaped individual reception, that is, "the medium is the message." In *Understanding Media: The Extensions of Man*, he described how the content was secondary to the technology, and that the technology controlled how we understood the stories, often in ways invisible to the audience. Moving through a discussion of various technological developments such as the light bulb or the train, he argues that these developments shaped our concepts of space and time, as well as our relationships with people. The technology dictated "the scale and form of human association and action," and the moving picture in particular altered society's view of itself (1964, 9). The early cinema gave Americans a self-concept as a nation of upstarts with plucky resolve and passionate perseverance. Busby Berkeley choreographed well-timed extravaganzas of beauty, while films such as *Casablanca* portrayed American traits of stoicism and loyalty. Durang, an avid moviegoer, particularly during his depression at Harvard University when he used his nightly movie outings as an escape, was inspired by the Frank Borzage film *A Man's Castle* to write *A History of the American Film*. The play, a "one-of-a-kind Depression [era] romance" with Spencer Tracy and Loretta Young, spoke to Durang because of the innocence of the characters: "I realized watching the film that these two 1933 characters seemed to represent a very positive view Americans had about themselves as both innately good and innately resilient in the face of adversity" (Durang 1997, 118). Durang was intrigued by this shifting self-image of America over the years, from the portrayal of American goodness and optimism in the 1930s and 1940s, to the sense of self-doubt and ambivalence of the 1960s, as indicated with the 1967 popular film *The Graduate*, whose main character lacks conviction and aspiration. Durang wanted to show how movies were "a prism of national consciousness" through a specific deployment of repeated character types that exhibit earnestness and strength early in cinematic history but whose fortitude deteriorates significantly following the Second World War. The first half of the musical follows the optimism behind the "Boy-gets-girl, boy-loses-girl, boy-gets-girl again" spirited motif, while the second half demonstrates war's harmful effect on relationships and social connections. More significant than this transformation, however, is the contingent nature of identity; even as Durang documents the cinematic shifts through history, he shows how dependent the national identity is upon the movies to not merely document, but to dictate character.

What made movies unique at representing a national identity is their ability to present a gestalt of Americana. This self-image of a country on the go was increasingly important to Americans as the nation increased its own industrial development after the turn of the century. As McLuhan wrote,

> The movies, by sheer speeding up the mechanical, carried us from the world of sequence and connections into the world of creative

configuration and structure. The message of the movie medium is that of transition from lineal connections to configurations. When electric speed further takes over from mechanical movies sequences. . . . We return to the inclusive form of the icon. (1964, 12)

Movies establish a particular set of personality traits for each character, and these characters in turn fit into a network of interdependent types; this network of character types replicates itself in multiple film genres. The five leading roles in Durang's play are nothing if not iconic. Loretta Young's character, an unassuming, but noble character type who is "pure of heart," repeats itself throughout various American films. As he tells Mel Gussow in an interview, "I realized she could be everyone" (Gussow and Mitchell 1977). In other words, her particular characterization became a set type in the American imagination, which the movies fed by replicating this type, or archetype, from film to film. Stanley Kaufmann, in fact, resorts to Jungian terms to describe the musical, perceiving it as a "burlesque of things that Hollywood had implanted in the world's store of images." He draws attention to legendary moments, such as James Cagney shoving a grapefruit into Mae Clarke's face, and notes how *Casablanca*'s lines have infiltrated the American collective repertory (Kauffmann 1978). Durang's cast of archetypes consists of Loretta, Hollywood's innocent and trouble-ridden heroine who endures a plague of misfortunes. Following her is the romanticized gangster figure, Jimmy; the tough-talking dame or temptress, Bette; the sweet-natured, "aw shucks" good guy, Henry or "Hank"; and Eve, the warmhearted, wisecracking, jokey best friend who never gets her man. These character types reappear throughout many movie genres, from the shanty-town romance to the gangster film to screwball comedy to a Busby Berkeley musical, incorporating America's current political or social history in the background. "Each archetypal plot," writes Clive Barnes, "each typecast character—ingénue, best friend, tough guy, idealist—is woven into this crazy odyssey of movie-going" (Barnes 1977). The repetition of such stereotypes requires that the actors not only be adept at playing multiple roles but also skilled at imitating the well-known actors in these famous parts. So, for example, Jimmy as the quintessential tough guy evolves from James Cagney to Orson Welles, then from Humphrey Bogart to James Dean to Marlon Brando as America's ideals of strong masculinity shifts. Hank, earnest and easygoing, begins as Henry Fonda, Jimmy Stewart, and Gregory Peck, before a transformation into Anthony Perkins in

Psycho (1960). Durang castigates Hollywood's own racist assumption of minorities by having a black actor play all the ethnic minority roles, from John Prentice in *Guess Who's Coming to Dinner* (1967) to the detective in *They Call Me Mister Tibbs* 1970), to the leading characters in the Blaxploitation films of the 1970s *Shaft* (1971) and *Super-fly* (1972), until settling on the driver in *Driving Miss Daisy* (1989).

Americans have a particularly self-referential relationship with their movies, understanding their own lives and circumstances through the lenses of their cinematic stories. Durang emphasizes this reflective quality by making the characters hyperaware of being in a movie. The opening scene harkens to D. W. Griffith's silent film *Intolerance* with a figure resembling Lillian Gish rocking a cradle behind which is a title projected onto the screen: "Out of the cradle, endlessly rocking . . ." (Durang 2003, 130). This symbolic overture underscored by the quotation from Walt Whitman signals from the start that the musical comedy will be allusive and referential—a pastiche. When the woman, after giving her child to an orphanage, dies and ascends to heaven, she, God, and the Virgin Mary congregate and remain visible as an audience to the unfolding action. Their presence as omniscient overseers, coupled with onstage theatre seating for the other performers, signals the self-reflexive quality behind this piece. "Does art mirror life or vice versa?" Durang's musical seems to ask, before falling decidedly on the latter option. The young child Loretta, upon leaving the orphanage, goes to a silent movie. She watches a minstrel singer first lip-synch to a sound track, but then his voice rings out authentically. The movie is *The Jazz Singer* (1927), the first to offer synchronized sound; now, the era of motion pictures has begun. Loretta meets, falls in love with, and shacks up with a tough guy, prompting a romantic duet, "Shanty Town Romance." Complications inevitably ensue: Jimmy and his past lover, Bette, are members of the mafia, involved with bootlegging during prohibition with the mob; Jimmy abandons Loretta when she discovers she is pregnant; and, after a shoot-out with the police, Loretta is accused of the murder, which results in a jail sentence of twenty-five years. When the gangster film terminates with a large "The End" sign in cutout letters lowered from the flies, everyone freezes position as if the film had ended, but are surprised to discover that they must still continue performing. Each time Loretta's life is punctuated with a seeming sense of closure, "The End" sign appears over the characters' heads and the action stops, but the closure turns out to be artificial. Rather, Loretta must continue with the action by carrying into the next movie.

The plot does not cohere around any central storyline. Archetypes who manifest similar behavioral traits appear and reappear among the various film genres. The stories are patterned on the interdependent relationships between these figures over different historical periods. The characters advance through gangster films as well as the melodramatic courtroom dramas, with resolutions for the film's stories, but not for the characters. Loretta's life intertwines first with a Depression-era chain-gang escape film, then a screwball comedy when she is brought home as one of the items the socialites were required to obtain on the scavenger hunt. She finds herself, looking dispirited in her convict uniform, among the high-class Mortimer family, whose stock list of characters consists of a "colored" maid, the society matron who collects foreign artists, her "madcap heiress" daughter "hungry for a man," and the put-upon father. The mix-up between the two film genres is comic in itself, especially the frivolity of their concerns in the face of Loretta's dire prison escape. She shouts her rebuke: "I want it over. I HATE SCREWBALL COMEDIES" (149) and escapes with a fellow prisoner, Hank, to his family's farm in a dustbowl Depression-era film that parodies *The Grapes of Wrath*, the 1940 adaptation of John Steinbeck's novel of the same name. There they meet Ma and Pa Joad, battered, yet stoic, trying to decide how to bury the grandfather whose body they keep in an old tire. Loretta must return to jail, but her sentence is transmuted during a scene of Christmas pardons issued by the Governor. Although her story ends happily her archetype must continue on to the next stage of her life, and thus she lands a job in Hollywood. Loretta joins a production crew on the set of a Western, dances in Busby Berkeley music, and later wins an Academy Award for Best Actress for her portrayal of true-to-life problems: "An alcoholic ex-ingénue who must overcome polio" (185). The back-and-forth shifting between Loretta's real life and her "reel" life equates to the self-referential relationship Americans have with their movies, ascribing elements they see on the big screen to their lives.

The musical demonstrates the persistence of these American archetypes under various guises as they transform from film to film to reflect the changing social contexts. "The movies have reflected their times with a terrifying accuracy and have, as a result, become a special kind of social history, a history that reports facts but requires interpretation," Clive Barnes noted in his review of the piece (1977). The heart-of-gold tough guy, Jimmy, moves through several permutations, from criminal gangster to capitalist lawbreaker to heroic soldier to war entrepreneur depending on each era's definition of heroism. Jimmy, married to Bette, has helped his wife to achieve a lead in the opera *Tosca*, based on his success at aggressively running a media empire in the fashion of Orson Wells in *Citizen Kane*. Haunted by the loss of his love, however, he tracks Loretta down at the Club Intimate. She has changed markedly, though, from the naïve waif to a sultry alcoholic, her lounge act replete with provocative songs, such as "Euphemism for Sale." Although aware it's a mistake, Jimmy takes Loretta to the opera debut of his wife; Bette, alerted to Jimmy's changing affections, attacks Jimmy, shooting wildly at his opera box and dragging Loretta on the stage as her hostage. When it is announced that the Japanese have bombed Pearl Harbor, America declares war, and Jimmy decides to enlist in the army. A large American flag appears, whose light bulbs are first gray, then illuminated in red, white, and blue as the musical changes to the modern era. Shedding the costume and the demeanor of a financial tycoon, Jimmy becomes the war hero, off to enlist in the army; the patriotic musical number "Off-to-War" fixes this noble image of him, despite the revelation that both Bette and Loretta are pregnant with Jimmy's baby. After he returns from the war and discovers Loretta has married another man, Jimmy becomes Rick Blaine, the role Humphrey Bogart played in *Casablanca*. In Durang's adaptation, Rick Blaine experiences moral qualms not from killing a Nazi soldier, as in the original, but from dropping the atomic bomb on Hiroshima. Despite the changes in cinematic roles, the same masculine iconic type repeats itself over and over as revealed by the consistent attributes of rebelliousness, anger, tough-mindedness, and inner nobility. His development through a number of different situations while still maintaining the same inner character demonstrates American preoccupation with a particular heroic type. Later, when he plays both Marlon Brando and James Dean, the character traits persist, but are warped; he stumbles about drunkenly and accidentally breaks Loretta's Oscar, bemoaning his remorse over dropping the atomic bomb. "You don't understan'. I coulda been a contender, I coulda been somebody" (187), echoing lines from *On the Waterfront*. Through the figure of Jimmy one witnesses how the cinematic heroes of the Greatest Generation have been transformed into dark horses burdened by lack of fulfillment.

Durang's musical also demarcates the shifting American ethos from before and after the Second World War as charted in the movies. In a scene from a dust bowl–era film, Hank offers his family the inspirational speech taken directly from *The Grapes of Wrath*: "I'll be wherever ya look. Wherever there's a fight so hungry people can eat, I'll be there. Wherever there's a cop beating up a guy, I'll be there" (151). As the police arrive, they shoot Hank and arrest Loretta, but Ma tearfully yet stoically insists she will remain strong, "Cause We're the People. They can't wipe us out, they can't lick us" (152) to the tune of Pa's harmonica. Both lines speak of an American populist philosophy, a sentiment about collective power founded in the hardworking folk of the earth. When Mickey, exhibiting the boy-next-door earnestness of Mickey Rooney, gushes about the reasons behind war, his words are resplendent with democratic idealism: "It's so that little kid in Kansas can grow up on a farm and be President or Senator or dogcatcher or whatever he wants to be" (166). Most of all, the Busby Berkeley number with cavorting women dressed as different vegetables and singing "We're in a Salad" presents America's frivolous innocence. Yet beneath this blithe exterior lies shameful origins of racism, xenophobia, and the irrational fear of communism. As the characters fly off to war, the characteristic integrity that has defined these early films recedes in the face of questionable values. The butler discusses placing the Japanese tutor in an internment camp, offering a direct commentary about American fascist policies. In a later scene, Loretta, Bette, and Eve, now performing as the Andrew Sisters, sign their popular war song "Don't Sit Under the Apple Tree (With Anyone Else But Me)," except they change "apple tree" to "atom bomb" and in so doing change a song about the fidelity of lovers to an indictment of the horrific violence committed on Hiroshima and Nagasaki. And the typical joyful narrative of soldiers' returning home from the warfront is likewise undercut by the harsh realization that neither they nor their relationships will ever be the same; when Clara exclaims, "I've been promiscuous," her lover Mickey responds, "I have no hands (*Hold up his handless arms*)" (179–80), and they question whether their love can survive promiscuity and amputation.

Durang tracks how the movies grow unhappier in conjunction with America's own progressively darker view of itself. In the second act, a pointed commentary is made about the reframing of basic American ideals. Ma Joad has been called in front of the House on Un-American Activities Committee, reported by her son, because of her repeated phrase, "We're the people." The fact that she has stitched this populist phrase on a red pillow sampler is proof for the judge to decide that she has communist leanings and to order her execution: "If we don't execute you, the next thing we know you'll be needlepointing *state secrets* to the Communists" (188). The farcical nature of his judgment quickly turns macabre when she is led offstage and the electrifying sounds and the flash of orange lights signal her demise. It is a strikingly sad scene considering this woman who stoically survived the dust bowl period is being executed at the age of 102 for a completely inconsequential act. The keen contrast between her innocence and the ignorant fanaticism behind America's Red Scare reveals yet another moment when America lost its moral footing. The scene is particularly significant in a play about American cinema because Hollywood's anti-communist blacklisting ruined the careers of many people in the motion picture industry.

The cinematic stories continued to underscore the problems brewing in the postwar era, particularly emerging psychiatric problems. Alcoholism rose to public attention, as did other social problems such as divorce and adultery, as well as psychiatric diseases like a nervous breakdown and schizophrenia. Durang's humor, however, does not invite sympathy: the character of Bette asks aloud, "What's a psychiatrist?" as her facial tic worsens (181). These cinematic narratives follow the earlier motif of self-help and resilience from the Depression-era films, except that these inflicted women are now superhuman caricatures for overcoming unbelievable odds. At the Academy Awards, each nominated drama reflects an actual social problem during the postwar era, grotesquely exaggerated. Bette has been nominated for Best Actress as an "unhappily married woman still in love with her former husband" until she receives shock treatments; Eve stars in a movie about "an alcoholic spinster shamefully in love with a Catholic Priest" (185); Clara has been cast "as a dimwitted socialite who can't cope with her husband's losing his hands in the war"; and Loretta, who in real life is an alcoholic stricken with polio, has been nominated for a film in which she portrays "an alcoholic ex-ingenue who must overcome polio" (185). Each of the these fictive scenarios refers to actual ordeal-survival films in the American repertory, such as *The Snake Pit* (1948), a film about a woman institutionalized in a mental asylum; or *With a Song in My Heart* (1952), a film about coping with life after a crippling accident; or *I'll Cry Tomorrow* (1955), a biopic based on Lillian Roth's actual struggle with marital and alcoholic problems. Loretta wins the award for Best Actress, and as she struggles to walk to get her award, the applause is thundering; the audience's congratulatory fervor reflects their own morbid fascination with stories about women transcending disabling problems. The fact that the actresses' own plights mirror that of their fictive selves highlights how Hollywood acts as a mimetic tool for real-life struggles, but Durang's satire goes deeper than that. The audience's applause correlates more to the degree of the abjection rather than the quality of the acting, suggesting a sadistic appetite for others' misery. The radio and later TV show *Queen for a Day* (1945–64), a type of confessional game show, was also driven by audience approbation of suffering. Contestants, always female, would provide emotionally charged stories of financial distress and self-sacrifice, and would be selected as "Queen for the Day" by how much pity her tale received, as determined by the "Audience Applause Meter." Durang's depiction of the Academy Awards Ceremony highlights America's fascination with frank self-pity and tales of lives gone terribly wrong, a far cry from the pluck and moxie of earlier films.

By the end of the musical, the American identity as competent and honorable has been completely eroded; the four central characters experience split identities and existential doubt. The overall question seems to be "who are we as Americans?" As the characters sit in a movie theatre, watching a biblical epic, Bette suffers from identity displacement; she has played too many characters in her lifetime. She wears a white-blond wig to emulate Marilyn Monroe, but when she does speak, in a Southern accent, she does not know who she is impersonating: "I'm trying to sound like Kim Novak in *Picnic*. Actually she didn't talk that way. It's more like Marilyn Monroe in *Bus Stop*. Do you think I look like her? Maybe I'm Carroll Baker in *Baby Doll*" (190). She runs schizophrenically through a variety of other roles: Elizabeth Taylor in *Raintree County*, Joanne Woodward in *Three Faces of Eve* ("Hello. I'm Eve White. Hi there, I'm Eve Black . . ." [192]), Linda Blair in the *Exorcist*, Sigourney Weaver in *Alien*, Diane Keaton in *Annie Hall*, Jodie Foster playing *Nell*. With a nod to 1970s popular psychology, she concludes: "I'm not quite sure who I am. I'm working on it" (197). For her part, Loretta longs for the lost innocence she possessed in her shantytown romance when her dreams were about a "proper" married life with children, a bedroom with two beds in it, and the obligation to "always have to keep one foot on the floor," in reference to the Hays Code regulating moral behavior in the movies. Now, she wanders into the movie theatre and propositions men, desiring to commit adultery. When Jimmy finds her and insists she come home, the two recreate an argument between George and Martha in Edward Albee's *Who's Afraid of Virginia Woolf*, complete with "killing" their imaginary child, but rather than murder just one child, it's twelve, a reference to the musical *Cheaper by the Dozen*: Loretta: "Go ahead! I've killed Ernestine." Jimmy: "I've killed Joel and Maxine!" (195). Hank, who has turned into the psychotic killer from *Psycho*, also fosters multiple identities: "Ma ain't dead. Are you, Ma? (*Speaks in a falsetto voice for 'Ma.'*) No, son, I'm fine. We're the people. (*Normal voice*)" (191). The rapid-fire quotations from various films, the dissolution of defined character, and the polyphony of voices suggest America's confused identity in the 1970s when the country lacked clear direction and a collective identity.

The late 1970s in America were shaped by a lack of trust in government leadership as well as an inferiority complex following atrocities in the Vietnam War. There was a general sense that traditional values were threatened and that bedrock institutions had lost their principles. In other words, the moment was well suited for the kind of emotional compensation disaster movies could provide. Nick Roddick connects the spate of disaster movies that appeared in the 1970s to the human desire for a new world order, after learning from the mistakes of the past, and Durang's characters long to start anew. In the last scene of *A History of the American Film*, a series of disaster films are projected on the screen behind the characters: *A Towering Inferno* (1974), *Tidal Wave* (1973), and *Earthquake* (1974). These movies all follow the same formula of a harrowing apocalyptic incident that leads to a therapeutic reckoning. As the last disaster movie plays, a true earthquake occurs and the movie theatre collapses around the characters; the characters, though momentarily stunned, take stock and move toward a cathartic resolution to begin again. As Jimmy says, "You know, I feel better after the earthquake. Sometimes you have to knock everything down in order to get a perspective on things" (196). Jimmy urges the cast to start a new race of people with the very traits that have defined them as a nation: to Bette he assigns nobility of spirit, to Hank, good-heartedness, and to himself, craftiness and resilience. He leads the chorus in song, locating in movies the specific traits that define American greatness: the spiritual values Spencer Tracy shares in *Boys Town*, the idealism associated with James Stewart in *Mr. Smith Goes to Washington*, and the racial tolerance behind Gregory Peck in *To Kill a Mockingbird*. However, the characters around him falter without the celluloid projections of themselves. Even as the chorus joins Jimmy in singing the "Search for Wisdom" song, they grow musically unaligned. Jimmy loses his ability to lead and instead lags behind the chorus, identifying the particular character traits a beat after the chorus has sung the line. The reality is that the past cannot be forgotten or edited out of history; earlier harms like the Japanese internment camps or the HUAAC have to be acknowledged, but the spirited singing of the chorus precludes them from accepting the ugly truths about America's wrongdoings. Furthermore, the exuberance is short-lived; as Loretta and Jimmy start to lead the chorus out of the movie theatre to begin a new life freed from the restrictive patterns of cinema narrative, the movie projector comes on and all the characters, despite Loretta's protests, mindlessly turn to the screen. Alvin Kernan points out in the *Cankered Muse* (1959) how a common convention in satire is to present a crowded canvas, wherein the victim stands in the midst of a turbulent mob alone in triumph or defeat, and Loretta is the perfect example of this device. In this final scene she stands among the insensate characters who sit mesmerized before the screen, willful in seeing myths about themselves. Reminiscent of the people chained to the wall in Plato's parable of the cave, these characters only understand a reality dictated to them by Hollywood. The determination and motivation they sing about are empty vows, as they lack the courage to forge their characters and personalities. The irony of this final musical number is in positing America's pioneering and independent spirit, only to witness the characters' escapist behavior of laziness, conformity, and passivity.

Although he satirizes Americans' relationship with their movies in *A History of the American Film*, Durang never adopts a negative ethos; he treats the usual fare of Hollywood moviemaking—the happy families, heterosexual romances, masculine loyalty, individual freedom, and rewards of honest labor—with joyful irreverence and even a nostalgic delight. It is only in the evening's accumulation of corresponding character types that Durang's commentary about the country's obstinate self-idolatry becomes obvious. Linda Hutcheon, referring to Woody Allen's parodic film *Play It Again, Sam* (1972), explains the American desire to emulate their heroes: "What is parodied [in Allen's film] is Hollywood's aesthetic tradition of allowing only a certain kind of mythologizing in film; what is satirized is our need for such heroicization" (2000, 26). Hutcheon's distinction is illuminating because it shows the satire behind Durang's playful parodies: his play criticizes how Americans need to fill themselves up with fabricated images of themselves. What began as entertainment turned into a recursive need for role models to emulate.

Mrs. Bob Cratchit's Wild Christmas Binge

Every Christmas, countless theatres around the United States stage versions of *A Christmas Carol*, a perennial holiday favorite despite its being set in England in the mid-nineteenth century. The story of Ebenezer Scrooge and his moral conversion, prompted by three spectral visitors who haunt him on Christmas Eve, represents the spirit of Christmas as embodied by ennobling suffering and unexpected generosity. When Pittsburg's

City Theatre commissioned Durang to write a Christmas play in 2002, Durang's response—*Mrs. Bob Cratchit's Wild Christmas Binge* (2006)—was a reimagining of the classical holiday tale as a satire on the values inherent within the American capitalist system. Instead of Scrooge turning over a new leaf and delivering gifts and a Christmas dinner to the Cratchit family, he and Mrs. Cratchit time travel into the twentieth century where their dispositions of selfishness and dishonesty reflect the status quo. Durang's play challenges the notion of redemptive goodness that American audiences associate with Christmas by spoofing one of the most cherished Christmas fables of all times, as well as giving a nod to other holiday classics that represent models of virtue, such as *It's a Wonderful Life*. By incorporating figures of American capitalist greed from the 1990s such as Kenneth Lay, Jeffrey Skilling, and Harry and Leona Helmsley, he makes a marked contrast between the idealized fictions people aspire to and to the real individuals Americans lionize. More than a yuletide mash-up, it is a pointed satire exposing the hypocrisy between the feel-good holiday narratives and the rapacious greed of corporate leaders, nestled into the capitalistic nature of Christmas itself.

Charles Dicken's *A Christmas Carol*, in which the hard-hearted Ebenezer Scrooge learns charity through the plight of a poor, disabled child, exists in popular imagination through numerous adaptations, from children's cartoons to the 1970 movie *Scrooge*, a musical with Albert Finney playing the eponymous role. As Paul Davis points out in "Retelling *A Christmas Carol*: Text and Culture-Text," *A Christmas Carol* has gone through countless iterations, and its iconic images, such as Tiny Tim riding on Bob Cratchit's shoulders, are etched into the public consciousness (Davis 1990). In composing this story, with its descriptions of food markets and festive dinners, carolers and Christmas trees, Dickens is often credited with giving the holiday its child-centric focus and its benevolent spirit of gift-giving. Moreover, he endowed the story with a sense of social justice which the British audiences appreciated, understanding the tale as a parable in beneficence in line with the original Nativity. Durang's satire does not attack Dicken's tale itself, per se, but rather the yearly performances of the story that peddle a system of egalitarian values that society espouses, but does not practice. Parody, as Hutcheon reminds us, involves a structural superimposition of the old text into the new, and Durang's adaptation of *A Christmas Carol* relies upon audience familiarity with the backgrounded text. The blinkered nostalgia surrounding contemporary performances of the play fosters simplistic attitudes about class differences, such that suffering betters a person, or that the poor should show gratitude, or that displays of human plight prompt benevolence from the wealthy. In subverting the tale, Durang deflates these hypocritical notions.

His parody relies upon a variety of alienation techniques. Characters break the fourth wall in order to emphasize the sentimental manipulation of the original tale; at one point Tiny Tim remarks upon his existence: "Unless Mr. Scrooge reforms his personality and learns to value Christmas, I can tell I'm going to die" (135). Characters draw attention to differences between the contemporary moment and nineteenth-century England. Scrooge addresses the ghost's African American racial identity, noting the absence of "Negro" people in 1840 London, while she, in turn, diagnoses Scrooge's tendency to mutter "bah humbug" as "seasonal Tourette's syndrome," admitting that such a condition did not exist back in 1843 (73). The anachronistic differences drive home the point that audiences cannot be nostalgic for an era for which they have no lived experience. In an aside to the audience, the Ghost threatens to beat up the badly behaved child actors backstage, but then acknowledges the audience's moral position against corporal violence: "But all you politically correct types don't like that" (74). The opening musical number, derived from the movie's initial sequence, involves the chorus singing "We Love Christmas," while pointing to imaginary holiday foodstuffs and gifts in fake merriment. By recreating the hackneyed gestures from community productions of *A Christmas Carol* and underscoring the corniness with such lyrics as "They come to town / They point at things" (76), the chorus reminds audiences of the original play's sentimental nature. Durang's play overlaid onto the original, what Hutcheon refers to as a "bitextual synthesis," reminds audiences that the yearly retellings of *A Christmas Carol* promote such a far-fetched belief in human goodwill that it obviates any need for social change.

The key allusion Durang superimposes onto his Christmas spoof is the Enron Corporation scandal, which occurred in 2001. As in the original Dickens tale, two men appear to ask Scrooge for a charitable donation, but instead of requesting donations for the poor in prisons and workhouses, these characters introduce themselves as Kenneth Lay and Jeffrey Skilling, who were two leading executives from Enron.[2] Enron's scandal represented greedy, dishonest executives, corporate ties to political administrations, and a lack of social responsibility—in other words, the kind of get-rich-quick scheme that many Americans tend to admire within the competitive framework of free-market capitalism. Scrooge upon hearing Lay and Skilling's plan to sell "energy units" to poor people, declare bankruptcy, and retire as millionaires is duly impressed and decides not only to join their team but to pay his employee, Bob Cratchit, in energy units and reduce his salary by half. Durang's allusion to this scandal seems a perversion of the Dickensian tale with its quaint notion of giving to the poor, but that contradiction is exactly Durang's point. The American financial industry's ability to finance political campaigns has retarded any fair distribution of wealth for the public good. While the free-market system seems impartial, in actuality, it is an affront to the country's democratic values of equal opportunities for all, and *Mrs. Bob Cratchit's Wild Christmas Binge* casts aspersions on sentimentalized tales that keep democratic values alive in fiction, despite actual practice.

Dickens's stingy, mean-spirited character of Scrooge would be at home in the United States' free-market economy, and thus Durang doesn't need to make any significant changes in his personality; his Scrooge never turns over a new leaf. Scrooge is particularly insensitive to scenes of others' suffering and refuses to accept responsibility for the Cratchit family's situation, even when the Ghost of Christmas Present asks him to empathize; Scrooge flatly states that Mr. Bob Cratchit shouldn't adopt homeless children he cannot afford to keep (97). The Ghost of Christmas Present invites Scrooge to witness selfless giving by traveling to Holland to watch a Dutch couple exchange gifts, O. Henry style, replicating his story "A Gift of the Magi." In the original tale, a husband and wife each sells a prized object in order to purchase for his or her spouse a Christmas gift; what they choose to purchase for the other is rendered useless by what they have chosen to give up: the wife cuts and sells her hair to buy her husband a chain for his watch, whereas the husband has sold his watch to purchase a comb for her lovely hair. However, unlike the characters in the Henry story who delight in their self-sacrificing love for each other, this couple decides to commit suicide because of the pointlessness of their gifts. The Ghost is irritated by the suicidal outcome ("I knew something was wrong when their names were Edvar and Hedvig" [110]), as well as the lesson Scrooge draws from this story, that "Christmas is stupid and makes us do stupid awful things" (110). As the play goes on, Ebenezer Scrooge proves more and more intractable. Visiting the Fezziwigs' Christmas party, the emphasis is not on joy, but on the excessive consumption associated with the season: "Be lively and frisky / You're gonna drink whiskey / . . . Get plastered and tipsy / And dance like a gipsy" (102), and Scrooge disgustedly watches Mr. Fezziwig collapse from a heart attack. Their ghostly stopover at the impoverished Cratchit house fails to alter Scrooge's disposition. As the Cratchit family begins to eat their Christmas meal, the extreme suffering makes the scene ridiculous. The swan that one child has caught and cooked is so overdone it is inedible; Little Nell, a character borrowed from another Dickens's classic, *Oliver Twist*, chokes on a nettle she has eaten out of hunger; and Tiny Tim begins to cough from consumption. Scrooge shows disdain rather than remorse; "Oh God, am I going to have to watch these pathetic children's death scenes?" he states as the Ghost tries to elicit Scrooge's sympathy from these scenes of stoic suffering. All the wrong notes are struck and the Dickensian message of compassion for one's fellow humans comes across as hollow and contrived.

Moreover, as indicated by the play's title, the star is no longer Scrooge, but Mrs. Bob Cratchit, who rebels against her subordinated identity as the long-suffering wife. During the opening musical number, Mrs. Bob Cratchit does not revel in the same Christmas cheer as the others do; the stage directions indicate, "*like her clothes, her nerves are threadbare*" (79). Back at home she reveals herself to be a suicidal depressive, overwhelmed with the number of children she is expected to care for. Not only do two children at her feet cry to be fed but there are twenty more children in the root cellar who are also starving. While in the traditional version she is a mild-mannered, solicitous mother, in Durang's musical she is openly exasperated with her condition and cruelly admonishes her children: "All children want to do is eat, it's disgusting. (*screams at them*) WHEN YOUR FATHER FINALLY MAKES SOME MONEY, THEN YOU'LL EAT! AND NOT A MINUTE BEFORE!" (91). Her sarcasm undercuts all attempts at sympathy for the family's health problems; as Tiny Tim hobbles in, carrying his crutch and announcing that he only fell twenty-four times, Mrs. Bob Cratchit yells, "Why won't you use your crutch, you stupid child?" (92). Her husband, Mr. Bob Cratchit, exemplifies noble suffering and shares how his fellow townspeople admire him for taking in foundlings, but Mrs. Bob Cratchit will have none of it: "I've had enough," she says, "wallowing in consumption, poverty, no food, no money, this isn't what I signed up for!" (136). When Mr. Cratchit brings in yet another orphaned child and announces a reduction in his already-low salary, Mrs. Cratchit has a breakdown; she escapes to the local pub, gets intoxicated, and throws herself off London bridge, only to be rescued by the Ghost, who returns her home, against her wishes. More and more she acts and speaks as if she is caught in the wrong play; she yells at her family: "Children, I've been out drinking and trying to drown myself in the Thames—you think I have time to be cooking for you??? God, when will feminism be invented so people won't just assume I'll be cooking all the time, and be positive and pleasant. I wish this were 1977, then I'd be admired for my unpleasantness!" (122). Even though the scenes of disappointment and distress at the Cratchit home are played for bathos, they have the opposite effect on Scrooge. The Ghost expects their suffering to rouse Scrooge's fine sentiments, and asks him, as they watch the scene unobserved, "Isn't this a sad family? Do you feel sorry for them?" Instead, the Ghost discovers that Scrooge admires Mrs. Bob Cratchit's brazen refusal to accept her impoverished status.

The stimulating of correct emotions based on watching the actions of others has a history in theatre, specifically in the eighteenth-century sentimental theatre which was meant to educate audiences in correct emotional responses, such as pity and sorrow, in order to influence the public's appropriate moral decisions. Many Christmas movies today are eagerly watched each year specifically because they inspire a "feel-good" quality associated with the holiday, such as *The Bells of St. Mary's* (1945) or *Miracle on Thirty-Fourth Street* (1947), and Durang alludes to the use of such filmic representations because of their ability to inculcate in Americans a communitarian and compassionate image of themselves. When Mrs. Bob Cratchit leaves for the pub a second time, complaining, "It's a horrible life!" she ushers in an allusion to *It's a Wonderful Life* (1946), as well as its starring angel Clarence, the divine emissary who saves George Bailey from committing suicide by helping him to appreciate the influence his life has had on his family and the town of Bedford Falls. The message of *It's a Wonderful Life* is decidedly community-oriented; however, Clarence cannot inculcate in Mrs. Bob Cratchit the same benevolent spirit. Turning to another popular sentimental story, CBS's televised *Touched by an Angel* (1994), Clarence seeks assistance from two fellow angels. *Touched by an Angel*, a TV series that ran in the United States for nine years, provided earnest, tear-jerking stories of angels who helped people overcome their problems by directing them toward God; its larger point showed that divine intervention could solve social problems. The two angels who assist Clarence determine that Mrs. Cratchit and Ebenezer Scrooge are in the wrong century. Their "solution" is to transport them to a luxurious high-rise Manhattan apartment in 1977 where their capitalist values find a better fit.

In their new incarnation as the socialites Leona and Harry Helmsley, Mrs. Cratchit/Leona supervises hotels, and Scrooge/Harry buys her expensive jewelry. Harry delights in the mean-spiritedness of his wife, such as when she fires one of her maids for forgetting to dust underneath the floorboards, alluding to Leona Helmsley's reputation for being the "queen of mean." Throwing a tantrum, she yells at the maid, "Christmas means nothing to me. You're fired, get out, get out!" She adds, "You're one of the little people" (153), a direct reference to Leona Helmsley's comments that the wealthy don't pay taxes, "only the little people [do]." The final song which the entire cast sings encapsulates Durang's larger point of the paradoxical place the productions of *A Christmas Carol* hold in a capitalist world. Bob Cratchit and his new, nicer wife sing about hard work, altruism, and being happy despite their poverty, while Scrooge and Mrs. Bob Cratchit sing arrogantly about their wealth: "We're so happy 'cause we're rich / (*Mrs. Bob Cratchit*) I'm short-tempered, I'm a bitch / (*Scrooge*) Still I love that she's so mean / (*Mrs. Bob Cratchit*) And his money is quite green" (155). While the Ghost's own confusion by the story's ending may correspond to the audience's reaction, the contradictory verses are a testament to America's own incongruous image as a politically egalitarian society that considers extreme income inequality as a natural and justified outcome of societal progress.

Toby Zinman, writing a review of the play in revival, commented about her own disturbed response to the play's bleak message that "rich, mean people are in fact much happier than poor, noble people" (Zinman 2012), but this is not Durang's point. Zinman seemed to have missed the irony of two texts placed side by side. "Both irony and parody operate on two levels," Hutcheon notes, "a primary, surface, or foreground; and a secondary, implied, or backgrounded one.... The final meaning of irony or parody rests on the recognition of the superimposition of these levels. It is this doubleness of both form and pragmatic effect or ethos that makes parody an important mode of modern self-reflexivity in literature" (2000, 34). Durang's argument is that the yearly fascination with Dickens's tale as a representation of the Christmas spirit feeds our own complacency regarding class inequality. The play operates on the perverse premise that observing poor people expressing gratitude gives others a positive Christmas feeling—that is, either Scrooge watching the Cratchit family or audiences watching the play should be moved enough to undergo a moral transformation. This belief absolves American guilt over class differences because of the purported generosity of the wealthier classes to assuage the poor's needs. Durang uses parody as a discursive strategy to attack a neoliberal ideology that gave rise to companies such as Enron and figures like Leona Helmsley, and his strategy works because of a culturally accepted image of a just and charitable society as depicted in *A Christmas Carol*. As dark as the message may be, *Mrs. Cratchit's Wild Christmas Binge* stands as a liberating gesture against the hypocrisy of the Christmas season.

Adrift in Macao

One of Durang's last parodies is *Adrift in Macao* (Durang 2009a), set in 1952 in the Portuguese territory of China known for casino gambling and shady dealings. This ninety-minute spoof on the film noir genre and the "exotic adventure" movie is pure entertainment; it is a thin boy-on-the-lam-meets-girl plot, filled with deliberately clichéd lines, smoke-and-dagger shenanigans, and a Trenchcoat Chorus that sings backup. Lureena, a platinum blond American chanteuse who has been stiffed by her recent man, lands in Macao and gets a job as a nightclub singer. Out of money and connections, she is hired by Rick Shaw, the owner of the Surf 'n' Turf Nightclub and Gambling Casino. Rick Shaw is not named after Rick Blaine in *Casablanca*, but after a play on words "rick shaw," the two-wheeled passenger carts that Lureena hails to transport her to a hotel. In accepting the job as lounge singer, she replaces Corinna, the opium-addicted, "second-banana" dame, who is none too happy to leave. Although she is comically drug-addled most of the time, she wrangles musically with Lureena in a lively scene of dueling solos when both singers try to perform their songs simultaneously, interweaving "Mambo Malaysian" with "Pretty Moon over Macao." Both women also compete for the attention of Mitch, a gruff drifter who seems to care for no one and is prone to long, brooding monologues which he delivers into the lens of an imaginary camera. He has been framed for a crime he did not commit and searches for the real murderer, Mr. McGuffin, in order to clear his name back in the States. Rounding out the cast is Rick Shaw's sidekick, Tempura, so named because he was "battered by life." The jokes are silly, lighthearted, and entertaining, indicative of Durang's own love of 1940s romantic-adventure films. The comedic actors have fun imitating the film noir style, hiding their eyes under the wide brim of a fedora, for example, or striking provocative poses under street lamps, the smoke from their cigarettes catching the light.

The score composed by Peter Melnick was highly praised for its parodic quality as well. The music consisted of a "tuneful pastiche of jazz vamps, saxophone squeals, and swingy close harmony" (Garvin 2007), and the numbers evoked "period music from Kurt Weill to big bands" (Isherwood 2007). Because of this reliance upon lyricism, melodies, and dancing to advance the narrative, *Adrift in Macao* cannot be fully discussed here, without access to the music, because the book and music are so fully integrated. For example, the opening prologue is a dumb show of film noir references set to atmospheric music: passengers in trench coats quickly debark, Rick Shaw surreptitiously hands off a Maltese Falcon, and a blond Barbara Stanwyck look-alike shoots her lover—all establishing the docks of Macao as an amoral locale. By the end of the musical, the audience is invited to sing along with the characters in a catchy tune, with large placards revealing the tongue-twisting lyrics of "Ticky Ticky Tocky Bangkok."

"Parody is a sophisticated genre," Linda Hutcheon argues, because of "the demands it makes on its practitioners and its interpreters" (2000, 33), but that is not the case in *Adrift in Macao*, where the audience is let in on the jokes. Characters pedantically explain to each other Alfred Hitchcock's use of a "MacGuffin" in his movies and make blatantly obvious allusions; large quotation marks seem to hover over each of their references. Lureena's opening song, "In a foreign city / In a slinky dress," acknowledges that most starlets in "exotic adventure" movies are in possession of stunning apparel designed more for cocktail parties than ease of travel. Allusions are not only verbal but visual as well, with actors appearing like famous black-and-white movie actors, such as Marlene Dietrich, or conveying the world-weary machismo of Humphrey Bogart. Moreover, the musical abounds in meta-theatrical references, drawing attention to the art of theatre. When Rick smirks "see you around" at Lureena, she nonchalantly responds, "Well, it's a small cast" (14). Later, Lureena refers to Mitch as "existential," but he disagrees: "No. I'm just a guy. Who's kind of hopeless and pursuing a pointless goal, knowing it won't work out but I gotta do it anyway," unintentionally matching her description. The actors openly address the musical convention taking recourse in song: "I mean, we saw a theme between us and we sang about it," offers Lureena. Even the unspoken rule that each character must have a song is observed when Rick Shaw sings about being denied his song: "They've given everyone a song / except for me. . . . I said to them, I am not amused / In this show I'm in, I am underused" (60). Rick Shaw's song is made all the funnier because it is not listed in the program (Stasio 2007). Finally, the prevalence of Asian stereotypes in

Western films is mocked; Tempura draws attention to how Westerners have typified the East as mysterious, repeatedly insisting "I'm very scrutable!" and periodically breaking out in gibberish: "A-koo, a-koo!" He has the last laugh at the end of the musical where he turns into yet another stereotype, this time a six-foot Irish man with red hair. Durang wrote *Adrift in Macao* as pure entertainment, meant to make people laugh, rather than a satire lambasting the problems in society.

In Durang's hands, parody serves as a useful tool for critiquing sanctimonious attitudes, although the outlandishness of his lampoons oftentimes belies his serious cultural critique. His frequent deployment of parody demonstrates how heavily literary history weighs upon his consciousness, either privately as seen in the existential dilemma facing the actor in "The Actor's Nightmare" (discussed in Chapter 3) or publicly, contributing to a flawed national mythology in *A History of the American Film*. In fact, his parodies reveal how the collective ideology is lodged within such cultural narratives, particularly the way in which the foundations of Western moral systems were shaped by stories. Much of America's identity and shared values are housed in the stories the country tells about itself; parody provides Durang with the perfect device not only to subvert the highbrow placement of literary or artistic work itself but to critique perpetuated, nationalist beliefs about America.. Retelling the stories that constitute the American self-narrative, he skewers these tales and reveals how these fictions hide a malfunctioning American psyche. He reminds his audiences of their shared, collective myths before his comedic scalpel begins to dissect these sacred cows.

CHAPTER 2
SEEKING IS BELIEVING

Durang's sensibility as a lapsed Catholic has shaped his plays. The old adage "once a Catholic, always a Catholic" applies in his case, in the literal and figurative sense. Literally, the phrase describes how a baptized Catholic, unless excommunicated, never really leaves the church because of the indelible mark Baptism places upon the soul. "A lapsed Catholic is simply another way of being Catholic," Richard John Neuhaus, a Roman Catholic priest, explains: "Catholic is a communal and sacramental given, not a choice. In sociological jargon, it is an ascribed and not an elected identity. You cannot get away from it; at least not easily, and maybe not at all" (Neuhaus 2006, 10). Figuratively, Durang did not fully escape from Catholicism, for he retains a cultural Catholicism that shapes the way he thinks. His frustration with Catholicism and organized religion can be traced through his works, particularly in his attacks against hierarchical institutions and dogmatic perspectives. As he expresses, "Even though I would not define myself as a believer anymore, I was, before I quite stopped believing, a serious Christian. During the Vietnam War, I felt that Christ actually meant for us to be pacifists. . . . I still have a lot of those beliefs. I just don't base them on the divinity of Christ anymore" (Durang and Wasserstein 1996). He ceased to be Catholic while speaking to a nun regarding the Vietnam War; she still felt hope despite the calamity of Vietnam War, and he realized he did not possess that confidence.

Durang stopped practicing Catholicism while at Harvard, but the early influences run strong, and his reactionary stance against such a monolith of institutional power is indicative of a lapsed Catholic playwright. Such "cradle Catholics," that is, baptized as babies, have internalized practices and beliefs that they work hard to expurgate as adults. As Neuhaus writes,

> Catholics of a certain age—those who can speak from personal experience about "the pre-Vatican II Church"—have tales beyond numbering of real or imagined instances of oppression, hypocrisy, pious pettiness, and intolerable constraints. Not surprisingly, in the

> company of such cradle Catholics, it is a mark of sophistication to have transcended "the Catholic ghetto." Dissent from official teachings—typically from teachings that do not sit well with the surrounding culture, and most typically from teachings touching on sexuality—is taken to be a mark of having grown up. (2006, 12–13)

Durang's maturation as a playwright or his "mark of having grown up" is reflected in his plays, which question many of the church's conservative and sexist teachings. The church is against the use of birth control, against homosexuality, and against the ordination of women; the church also insists that its priests and nuns be celibate. Authority of the church is absolute; the church is not a democracy but is constituted by the sovereign will of Christ. Even the emphasis on individual culpability is extended so far as to imply that the agony of Christ is the personal responsibility of Catholics. Durang's plays reflect an attack on such doctrinaire beliefs, whether it be a direct satire against religion or against irresponsible authoritarianism.

Although his plays are critical of ecclesiastic authority, there is still a theological longing for a replacement of Christianity, which appears mostly in his later plays: *Laughing Wild* and *Miss Witherspoon*. Robert Brustein writes: "Underlying Durang's sometimes vitriolic satire lies a painful religious apostasy. Reared as a pious Roman Catholic Durang gradually learned that God often doesn't answer prayers. . . . As a result of this discovery Durang's early Christian piety eventually gave way to a profound disenchantment, his lost innocence pushed aside by a lacerating sense of the absurd" (Brustein 2015). His own "will to hope" even in the face of despair is born from his early upbringing in the Catholic Church and the learned practice in prayer and the belief in miracles; the rejection of this results in the anger of his early plays. Nicolas Martin, who won an Obie for directing the New York production of *Betty's Summer Vacation*, attributes the sense of disappointment in Durang's pieces to his religious formation: "Chris's belief that life really ought to be better than it is" is obvious in many of his works. "He's very Irish Catholic and that moralism" distinguishes Durang's dramadies from those of "slash-and-burn satirists" (Dezell 2001). The education Durang received at Delbarton, led by Benedictine priests, encouraged a form of existentialist questioning; he remembers reading under their tutelage *The Myth of Sisyphus* (1942), Albert Camus's philosophical essay about human response to an absurd world. Durang writes as someone who originally conceived of the world as a well-ordered place and then woke one day to realize that this sense of order was lost. This early Christian formation prompts the existentialist determination of his later plays, as characters make choices to pass beyond the void and engage in a spiritual transformation. Later plays, such as *Laughing Wild* and *Miss Witherspoon*, show characters searching for meaning in a world seemingly adrift, in sharp contrast to the earlier plays that feel madly liberated with the upheaval of organized rules. In these plays, the absurdist theatre acts as an affirmation of life wherein characters believe they can transcend their situations. In this way, Durang's early and later works are merely two sides of the same philosophical coin: a mocking repudiation of the belief in God, and a search for some organizing schema to replace the previous plan.

The Nature and Purpose of the Universe

When Durang offered his challenge to Western literature, he went head-to-head with Doestoevsky's famous novel, *The Brothers Karamazov*; in his next play, in taking on God, Durang parodies the Book of Job. *The Nature and Purpose of the Universe* is Durang's attack on the Catholic Church's valorization of suffering. He modernizes the prominent biblical story where the righteous Job loses everything in order to test his faith. What Durang does is to illustrate the Catholic belief that suffering is required of Christians, and that it is part of God's plan. One is hard pressed to avoid stories of stonings, beatings, flayings, and crucifixions in the early church's history; medieval churches are filled with the depictions of saints holding the gruesome objects of their torture or severed body parts. Underlining this fascination with violence is the proof of their Christian fortitude and faith. The church's teachings direct Catholics to likewise accept their suffering as part of this stoic tradition, as an exemplum of their faith in Christ. In the "radio version" of *The Nature and Purpose of the Universe*,[1] an announcement at the beginning mentioned the names of several Catholic schools: "Our Lady of Perpetual Sorrow School," "Our Lady of Tears School for Boys," or "Our Lady of Agonizing Suffering." Although the last one is fictitious, these epithets for the Virgin Mary remind Catholics of the suffering she experienced as Jesus's mother, and instructs Christians that they are meant to suffer similarly. In *The Nature and Purpose of the Universe*, the religious figure, Sister Annie, directs Elaine to follow her duty unquestioningly because it is the "will of God": "You are supposed to suffer, you stupid, stupid woman!" (Durang 1995, 256), she says while slapping her. This plot, wherein a woman accepts her torture at the hands of others, has a corollary within the church's theological premises and artistic traditions. Durang's play, in questioning the nature and purpose of the universe, asks one of the most difficult questions: Why would a benevolent God want suffering?[2]

Durang structures *The Nature and Purpose of the Universe* as a parodic treatment of the Book of Job, a detail missed by some reviewers of the play. Richard Eder believed that Durang was making fun of mediated representation of the typical American family, writing, "His satiric eye is fixed on a movie or television screen or a book or a stage. Instead of life, he parodies representations of life, in this case, a soap opera" (1979). Eder's review, as well as those of the play's 1997 revival, did not mention the Book of Job (cf. Eder 1979, 15; Deffa 1997; Gluck 1997); absent is the Catholic worldview that forms the basis for Durang's attack. Ignoring that Durang's version derives its meaning from the Book of Job, as its backgrounded story, is to risk misunderstanding the play. As Linda Hutcheon reminds us, the final meaning of parody rests on the recognition of the doubleness of form (2000, 34). The Book of Job, one of the Wisdom books of the Bible, follows a story of unusual personal devastation in order to test one man's faith in God. Job, a pious and wealthy man, experiences a series of sudden, devastating misfortunes; he loses his entire livestock, along with his farmers, servants, and shepherds, and all of his children die in a sudden natural disaster. He next develops ulcers that cover his entire body, but rather than "curse God and die," Job shows steadfast faith in accepting both the good and bad fortunes from God. At the end, God rewards Job tenfold for his faith by reinstating his immense fortunes and his livestock, and giving him ten more children. This compensatory ending does not sit right with Durang, who concludes his tale of suffering without any justification for human pain.

Durang turns to the Book of Job because it emblematizes the ethos of redemptive suffering; it is a narrative structure disposed toward torment and sorrow. Contrary to more recent church teachings that advocate people follow their own "conscience of morality" (i.e., personal wisdom informed by the church's theology), in the 1940s and 1950s Durang grew up witnessing priests who were strict moral leaders and exercised dictatorial rigidity over people's souls. Durang shares a personal story illustrating how Catholic dogma constrains individual lives:

The impetus for [*The Nature and Purpose*] was the suffering of a friend of my mother's—a lovely woman, age twenty-five, who had five children and an alcoholic brute of a husband. She had asked the local parish priest, a nice and admirable man in most respects, if she could perhaps use birth control to protect herself in case her husband raped her in a drunken rage: the priest thought about it over dinner, then said no. The husband did force himself on her, and she had a sixth child. (1983, xii)

Durang's own personal experience with priests characterized them as strict, unfeeling moral leaders who taught a kind of masochistic acceptance of life's travails as a form of spiritual observance. When his parents divorced, for example, his grandmother told his mother: "Don't change your life. Christ suffered on the cross. This is your suffering" (Keating 1988). That the priests' stoic philosophy was passed on to their congregants who in turn passed it onto each other troubled Durang.

Naming his family the "Manns" indicates the allegorical nature of *The Nature and Purpose of the Universe*; they stand in for humankind. It would be understatement to call the Mann family dysfunctional; the family violence borders on sociopathic. Eleanor Mann, the wife and mother of three boys, suffers great emotional and physical pain throughout a play of thirteen scenes, one scene shy of the Stations of the Cross. Her life is an endless drudgery of housework and homemaking, but it is the emotional and physical battery that constitutes her Job-like agony; she is mercilessly beaten by her family members, belittled by neighbors, raped by a houseguest, and finally experiences the death of her most vulnerable son. No one comes to her aid. Steve Mann, her husband, constantly heaps indignity upon his wife; he tells her, "Really, you are the worse wife and mother I've ever seen. You deserve an amateur hysterectomy" (Durang 1995, 247). Donald Mann, her oldest son and a pimp and drug pusher, puts her in harm's way when he brings a client to the house who mistakes her for a prostitute and rapes her. Gary Mann, her gay middle son, also treats her with contempt. She devotes herself to her youngest son, Andy Mann, who has lost his penis in an accident involving a reaper. The family's Catholic background is revealed early when the husband reassures Eleanor that "God provides," even while reprimanding her as a "whore of Babylon" for protesting her sons' abusive natures. And just like Job, she is repeatedly sent various trials to test her faith, as acknowledged by the onstage narrator: the neighbor, Mrs. Ackerman, stabs Eleanor with a hypodermic; the school secretary blames Eleanor for her children's bad behavior; and the Census Reporter, who arrives at the house to collect data about the Mann family, concludes that Eleanor "leads a lousy life" (251), berates her for her lack of friends, personal attractiveness, housekeeping and parenting skills, and shouts: "WHY DO YOU CONTINUE LIVING, MRS. MANN? WHY DON'T YOU DO YOURSELF A FAVOR?" (252). Her mean-spirited comment echoes Job's wife's suggestion that he should "curse God, and die."

Eleanor's only reprieve is a visit by the Fuller Brush Man, a door-to-door salesman who speaks kindly to her about God's benevolence and promises an end to her suffering. The same man also plays the onstage narrator, Ronald, who narrates Eleanor's tragic life, relaying her predicament disinterestedly, but not unsympathetically. Ronald, dressed in a tuxedo and recounting the setting with an air of sentimentality ("The frost was on the pumpkin and a nip was in the air" [234]), undercuts the violence through his charm. He provides prescient explanations at the beginning of each scene, informing the audience of how God will send Eleanor trials through various agents. Such comments send a reassuring, though deceptive, message that God has a rational plan. Ronald himself, as an agent of God, appears as an angelic mediator who can advocate on Eleanor's behalf, or a trustworthy figure who bears witness to her suffering. The hope that Ronald/Fuller Brush Man provides Eleanor is one that audience in the theatre wishes to believe, too, based on the Book of Job's narrative pattern of suffering and redemption; after all, as one of Job's visitors reminds him, suffering is rendered for a purpose: edification; "with suffering, too, [God] corrects man on his sickbed, when his bones keep trembling with palsy" (Job 33:19). After another unnaturally cruel scene where Eleanor has been raped for three hours, her eldest son beats her and her husband slaps her for neglecting to make dinner and clean the house, Ronald's reassuring words come as a relief to both her and the audience. But Durang deliberately misleads the audience with the character of Ronald. It is all the more devastating to discover at the play's end that the Fuller Brush Man is not really an agent of God; he has deceived her and the audience into believing her suffering would lead to vindication. The plot takes a turn for the worse, when her husband, Steve, along with a radical nun in his parish kidnap the Pope on the Pope's visit to Weehawken, New Jersey. Because the two accidentally shoot and kill the Pope as well as the youngest son, Andy, the whole family must move to Iceland. Grieving over the death of her son, Eleanor hopes to end her life in a slaughterhouse, but God "saves" her for more suffering; the final lines of the play, as Eleanor comprehends that her anguish will continue, are her pleas for her killers to end her torment, screaming, "I don't want to live. Please kill me. Kill me!"

Grotesque comedy is an ideal choice for painting authoritarian harm, and the violence in this play is particularly sadistic in order to encapsulate Durang's satire on the Catholic Church. There is no better precedent in the theatre for the untrammeled power of authority figures than King Ubu by Alfred Jarry, a clownish figure who enacts horrific crimes in a primal, exaggerated, yet hilarious fashion, and Durang similarly capitalizes upon this eroticization of the pain that the powerful can inflict upon the weak. While the men in the Mann family constantly abuse Eleanor, at school, Andy, who has lost his penis and thus is both disabled and emasculated, suffers humiliation from the teachers. Summoned to school for a parent-teacher conference, Eleanor finds "*[the school secretary] at a desk, ripping up papers and/or shooting rubber bands into the air. Andy's shirt is off, and Coach Griffin is whipping him on the floor*" (240). The Coach insists that "no boy without a male organ" can participate in his gym class; later Andy is punished sadistically for an indiscretion by being forced to wear girls' clothing for a month and the nurse takes Andy's temperature rectally "in order to humiliate him" (252). Those in authority do not have any justification for their disciplinary methods; rather the scenes of sexual humiliation read as fetishistic release all the more sickening for abdication of responsibility toward children. Even those espousing to moral leadership are either dangerously infantile or ineffectual, such as Sister Annie de Maupassant, who throws glitter in the air to declare herself "the true and only Pope," or the Pope who idiotically sees the smog as "a symbol of evil in this world." As a writer of grotesque comedy, Durang wields the dramatic form to examine paradoxical thinking; tragedy presupposes a moral code with a responsible sense of leadership and law, whereas comedy presents the world as morally irresponsible and chaotic.

In an attempt to dismantle the Catholic valorization of suffering, Durang's black comedy illustrates the masochistic mentality constructed by accepting suffering as a necessary spiritual observance. The amount of physical violence inflicted on Eleanor cannot be overstated, even while it is framed as comic by its exaggerated quality and Durang indicates that the violence must be "generalized"—that is, the actress does not act as if she is physically harmed. Richard Eder in his *New York Times* review questions the use of violence based on his unsettling reaction:

> There is a suggestion of the distasteful.... It is not in the play's subject matter but in the nature of theatre itself. Like it or not, there are human beings on stage. Ellen Green [the actress who played Eleanor] is playing a totally burlesque mother, and the abuse she is constantly subjected to is often hilarious. And yet it becomes too much: The second or third time that she is reduced to weeping helplessly on the floor, it is a woman that we see, weeping helplessly on the floor—and to no purpose. (Eder 1979)

The sense of shocked sadness Eder speaks about in watching the performance is part of the experience of the grotesque. The comedic grotesque is, according to Wolfgang Kayser in *The Grotesque in Art and Literature* (1963), primarily a mode of reception, as Eder proves by his reaction as a form of alienation. It in an expression of our failure to orient ourselves in the physical universe, to laugh when we should feel distressed. Durang thus manipulates the audience members into an uneasy form of detachment in order to interrogate the harmful premise associated with Catholicism that admonishes people for avoiding their destined suffering. As Sister Annie proclaims, "Like some great spider, God weaves an immense web in which to trap us all and then in a fit of righteous rage, He eats us. The Eucharist at last finds its just and fitting revenge" (255).

Moreover, Durang constructs such exaggerated violence so that audiences will laugh at "how *preposterously* awful Eleanor's life is" (262; emphasis in the original); in other words, the play targets laughter at the absurd premise that a painful life is a warranted good. A short summary of the stage directions reveals the many acts of battery directed toward her: Donald "*hurls her to the ground*"; Donald "*kicks her*"; Steve "*kicks her*"; Donald "*hurls his mother to the ground*"; Donald "*pushes her slightly*"; Donald "*kicks her a little*"; Donald "*hurls her to the ground*"; Donald "*slaps her face lightly but continually*"; "*Steve pushes Donald away and gets on top of Eleanor, slapping her*"; Steve "*kicks her*"; Steve "*throws her to the ground*"; and Steve, Donald, Gary, and his boyfriend, Ralph, "*kick her lightly on the ground*"; at one point Steve tells his wife to kneel on the ground as punishment for her messy housekeeping skills and kicks her. The violence is constant, but burlesque. In the opening scene, when Donald yells at his mother for his missing hypodermic needle, he hurls her to the ground, calling her slut, slattern, trollop, and tramp, while the youngest son plaintively states, "We need more sugar, mom, for the cereal" (235). The exaggerated response to the loss of a needle, the antiquated terminology ("slattern and trollop"), and the youngest son's mundane request makes the violence stylized and farcical. The incongruity of Donald yelling "Can we have no peace in the morning? Is there no civilization left anywhere in this stupid house?" (236) while kicking over a table and hurling his mother to the ground signals a violence that is childishly perverse.

Humor theorists have argued that black humor may provide a form of relief; for the person telling the joke, there is a sense of mastering the horror of the situation. Durang felt an emotional release writing the play, almost as if the play were a response to the depression lifting. In his Author's Notes to the play, he describes the play "flying out of [him], with this enormous energy and glee" and that the experience of writing the play reversed his own feelings of hopelessness "about life and love and relationships and people's inability to find happiness." In writing the play, he no longer felt overwhelmed by his pessimism and in fact he found "the excess of suffering funny" (230–1). Creating a play wherein violence is inflicted upon a weak character served as personally cathartic for him regarding his family dynamic: "I saw people being horrible to one another, over and over and over. So, the sort of endless suffering that the housewife goes through in 'Nature and Purpose of the Universe' seemed gruesomely and gleefully too much. It felt like an exorcism, writing it" (McGill 1982). Michel Schweich, a psychoanalyst working with psychotic patients in France, when discussing the treatment of psychopathic rage notes how laughter signifies a development toward cure: "Laughter appears . . . at the moment that the subject in his aggressive encounter with the world . . . discovers and rediscovers an intermediary which allows him to render that aggressivity acceptable. . . . Laughter allows the patient to pass beyond an impossible aggressivity, a paralyzing anxiety, in an activity that is eminently pragmatic and joyful" (qtd. in Gutwirth 1993, 133). Short of calling Durang's creative laugher psychotic, there is a noteworthy connection between his release of his familial anger through black humor that results in abating his depression. Witnessing another's pain paradoxically provided him a critical distance from worrying about life's circumstances: "I found the energy and distance to relish the awfulness of it all. This 'relish' is something that audiences do not always feel comfortable with, and I find that some people, rather than simply disliking my work, are made furious by it" (1983, xii). The point behind many of his plays is not simply to depict suffering, but to get at the incongruous belief system behind suffering, particularly the practice of abjection inculcated by the Catholic Church.

Sister Mary Ignatius Explains It All for You

Humor, according to Freud, is the method by which the individual saves himself from feeling great pain caused by a terrible situation, either by deflection or mastery of the situation. In Freud's 1927 article "Humor," he identified the liberating component of humor as "the victorious assertion of the ego's invulnerability":

> The ego refused to be distressed by the provocations of reality, to let itself be compelled to suffer. It insists that it cannot be affected by the trauma of the external world; it shows, in fact, that such traumas are no more than occasions for it to gain pleasure. (1961, 162)

Durang, writing *Nature and Purpose of the Universe*, used humor to triumph over a damaging Catholic education and experienced the "peculiarly liberating and elevating effect" that humor can provide (1995, 162). Durang's one-act play *Sister Mary Ignatius Explains It All for You* (1979) is another attempt to liberate himself from his disappointment with his Catholic faith in the face of his mother's suffering and death from cancer. Watching the films of Frederico Fellini, Durang witnessed how a dramatist could make Catholicism a topical and intrinsic part of his storytelling. His intellectual disillusionment with Catholicism resulted in the humorous contradictions of Sister Mary, the nun who purports to "explain it all."

Sister Mary Ignatius Explains It All for You is Durang's watershed play, as it brought his work to national prominence when it won him—at the age of thirty-two—the Obie Award for Best Playwright (1980) and Elizabeth Franz an Obie for Best Actress. His play about a gun-toting nun who is revisited years later by her vengeful students had the longest New York run of any of his plays, allowing him the means to make a living full-time as a creative writer. Durang took his disillusionment with the Catholic Church and positioned it within an educational setting, casting the teacher-student paradigm as an abuse of power, as Eugène Ionesco did in *The Lesson*. Durang's play subjects Catholic education to a sharp critique and satirizes its authoritarian stance of presenting doctrinal teachings as if they were absolute truths. While he was growing up, Catholic theology was taught not as an interpretation of biblical writings, but as fact. Thus, he created the imperious Sister Mary Ignatius, who stands in front of the classroom and delivers information similar to what Durang heard in Catholic school from the ages of seven to thirteen. Sister Mary lectures to the audience as if they were her students, informing them about heaven, hell, and purgatory as if these places were real, and then breezily explains, "You can expect to be in purgatory for anywhere from 300 years to 700 billion years" (Durang 1995, 381). The specificity of the numbers humorously emphasizes the purported definiteness of the afterlife. The second half of the play turns dark when her former students hold Sister Mary responsible for their emotional and psychological pain and threaten to kill her. In defense, Sister Mary shoots two of her students with a pistol, a gesture which—although extreme—points to the significant harm the church has inflicted upon people's sense of self-worth.

The play relies upon the traditional teacher-student dynamic of an authority figure having power over the vulnerable and innocent (Hardin 1999). Breaking the fourth wall, Sister Mary lectures the audience about various topics of Catholic doctrine: mortal and venial sin, the Ten Commandments, birth control, abstinence, saints, prayers, and homosexuality ("the thing that makes Jesus puke"). She alternates her lecture by answering questions purportedly submitted by audience members, correcting their understanding of the Immaculate Conception, for example, as well as giving her opinions about "modern day Sodoms [such as] New York City, San Francisco, Amsterdam and Los Angeles" (389). When her young student Thomas appears, she catechizes him through a manipulative pedagogy, asking him questions and rewarding his answers with cookies. In other words, Thomas ingests dogma along with her treats. Her teachings grow suspect, both because of the errors Thomas makes and the contradictory quality of her information. When she asks Thomas to spell "ecumenical," he misspells it with a "k," yet she rewards him nonetheless. Questions such as "Who made you?" are innocent enough, but asking about the ninth commandment and rewarding Thomas's robotic reply that it "forbids all indecency in thought, word and deed, whether alone or with thy neighbor's wife" (384)[3] reveals a form of moral brainwashing. As she lectures on "mortal sin," as "the most serious kind of sin you can do," she lumps all kinds of actions together: "murder, sex outside of marriage, hijacking a plane, masturbation," implying that sexual inclinations are criminal activities. While equating the act of masturbation to hijacking a plane may seem an oversimplified rendering of Catholic morality, her list of grave offenses is, in actuality, technically correct.

The lecture moves out of Sister Mary's control when she reads aloud questions that expose paradoxes inherent within Catholic theology. Sister Mary's pronouncements come straight from the Baltimore Catechism, a Catholic school text in use for over seventy-five years. The question-and-answer format of the Catechism presumes a theological certainty regarding such matters as sin, the sacraments, and God's grace. However, when the church revised some of its beliefs with the Second Ecumenical Vatican Council in 1965, it revealed theology as a constructed body of knowledge, rather than divine truths—an actuality that Sister Mary cannot comprehend. For example, Vatican II eliminated certain practices, such as the prohibition against eating meat on Fridays, which was previously considered a mortal sin. Rather than be concerned by this revision of sin and its subsequent punishment, Sister Mary righteously claims that "people who would eat meat on Fridays back in the 50s tended to be the sort who would commit other mortal sins, . . . many of them are in hell for other sins" (388). She handles the theological theory of "limbo" in similar fashion; whereas early church fathers taught that the souls of unbaptized babies spent eternity in an intermediary state, contemporary Catholic thinkers have dismissed this concept. Sister Mary, struggling to understand such theological reversions, imagines a scenario where "unbaptized babies are sent straight to purgatory where, presumably, someone baptizes them and then they are sent on to heaven" (388). Because she cannot lose her own sense of security and acknowledge that theological authorities were ever wrong, she instead depicts the afterlife as a quality-control assembly line. But when she receives a question such as "If God is all powerful, why does He allow evil in the world?" (385), she merely skips over it. The doctrinal method of teaching theology demands a certain logical inconsistency that cannot be sustained pragmatically; the presence of evil and suffering in the world cannot be explained through her rote teaching methods.

Sister Mary soon finds herself challenged by the arrival of her former pupils. The visit is a therapeutic gesture for the students, for they wish to repudiate a figure from their childhood who maintains a monstrous presence over their conscious lives. They arrive dressed as actors for a Christmas pageant, Mary, Joseph, and the two halves of the camel, reverting to their earlier selves. Typically, children only perform the nativity, but this pageant involves both Christ's birth and crucifixion. Conflating the birth and death of Jesus into one pageant appears anarchistic; the moment they nail to the cross the baby doll that represented Jesus in the Nativity is especially grotesque, and Durang's stage directions highlight this fact: "*The cheery, happy expression of the blond-haired doll looks eerie and incongruous hanging on the cross.*" In the hands of adults, the scene "*seems disturbing and inappropriate*" (396), almost like an ecclesiastical ritual that has been profaned. After the costumes come off, the adults reveal the traumatic circumstances they have suffered due to Sister Mary's teachings. Aloysius has bladder problems because Sister Mary would not allow him to use the bathroom during class; Gary, although comfortable as a gay man, worries about his homosexuality in the eyes of the church; Philomena, who now has a child out of wedlock, recalls how Sister Mary physically punished her for not doing her homework; and Diane acknowledges that she has had two abortions. Sister Mary lambastes Philomena, Diane, and Gary as having committed mortal sins, but compliments Aloysius for having "turned out well" because he has a family. When Aloysius admits to being an alcoholic, contemplating suicide, and beating his wife, Sister Mary rationalizes his behavior, saying, "Within bounds, all those things are venial" (401).

Sister Mary's theological teachings come under more serious criticism when Diane questions God's involvement in her mother's terminal illness and her suffering for almost two years. Furthermore, Diane was raped on the day of her mother's funeral, a set of coincidental circumstances that she finds all the more outrageous in the face of the universe's silence. These horrible events led Diane to see the teachings of Sister Mary as suspect; the logical assurance in which Sister Mary taught theology was undermined by the "randomness" of the wicked events. "I became angry at myself," she explains, "and by extension at you, for ever having expected anything beyond randomness from the world" (406). Diane scrutinizes the seemingly rational perspective of God's actions in light of her mother's death, and she sums up her degree of frustration with the church's teachings. Catholicism, as taught by Sister Mary, offers no explanation for Diane's mother's intense pain and Diane's rape, even while it purports to offer causal explanations. Her real rage, as Frank Rich notes, "is aimed at God, whose silence to their suffering renders them more impotent than even the autocratic Sister Mary does" (Rich 1982a).

Satire exists to regulate those tendencies toward abuse of power, and *Sister Mary Ignatius* fulfills this task. In this comedy, the people do not win against the clergy. The students' method of humiliation, to return and point out to Sister Mary that her dogma can provide no explanation for rape, cancer, or alcoholism backfires; Sister Mary remains undaunted in her convictions. She reveals herself to be powerfully in control, first by shooting Diane and then by shooting Gary. Philomena runs away and Aloysius is left standing on the stage, in desperate need to relieve himself, with the young Thomas holding him at gunpoint. The Catholic Church remains standing, in the guise of the next generation, while around her are her victims: dead, or having fled, or in suspended discomfort. The ending of the play does not illustrate subversive comedy, but rather the Theatre of the Absurd's bleak acknowledgment of the priority of authoritarian rule. "If a satirist presents a clergyman," Northrop Frye writes about satire, "as a fool or a hypocrite, he is primarily attacking neither the man nor his church. The former is too petty and the latter carries him outside the range of satire. He is attacking an evil man protected by the prestige of an institution" (1944, 79). In light of Durang's large polemic against authority figures, Frye's point makes sense: Sister Mary is an emblem of oppression rather than an actual representative of the Catholic Church. As if concurring with Frye, Leonard Appling Troy sees the Religious Right as Durang's satirical object rather than the Catholic Church; he claims that "the absurd behavior of the title nun is misinterpreted as anti-Catholic rhetoric rather than as a metaphor for a larger socio-political critique of authoritarianism which supersedes orthodoxy" (2010, 12).

While this alternative political target is important to consider, it removes the singular contradictory wickedness of a character such as Sister Mary. Frank Rich termed her "the most chilling character in the Durang canon" (Rich 1982b). In performance, her particular insanity comes alive; Lawson describes the "quivering self-righteousness" of Elizabeth Franz's performance, while Rich comments on her gleeful accounts of violence done to others: "As she lectures her students on the 'physical torments' of hell, her voice quivers with self-contentment, her mouth curls heavenward in a self-righteous smile" (Rich 1981). Durang offers a glimpse into her upbringing as a product of Catholic hegemony: she was one of twenty-six children because of the Catholic Church's prohibition against birth control, and her father's welcoming drunk, homeless men into their home was in line with Christ's precepts of charity and love. For Jack Kroll, what makes the character particularly frightening is how "Sister Mary's belief is stronger in its visionary mania than the ravaged rationalisms that oppose it" (Kroll 1981). Sister Mary is a powerful figure precisely because she is a familiar *type*, a religious zealot, who manically holds to her convictions. She is a flesh-and-blood character with whom the students had a relationship, and not merely the symbol for an institution. Otherwise she would not have such a crippling psychological power over her students.

William Alfred, Durang's playwriting teacher at Harvard, once warned the young Durang he might make people mad, and the prediction remains strikingly prescient. It is hard to imagine what made Durang's play so controversial, appearing only a decade before musicals and plays like *Nunsense* (1985) and *Late Night Catechism* (1993), or movies like *Dogma* (1998). Moreover, when *Sister Mary Ignatius* first premiered, it was one of a handful of plays questioning the teachings of the Catholic Church, as noted by Reverend Robert E. Lauder in a letter to the *New York Times*.[4] Offended audience members walked out of performances of *Sister Mary Ignatius* in NYC, and the play was picketed by Catholic organizations during its 1981 Los Angeles run. Even his aunt, without having read the play, left a message on his answering machine, saying, "You have created a sacrilege. If you look up sacrilege in the dictionary, you will see that is what you have done" (Johann 2016, 107). Boycotts and protests grew during its regional tours, such as those in Detroit and Boston. In West Palm Beach, Florida, plans to produce the play were canceled by the Stage Company; the theatre's artistic director admitted, "We have chickened out due to a storm of threats, apprehensions, and untoward fears" (Mitgang 1983). The Nassau Community College's Theatre Department in New York produced the play in spite of pressure from the local chapter of the Catholic League for Religious and Civil Rights; the college's leadership permitted the performance to proceed in the name of academic freedom. The protest that drew the most attention involved a production put on by the St. Louis Theater Project Company in 1983. The local chapter of the Catholic League for Religious and Civil Rights requested that the group not produce the piece, and Archbishop John L. May joined in, branding the play a "vile diatribe against all things Catholic" in the *St. Louis Review*, the Archdiocesan weekly newspaper. The Anti-Defamation League of B'nai B'rith and the National Conference of Christians and Jews joined his denunciation, while the Missouri State Senate threatened to remove financial support from the Missouri Arts Council, who had helped finance the production. In the end, the $60,000 cut proposed was restored, but the Missouri Arts Council received a legislative "letter of warning" advising them against giving money to groups that discriminate against religious denominations.

As a product of the 1960s, Durang grew up in a spirit of open debate and was genuinely confused by the controversy regarding the play *Sister Mary Ignatius*. He was alarmed about the letter of warning the Missouri Arts Council received and what it could portend for future artists: "[The letter] puts quite a burden on the Missouri Arts Council. I still feel that it is intimidation" (Mitgang 1983). He considered the turmoil part of the conservative backlash against indecency in the arts that culminated in the reduction of funding to the National Endowment of the Arts in 1989, which he explored more in his play *Sex and Longing*. He explained his astonishment regarding the protests in an interview with the *LA Times*: "I didn't expect people to be so upset and I didn't expect anybody would get involved and say you shouldn't put it on. I honestly felt if you don't agree with someone you say, 'I don't agree with that,' but it's rare someone would try to stop it" (King 1990). Based on the protests, Durang got more involved in issues of censorship, such as joining PEN, an international writers' organization devoted to human rights and freedom of expression, and with the Freedom to Read Foundation, an organization that protects and supports the rights of libraries to provide controversial books and information to the public. As Durang mentioned a few years later, "My play attacks ideas taught by the conservative Church to me and to countless others. . . . If we are not allowed to criticize ideas, I don't know what the use of free speech is" (Durang 1985b).

Laughing Wild

Although the play *Laughing Wild* (1987) is not autobiographical, Durang notes that the play's thematic search for "meaning" is one he personally intuits. Growing up Catholic, he was taught about a paternalistic God with predestined plans for his life, and a team of guardian angels and saints to assist with these goals. When he became an atheist in college, he had to abandon this belief system, but had nothing in place to compensate. The New Age philosophy circulating at the time, a kind of "secular humanism married to a sense of magic" (1997, 378), directed people to turn inward and access the forgotten wisdom or intuition locked within themselves. Durang refers to the Narrator's quotation from Thornton Wilder's

Our Town, "Most people believe in their bones that something is eternal," as something that deeply resonated with him (Dezell 2005). Durang wrote *Laughing Wild* for himself and E. Katherine Kerr; they performed it together in New York in 1987, and he performed it again in 2005 at the Huntington Theater Company in Boston with Debra Monk. The male character, called Man, corresponded with his identity: a lapsed Catholic, looking for a faith-practice and finding it (with some reservations) in New Age philosophy, and openly avowing: "I'm starved for some meaning. . . . I'm tired of being an existentialist" (Durang 2003, 400). As a testament to the search for life's meaning, the play situates this search not in the reflective space of nature, but in an urban environment. Set in the busy, crowded metropolis of New York City in the 1980s, *Laughing Wild* holds the cityscape as responsible for the sense of modern alienation people feel. John Beer identifies urban angst as the key theme: "*Laughing Wild* depicts an anarchic New York tottering between depression and manic exhilaration" (Beer 2007). The calamitous event that begins the play is the chance encounter between the Woman and Man in the supermarket, when the Woman strikes the Man for impeding her ability to reach for a can of tuna fish. The psychological tensions that ensue from living in close proximity with others become the gist for their spiritual quest.

The play is structured as two alternating monologues by the Woman and Man, with a third act where the two characters enter one another's dreams. The monologue format serves as sanctioned self-analysis, which allows for a stream-of-conscious format. The Woman is certifiably insane, as indicated by her anger, her gestures of random violence, and her time spent in institutions. The Man is worried and depressed, but functioning; he has a job and seeks to empower himself through positive thinking. Their similar frustrations and anxieties about living in New York and their longings for connection suggest they are more alike than different. Durang seems to borrow a page from Freud's *Civilization and Its Discontents*, as the sum of their speeches consist of navigating a world despite the presence of others intent on creating obstacles and thwarting their desires—such as accessing a can of tuna fish in the grocery store. Unable to express her simple request, the Woman starts to cry out of frustration, then she hits the Man's head with her fist, knocking him to the ground, and yelling, "Would you kindly move, asshole!!!" (380). After describing the confrontation, she enumerates the list of her frustrations; she competes with others for a taxi cab; she fights with a cab driver who refuses to take her uptown; and she envies people who are happy, like the teenagers who come into the city from New Jersey. She ratchets up the level of animosity in each episode, threatening to kill a fellow grocery shopper for taking her cab, for example, even while simultaneously yearning to "recapture the feeling of liking to be alive" (418).

The Man, for his part, is a "normal" individual who suffers from anxiety. Dressed in gray, reciting new-age mantras, he shares with the audience secrets for positivity based on a recent workshop. Having participated in a New Age ceremony in Central Park known as the Harmonic Convergence, he relishes the connection he experienced with the crowd chanting "ohm," and seeks to recreate these feelings of community. Although he provides no direct attribution, his attitude of personal responsibility for his well-being can be traced to movements during the 1960s and 1970s such as Norman Vincent Peale's *The Power of Positive Thinking* (1952), or the Erhard Seminars Training (EST), a form of group therapy. However, as much as he promotes this practice, he struggles to reframe positively the interaction with the Woman he met in the tuna fish aisle, who punched his head for no apparent reason. He insists that humans can change their thinking patterns, yet moments later admits that he is unable to reframe the Chernobyl Nuclear Power Plant disaster, or the news story of a fourteen-year-old student who shot his substitute teacher, or other horrific world events; "I don't know how to cope with that" (394), he flatly states. Frank Rich sees both characters as struggling "to dispose of their underlying ontological rage—whether aimed at God, parents, or authority figures of church and state—so they can relieve their anxiety and resume living with some modicum of hope" (Rich 1987).

Rich is on the mark: in addition to the characters' search for spiritual meaning, the play targets authority figures, especially dictatorial individuals and groups who attempt to legislate public behavior. Ironically, Rich was one of the figures Durang wished to attack; in writing the play, he funneled his frustration toward Rich's bombastic theatre reviews in the *New York Times*. "Some days I want to kill Frank Rich," Durang writes in the play's afterwords. "He represents this Great Deaf Ear I must somehow get through to in order to reach a theatre-going public" (419). By satirizing other authority figures in the play, Durang attacks the monopolizing power that Rich possesses over the public's perception of a play and ultimately the play's commercial success. The Woman and Man offer harangues about authority figures whose elevated public positions give their opinions greater weight, even if these opinions are harmful or erroneous. The characters speak about specific people who determine the values and the opinions of society; the Woman resents Mother Teresa, whose 1979 Nobel Prize speech spoke out against abortion as the greatest evil of our time, Dr. Ruth Westheimer, a sex therapist known for her frank radio talk show, and Sally Jesse Raphael, a sensationalist TV talk show host for eighteen years; "Why does [Raphael] think she's interesting, or that we should listen to her? Why does she have all this self-confidence?" (384). The Man, as a homosexual, speaks about the legal and societal prohibitions against homosexuality, stressing how painful this disapproval is for him. He cites a 1986 Supreme Court ruling *Bowers v. Hardwick* that criminalized oral and anal sex between consenting adults in private, supporting the constitutionality of the Georgia sodomy law. He attributes this ruling to the Religious Right's conservative moral code and their biased construction of God; in humorous fashion, he imagines an anecdote about God using AIDS to punish homosexuals, drug addicts, hemophiliacs, and Haitians, "Anything beginning with the letter 'h'" (399). The Man mentions the Meese Report, the study issued under President Ronald Reagan to restrict the use and production of pornography, as another example of high-profile figures unjustifiably determining the moral behavior or curtailing the sexual desire of others. Much of the anger and anxiety the Woman and Man feel comes from feeling judged by others. While these political figures seem to represent the vox populi, in actuality they dominate the lives of others by their conservative and limited thinking.

In an attempt to escape from authoritative control, the Woman and Man become authority figures themselves in a surreal, fantastic dreamscape of Act 3. Essentially, the two characters enter into or appear in one another's dreams. They take on the role of their nemeses: the Woman, after killing Sally Jesse Raphael, becomes a talk show host, and the Man enters as the Infant of Prague, the ornate, iconic Catholic representation of the Christ Child. Each character replicates the dictatorial behavior of their namesake. The Woman speaks boldly about her strong political beliefs about nuclear proliferation and the ozone layer, sexual education encouraging the use of condoms, and the AIDS crisis. The Man, now the Infant of Prague, and looking like an "outsize, comical chess piece" (Oliver 1987) in his regal robes of gold and red, speaks pontifically on behalf of the Catholic Church. He absurdly mimics the conservative viewpoint of the Religious Right, pronouncing that sexual intercourse is only for procreation, that teenagers should repress their sexual urges until marriage, and that people who are at risk for AIDS should refrain from sex. The Infant of Prague, an iconic statute in Durang's house as a child, has lost its cultural significance. A seventeenth-century artistic rendering of Christ as a child, the statue is meant to show Christ's inner, princely beauty through the ornate clothing, but no one today is familiar with this figure, which is why Durang chose the figure. Thus this outdated, incomprehensible icon serves as the perfect purveyor for outdated, inappropriate doctrines, such as mandating sexual abstinence for teenagers. Replicating the play's initial confrontation over a can of tuna fish, the Woman unleashes her frustration with the Infant of Prague and knocks him over, releasing the frustration many feel toward the regulation of morality by impudent authority figures.

Humor plays a key role liberating oneself from the judgmental voice of society. The Man admits to needing a pleasurable belief system to sustain him through life, in ways that positive thinking or existentialism cannot. Although an "ad hoc existentialist," he realizes that he is hungry for some uplifting spirituality; "It's hard to be joyful when you're an existentialist," he admits. "Albert Camus was not a laugh riot" (400). On the other hand, the Woman has the ability to step outside of her own tragic situation and to perceive it as funny. When a street musician offers to help her out of the gutter, she instead requests him to play "Melancholy Baby," as an appropriate song for the moment. Separating herself from her pain, she finds her comment "oddly appropriate to the circumstance" (382) and makes an allusion to the line "laughing wild amid severest woe," a poem by Thomas Gray which Samuel Beckett also quotes in *Happy Days*. She draws a similarity between Winnie and herself as isolated individuals, either by the physical barrier of a mound of sand, or the emotional barrenness of the urban environment. While her wit sustains her, it is only by forming a connection with another can she remediate her feelings of loneliness.

The plea for empathy, to be understood by another, is repeatedly heard throughout the play. The Man asks for empathy with respect to his sexual orientation, yet he finds he must fight against his own unempathetic urges toward others. While participating at the Harmonic Convergence, a public ceremony for a new world order, he discovers that his judgmental nature is antipathetic to human connection. When participants in the ceremony began to voice their intentions for a new world order, the Man found himself irritated with the banality of their comments: "I just wanted instant transformation of the planet, and I didn't want to take potluck of listening to any strangers in the crowd say how we should go about it. . . . When you're judging people, you certainly don't feel a sense of unity, do you?" (402). Holding judgment in abeyance seems to be the key toward human connection, as the play illustrates. For example, the play's monologue format invites audience members to step into another's interior landscape, from the play's opening line, when the Woman indicates her desire to be understood by others: "I want to talk to you about life" (380). One critic notes his own discomfort in relating to the Woman's speech: "It's unsettling to find yourself agreeing with her about something, such as her attitude toward performers who bully the audience into singing along (she cites Diana Ross and Pearl Bailey), and then to hear her add: 'I want to see them killed.' Whoa" (Shirley 1989). Monologues as a genre require a sustained act of listening, as well as the capacity to reserve critique. In discussing the monologue's form of public address, Jennifer Beth Philips illustrates how the play "creates the possibilities for a brief, empathetic community to form" (Philips 2008, 215), and the audience does listen to both characters longer than they would listen to a typical stranger. In a final dreamscape scene, the Man's patience is put to the test as he tries to lead a fictitious crowd in Central Park in a shared chant of "ohm," while the Woman interrupts his attempts, by making car alarm noises and dancing outlandishly. Trying to meditate despite her cacophony, the Man finally screams at her to "SIT THE FUCK DOWN!" and her noisemaking stops. His quest for communion with other people has been thwarted precisely by another person, showing a basic paradox: humans make it difficult to connect with humanity. However, when the Woman begins to cry, he reaches out to her with a simple question: "What's the matter?" (417). Because of his gentle inquiry, she is able to express her pain and calm down. The Man leads the Woman and crowd, which has now become the audience, in a gentle exercise of collective, communal breathing. Breathing, like laughing, connects people to their bodies and to each other, emotionally, energetically, and without incurring judgment or beliefs.

Sex and Longing

After reflecting upon the censorship battle that occurred in St. Louis regarding *Sister Mary Ignatius*, Durang wrote the play *Sex and Longing* (1996), which premiered at the Cort Theater in New York City. Religion in America at the time was dominating public discussion, and its political role had grown considerably since the early 1980s when the Moral Majority was first formed. The Christian Right, comprised of mainly white fundamentalist Christians, was and still is a social movement that attempts to mobilize evangelical Protestants and other orthodox Christians into conservative political actions. Republican strategists drew upon these evangelical voters as core members of the party coalition and worked to ensure that favored candidates won party nominations. Becoming a faction of the Republican party, the Christian Right used its leverage to move the party's platform to the right on social policy, such as banning legal abortion, eliminating laws that protect gay rights, reducing the amount of sexually explicit material in the media, and promoting religion in public life, such as school prayer (Wilcox 2011). While the Moral Majority in the 1980s was seen as a relatively innocuous beginning to the modern-day Christian Right,[5] by the spring of 2000 the Republican-controlled Congress had given the Christian Right a few policy victories, such as The Defense of Marriage Act (DOMA), which allowed states to refuse to honor same-sex marriages performed in another state.

Among Western democracies, the United States is uniquely characterized by how significantly its politics is infiltrated by religious discourse. Durang considers the Christian Right's point of view on sexual morality as dangerous: "I do feel that the Christian-right viewpoint on, say, sex education, is hysterical, psychologically unbalanced, and harmful to people and causes death" (Durang and Wasserstein, 1996). Durang's play *Sex and Longing* speaks directly to the impact the Religious Right has on imposing a narrow morality on all Americans. The play satirizes how the members of the American Religious Right will stop at nothing to regulate the sexual desires of other people in society, and it dramatizes this tension as a conflict between a nymphomaniac and two right-wing Evangelicals, a minister and a Congressman's wife. Over the course of the three-act play, Lulu Dubois, the nymphomaniac, ends up as both a target and a martyr: she is attacked by a sexual predator, saved by the minister who in turn molests her, and is used as a cause célèbre for the Religious Right. The play was not a critical success and Durang refused to have it published, yet this chilling comedy illustrates the Religious Right's attempt to control and legislate the sexual desire of others.[6]

The main character, Lulu Dubois, is the physical embodiment of sexual hunger. Played by Sigourney Weaver in the original production, she stalks about the stage in lingerie, calling out, "Sex here! Anyone want sex? Sex! Sex! You there? Anyone?" or lolls about on her bed, moaning, "Sex and longing." It is not clear whether she is meant to be understood realistically or allegorically, as she bears names that symbolically connect her to other libidinous literary figures. Frank Wedekind created the prostitute named

Lulu, an early expressionist femme fatale, played in silent films by Louise Brooks, whose sexual attractiveness led many men to their downfall. It is telling that Wedekind considered this character "not a real person, but the personification of primitive sexuality." Her family name Dubois comes from Blanche Dubois, Tennessee Williams's Southern belle whose suspected history of earning a living by providing sexual favors forced her out of polite society. Durang's character of Lulu Dubois was a Washington socialite, known as Sadie Thompson, before turning to prostitution. This second name alludes to another literary prostitute, this time from W. Somerset Maugham's "Rain" (1921), a short story made into several movies and a musical, about the sexual frustration Sadie elicits from a missionary intent on redeeming her. Durang's Lulu Dubois thus symbolizes the libidinous drive that the conservative sector of society wants to control.

The exaggerated depiction of this character's sexual behavior makes her both comical and unrealistic; she complains that a recent group encounter with twelve to fourteen men left her feeling unsatisfied. Her gay roommate, Justin, commiserates with her need for constant sexual fulfillment, although he requires sexual intimacy at a lesser rate: only once every three hours, instead of every fifteen minutes. The two of them have collaboratively written a memoir, "Explicit Photographs of the Last 300 People We Slept With," perhaps an allusion to the 1990 National Endowment for the Arts controversy regarding public funding for the work of four sexually explicit artists. Lulu has very little character development; at times she appears to repress a threatening memory about her parents from her childhood, but the play never develops the psychological connection between her past trauma and current sexual proclivities, and offers no explanation for her extravagant libido. Critics have noted this lack of character detail as both a drawback and a component to understanding the symbolic nature of the play: "Her emptiness makes her the perfect target for madmen of all stripes," writes Greg Evans in *Variety*, "from a sadistic serial killer with a penchant for dismembering prostitutes to a sex-obsessed preacher so determined to clean up New York that he petitions the city fathers to pass a zoning ordinance against Lulu" (Evans 1996). Lulu is first and foremost an emblem of untoward sexual behavior that the Religious Right wants to tamp down.

The play's counterpart to her sexual obsession is found in the two religious conservative characters whose compulsion to control the sexual lives of others makes them join forces: Mrs. McCrae and the Reverend Davison. The prudish Mrs. McCrae, along with her husband, the right-wing senator, Harry McCrae, share children and political conservatism, but little else. She appreciates the political power he wields, and urges him to advocate for particular moral issues, such as compulsory prayer in school and the death penalty for anyone engaging in sex with a prostitute. Unbeknownst to her, her husband solicits the services of prostitutes, a blatant indication of the Religious Right's hypocrisy. Reverend Davidson, a character both ominous and prurient due to his own repressed sexual urges, first appears onstage praying to a large statute of the crucified Christ, suspended from the ceiling; his worship appears masochistic in the presence of the domineering crucifix. Mrs. McCrae and the Reverend Davis work together to organize a Senate Subcommittee against obscenity in the literary arts. They hold meetings to solidify their plans to amend the Constitution in order to "redefine America so it is based on Christian morality" (20). Mrs. McCrae pledges her husband's help with Reverend Davidson's mission, and she aligns herself firmly with his cause. Discussing illicit behavior in general, they focus on Lulu Dubois as one of Washington's "fallen" women, especially in light of the explicit memoir she has written. Consequently, a concrete step toward implementing their political agenda, they formulate a scheme to "save" Lulu and return her to her former identity as Sadie Thompson. They invite her to visit them, which she does reluctantly, wearing nothing but a large bed sheet wrapped about her body, sulking and slouching in her chair like a recalcitrant child. As one method of reforming her, they lecture her morally, with such lines as "Saint Paul teaches us that sex is bad," but she escapes from their clutches and returns to pursuing strangers on the streets for sex. A murderer enters from the shadows, and the comical atmosphere of the play turns threatening; Lulu is engulfed by repressed childhood memories of when she was physically menaced. "I'm not here, I'm not here," she screams as the knife-wielding attacker severs the muscles in her arms. The timing of the event, after her refusing to reform to the moral demands of Mrs. McCrae and the reverend, seems to indict her own risky sexual behavior for endangering her, made all the more so when the Reverend Davidson appears, shoots the attacker, and prays over Lulu's inert body, except he refers to her as Sadie Thompson.

While initially the reverend appears to be her savior, both he and Mrs. McCrae intend to redeem Lulu/Sadie and use her in order to advance their political agenda. The Reverend Davidson houses Sadie after her attack at his home, but his charity is suspect. He announces that he is "healing her soul" during her physical rehabilitation, but he is in actuality psychologically tormenting her: he throws away flowers sent by her former partners, and he prevents her friend Justin from visiting, making her feel abandoned by her friends, and he leads her to understand that her sexual promiscuity resulted in her current pain, referring to the attack as God's punishment or the "wages of sin." With the purported goal to redeem her soul through acquiring social graces, he and Mrs. McCrae host a tea party, wherein they expose even more of their own moral hypocrisy and frustration. The reverend's repressed sexual deviance is evident from his deep-seated anger; he snaps at Sadie when she protests their labeling her a prostitute, and when Mrs. McCrae talks about her children, he brusquely reprimands her, "Men are not expected to be interested in children." His description of the punishment for pedophiles is so vivid—"They should be castrated, put on a spit, and roasted over a fire"—that it points to his sadistic leanings. Mrs. McCrae, though appearing a society matron, reveals herself to be physically and psychologically abusive: she hits and humiliates her children to instill obedience. Two of her children "turned out beautifully. They cower when I enter the room," she remarks, and mentions having disowned her youngest child, because he is gay, a testament to her moral rigidity as a Christian rather than a parent's unconditional love. As an example of her children's absolute obedience, she describes their willingness to kill if she ordered them to. Not to be undone by Sadie's moralistic queries, she reassures her, "I wouldn't kill people unless God told me these people should be killed." In so saying, Mrs. McCrae reflects what Christian activists believe is their role: to protect America from loss of God's favor by acting like religious warriors. The conversation that transpires during the tea scene is rife with moral hypocrisy; as David Sheward writes, "One minute the trio are exchanging pleasantries about the weather, and the next they're debating which segment of society could justifiably be exterminated" (Sheward 1996). But Mrs. McCrae's double standards are lighthearted in comparison to the reverend's pretense; after Mrs. McCrae leaves his house, he molests Sadie. The image of a woman without the use of her arms being tormented by a man is horrific; furthermore, the words she again speaks to disassociate herself from the abuse—"pretend it's not happening, pretend you're not here"—implies a history of sexual abuse.

Act 2 turns burlesque in tone and demonstrates the abuse of power in the hands of the Religious Right. A congressional hearing is being held in order to amend the Constitution to allow for greater religious investment; Mrs. McCrae and the reverend present their arguments to amend the Constitution in order "to put America back on track." They specifically ask for three amendments: to abolish all abortions, to enforce public prayer, and to forbid sexual behavior outside of legal marriage, and they also include a provision to apply the death penalty to any men who seek prostitutes, a condition that worries Senator McCrae as he presides over the hearing. The congressional hearing, however, is a farcical circus: a large American flag flies in the background, but with a trick of a see-through scrim, the lights change to reveal Reverend Davison's crucifix superimposed upon the flag, symbolizing the conflation of the church and the state that the First Amendment explicitly denies. Mrs. McCrae cheerily disavows any unconstitutionality of the proceedings: "God should be in our thoughts; he is on our pennies." Moreover, the legislators are inflatable sex dolls that listen placidly to the speeches; they occasionally lose tumescence and must be propped upright—like marionettes—by ropes that are connected to a pulley system in the ceiling. The responsive movements of the legislators-as-blow-up-dolls make them appear to be controlled, literally, by the church as their ropes connecting them to the ceiling pass behind the crucifix-imposed flag. For his part, Senator McCrae is an immoral buffoon; he arrives late to the proceedings because of his drinking and adulterous affairs, and makes egregious Freudian slips revealing his own self-gratifying practices. At one point, he drunkenly wonders "what would Christ want," and the reverend brings Christ to testify upon the congressional floor. The preposterous gesture of Jesus Christ showing up as a key witness at a legislative hearing provides the perfect analogy to the Religious Right's habit to state God's opinion on contemporary matters as if it were factually available. The character of Jesus speaks in favor of capital punishment, an apparent contradiction in light of his own death, and advocates cutting the capital gains tax, which is at odds with his more charitable proposals in the Gospels. When questioned as a witness, he states he is against homosexuals, school lunches, and condom use by teens: "If teenagers are not willing to practice abstinence, then they deserve to die [from AIDS]," he unmercifully pronounces. As Lulu/Sadie pointedly comments, "This man isn't Jesus. He's a Republican."

While the proceedings begin humorously, the grotesque absurdity of totalitarian power in the hands of the Religious Right becomes clear. Reverend and Mrs. McCrae have subpoenaed individuals as evidence for their proposed amendments, such as Justin Stewart, Lulu's friend from the first scene. As part of his "testimony," Justin is strapped to an electric chair and electrocuted while being shown images of men, reminiscent of the aversion therapy that was done to the central character in *A Clockwork Orange* to stop his violence by associating a particular stimulus with pain;

however, this procedure is intended to stop Justin's homosexual urges. The second witness, Lulu-now-Sadie, described as a "modern day Mary Magdalene," testifies in front of Congress and talks about forgiveness and her sin of sexual compulsion. When she starts to describe what the reverend does to her at night, he chloroforms her. At the end of the hearing, Jesus takes off his clothing to reveal he is the same murderer who maimed Lulu earlier; having met the reverend at a Bordello, he was given information to find and kill her. Thus Durang's point, about how "the Christian-right viewpoint" is harmful to people and even causes death, is dramatically fulfilled: a man is electrocuted to rehabilitate his sexual desire by Christian representatives; Sadie is gagged when she tries to speak against her sexual abuser, a minister; and a Jesus imitator murders a woman confined to a wheelchair—all before the nation's highest political body. In the final scene her body transcends the material confines of the earth and she arrives in heaven. As a ghost, Sadie visits Justin to tell him, "I do have a soul, I do have a spirit," delighted to be disconnected from the desperate longing that possessed her body. Moreover, now that she is able to recall the repressed traumatic memories of her parents' murder, she understands that her sexually aberrant behavior was not within her control. In this way, Durang does not allow the play to end with the Religious Right triumphing over Lulu/Sadie; instead she is vindicated from the conservative Christians who disparaged her.

Durang's play *Sex and Longing* demonstrates an abuse of power over people's emotional and behavioral lives that is so wrong-headed as to be frightening. Several reviewers complained about the play's sketch-like nature, such as Vincent Canby who described it as "a shapeless amalgam of absurdist theater, satire and parody" (Canby 1996). It is important to realize that as a satirical play, none of its characters are meant to be realistic characters, but instead cookie-cutter stereotypes, such as the macho cop who is a repressed homosexual; the hypocritical senator; the prudish wife; the lecherous preacher, as Canby himself notes. Durang does not position Lulu to garner audience sympathy; sympathy for a main character would only lessen the play's ideological attack. Rather he requires the audience to maintain a critical distance from her personal plight in order to understand the politics behind legislating morality. After he wrote the first draft of the play, he received a phone call alerting him to the fact that several conservative congressional leaders and Christian evangelical groups had crafted a broadly worded Religious Equality Amendment to the Constitution that would permit student-led prayers in public schools and government aid to parochial schools. Act 2 of his play depicting a congressional hearing to change the Constitution was eerily prescient. John Heilpern, in his review, underscored the play's coincidental plot alongside the real congressional hearings, remarking how "the censorious reality is actually ahead of the imagined satire" (1996).

Miss Witherspoon

As the previous plays have shown, various kinds of longing shape human lives: the longing for happiness, sexual fulfillment, connection to others, or meaning and purpose. Durang's personal need to fill the void that Catholicism left can be partially traced through the yearnings expressed by his characters over the years; however, he explicitly addresses this longing with the character of Miss Witherspoon. Matthew Murray, in his review, pronounced this play as marking a transition in Durang's life: "It's taken nearly 30 years, but it's finally happened: With his new play *Miss Witherspoon* at Playwrights Horizons, Christopher Durang has officially become a full-blown optimist. . . . Miss Witherspoon's journey is Durang's journey, from disbelief to acceptance, from what most assuredly is not to what just might possibly be" (2005). Leonard Jacobs also sees a resonance between the lead character and Durang: "For Veronica, and maybe for Durang, it's a whole new journey" (2005). With *Miss Witherspoon* (2005), Durang offers a different view on religion than that of the impassioned 28-year-old who wrote *Sister Mary* or the baby-boomer character he played in *Laughing Wild*, who relied upon New Age philosophy, meditation, and self-help programs. *Miss Witherspoon* may be Durang's most didactic play, in which his own evolving faith-based perspective determines the lesson the main character learns.

Miss Witherspoon was originally composed as a five-minute monologue for a festival of short plays to mark the first anniversary of the World Trade Center disaster, and a generalized fear of disaster underlies the play. The one-act play begins as a typical Durangian dark comedy about catastrophic disasters, unhappiness, and suicide. Albert Camus's absurdist question from "The Myth of Sisyphus" hovers over the play: "Judging whether life is or is not worth living amounts to answering the fundamental question of philosophy." The main character commits suicide within the first scene, yet the artificial quality of the set, with its cerulean Magritte sky and golf-course-green lawns, as depicted in the production at Playwright's Horizons, makes her pain seem existential rather than tragic. On the phone with a friend, Veronica, referred to only as Miss Witherspoon to emphasize her single status, confesses her feelings of hopelessness. She is lonely, having broken up with her boyfriend, and refuses to take medication prescribed for her depression. She is also terrified by natural and manmade disasters: nuclear waste, terrorist attacks, anthrax, hurricanes, tornadoes. Chicken Little randomly appears, running and screaming "the sky is falling!" presaging the collapse of large pieces of metal debris into Miss Witherspoon's backyard. Durang combines the World Trade Center's collapse with Skylab's risky return to earth in that both events reflected a sense of the helplessness in the face of cataclysmic harm. Skylab, an unmanned space station that NASA placed into orbit, was due to reenter the earth's orbit in 1979, but the scientists were unable to determine where it would eventually land; the scientists estimated a 1-in-152 chance that a human being would be hit by falling debris (Coates 1979). The sense that the US government irresponsibly endangers people's lives disturbs Miss Witherspoon: "And the experts didn't think it through, I guess. Sure, let's put massive tonnage up in the sky, I'm sure it won't fall down. Sure, let's build nuclear power plants, I'm sure we'll figure out what to do with radioactive waste eventually" (Durang 2006, 8). Her opening monologue details her vision of a world of catastrophic circumstances, yet her capricious banter invites laughter even as she expresses her fear. "Fear," as Bakhtin has explained, "is the extreme expression of narrow-minded and stupid seriousness, which is defeated by laughter" (Bakhtin 1984, 47). Her fear of the government irresponsibility is valid, but it can be conquered by humor.

After she kills herself, Miss Witherspoon finds herself in the Bardo, an intermediary spot between dying and being reborn into a new life. The Bardo, a concept from Tibetan Buddhist eschatology, offers the deceased person the space to achieve transcendence by recognizing his or her true nature, or, failing that, to reenter into another cycle of rebirth and life. She is helped in this process by three "mahatmas" or wise teachers who appear: Maryamma, Jesus, and Gandalf, each one representing Buddhism, Christianity, and Western esotericism. Maryamma, an Indian woman dressed in a sari, serves as Miss Witherspoon's chief foil; she is frustrated by Miss Witherspoon's refusal to be reborn and explains to her the necessity of returning to earth. In Buddhism, rebirth is required; it is a link between one life and the next which creates a continuity of consciousness. Maryamma insists Miss Witherspoon's rebirth is required to clean her aura, which is "murky brown" and "tweedy," like that of a bothersome character in an Agatha Christie novel. But Miss Witherspoon is reluctant to return to earth: as she tells the spiritual guide, "I didn't like being alive. I don't trust it." Although fundamentally pessimistic—she admits she found it "hard to get on the hope bandwagon"—there is a likeable quirkiness to her character. Played by Kristen Nielsen, the actress conveyed a grounded emotional quality to a role that might have been misinterpreted as one-dimensional. As Ben Brantley describes her, "She has willed herself to be a tough, brittle cookie. . . . But every so often she registers the real terror and pity of the way of the world, and her irony turns into agony. Ms. Nielsen's eyes go wide at such moment and her voice becomes a wounded bleat" (Brantley 2005). Miss Witherspoon and Maryamma engage in loopy philosophical duels about spirituality. At one point Maryamma tells her that she was married to the soul of Rex Harrison before he was Rex Harrison: "In your last life you kept recognizing him when you'd see the actor Rex Harrison, but you were actually recognizing your husband from 1876, not the person who won the Oscar for *My Fair Lady*" (22). Miss Witherspoon's nihilistic arguments are hilarious in their belligerence against the dry wit of Maryamma, who cleanly cuts her adversarial views on reincarnation.

Miss Witherspoon returns to life on earth three times, depicted as her flying through air while a wind blows her clothes and hair about. The first two times, she refuses to live out the life assigned to her, and kills herself. First, she reincarnates as a baby to a wealthy, loving couple. Placed in a bassinette, with her adult head showing, her parents coo over her, alternating their baby language with worries that their dog, jealous over the new baby's arrival, will bite. Miss Witherspoon, quickly apprehending a novel solution to ending her current life, successfully encourages Fido to attack her and dies. When next she appears in the Bardo, an incredulous Maryamma asks her, "Did you just commit suicide at two weeks old?" (20). Although Miss Witherspoon is pleased to have control over her life, Maryamma explains to her the concept of karma: the repercussions of her actions will cause the couple to suffer such guilt that they will spoil their next child, who will grow up to be an irresponsible teenage driver and kill two people in a drunken car accident. Her second incarnation on earth is, again, as a newborn baby to a lower-class couple who are decidedly "trailer trash." Played by the same actors as the previous well-heeled couple, these parents are angry, drug-abusing, low-life vagrants, who, instead of adoring their baby, treat her like a tiresome burden. As the young Veronica grows up in the family, her situation gets progressively worse. Her father has an overdose and dies, and her mother emotionally and physically abuses her, calling her "pig" because she is overweight, or slapping her when she does her math problems incorrectly. The school system offers no salvation for Veronica; even though the guidance counselor witnesses how the mother treats Veronica, she cannot change her situation. Veronica, confessing to feelings of suicide, purchases pills from a Sleazy Man she meets in the park, has an overdose, and dies.

During her third rebirth, Miss Witherspoon takes the form of a dog and experiences pure joy in this manifestation; she fetches balls for her owner or jumps joyfully upon his return from work. Miss Witherspoon confesses to Maryamma upon her return to the Bardo: "I don't remember worrying and thinking ahead. I just seemed happy in the present" (40). In saying so, she conveys the attribute that Buddhists aspire to: the elimination of desire and craving. Furthermore, she learns about karma when Maryamma reveals the details behind Miss Witherspoon's death. The car that hit her was driven by the drunken teenage boy whose parents raised him indulgently due to their guilt over their first baby's death, that is, Miss Witherspoon. Her self-centered action of suicide had repercussions to both herself and others, which is evidence of how karma works; karma is a principle that connects past actions to future events. Defending herself, Miss Witherspoon refuses to associate herself with their actions and insists she not be considered "bad" or "guilty." Maryamma, however, corrects her thinking: "The lesson is never: I am bad. At our core we are not bad. The lesson can be: I should not commit suicide. It could be: I must be aware that my actions have an impact on other people" (42). It is clear that Miss Witherspoon has much to learn over her multiple reincarnations, including not to seek escape via suicide. As Maryamma tells her, she was placed within this life for a reason: "Your soul makes the choice of the life that will teach you the lesson you need to learn. . . . And you keep killing yourself, that doesn't make good karma. You don't get ahead with suicide" (33).

Repeatedly, the spiritual guides encourage her to make the world a better place by working on behalf of others. Jesus, played by a black woman in a flowered dress and a Sunday-morning going-to-church hat, shares with Miss Witherspoon her own teachings such as being merciful and spreading peace, refraining from judging others, and not being materialistic. Miss Witherspoon agrees but has no interest in motivating people to act morally, prompting Jesus, to plead with her: "If you're in agreement, why won't you help?" (56). Gandalf, the wizard from J. R. R. Tolkein's book *The Lord of the Rings*, advocates moving people more quickly through their reincarnation stages in order to save Middle Earth. As a fictional character from popular culture, his appearance speaks to contemporary society's need for spiritual guidance in any shape or form. Whereas Jesus provided teaching on spirituality and compassion, Gandalf offers Miss Witherspoon an abbreviated history of human sociological development, illustrating how humans formed tribes for survival, but consequently turned to tribal warfare when they began competing for goods. He summarizes the problem with humanity as one of internecine combat; as people advance in technologically more sophisticated warcraft, they cannot see the damage they cause other humans because they have failed to evolve spiritually. While Miss Witherspoon respectfully listens to the arguments made by the spiritual guides, she does not recognize her role in the larger fabric of humanity. She repeatedly insists that she would prefer a state of "nothingness" where she would no longer have to think or make choices. She recommends that the afterlife should simply be like a television after it has been unplugged, "Nothing going in, nothing going out" (35). What she does not understand is that this model does not lead to enlightened consciousness.

The Bardo, as traditionally understood, offers to the deceased individual hallucinations or visions by which he or she is compelled to choose his or her rebirth. Miss Witherspoon begins to experience a series of flashbacks that are shared with the audience. The Voice announces that she has left the Bardo and entered the so-called Jewish model of the afterworld, which the characters have jokingly referred to as "the General Anesthesia Afterlife" (44). Instead of nothingness, however, she sees scenes from her previous life with her low-class, abusive parents. The same scenes enacted previously are presented again, but in an eclipsed manner, as if someone were fast-forwarding a DVD player: the Mother calling Veronica a "fat ass," the father overdosing, the Mother slapping Veronica for not knowing her multiplication tables, and the visit to the teacher. However, at the end of these abbreviated scenes, a new scene emerges, based on the suggestion Maryamma offered that Veronica could have sought the teacher's assistance and attempted to change her life rather than resort to suicide. In a scene reminiscent of Henry Higgins teaching Eliza Doolittle to speak, from G. B. Shaw's play *Pygmalion*, Veronica is shown benefiting from her teacher's instruction and elevating herself through education, progressing so far as to become the Commencement Speaker for her graduating class. During her speech, she addresses the volatile nature of their world, mostly due to human-inflicted harm such as global warming. As an earthquake begins, Veronica encourages her audience to stay calm, and in her ability to guide them she emerges as a leader, fulfilling what Jesus has asked of her: to assist others. She returns to consciousness in the Bardo with a new understanding of her purpose, and her ability to envision an alternative ending to her own story moves her toward enlightenment.

For a Durangian play about suicide and death, the end is remarkably upbeat. The three spiritual guides are successful at convincing Miss Witherspoon to help people to "move past their tribal mentalities and to embrace their interdependence" (61), and she returns to her earlier life with the upper-class parents, appearing once again as a baby in the bassinette. Several critics pointed to the unexpected resolution at the play's end; Eric Grode remarked that "the upbeat resolution is also a bit cozy" (2005), while Marilyn Stasio was more arch in her disappointment: "Perennial bad-boy Christopher Durang has mellowed to a fault in his uncharacteristically benign comic fable about spiritual redemption in an age of anxiety and despair" (2005). However, as a comedy, the play's ending confirms the genre's social or communal dictates, providing a vision of the "way things should be" as Northrop Frye once observed about Shakespearean comedy. Affirming her decision to live life, Miss Witherspoon does not permit the dog to bite her this time, instead yelling at the parents, "GET THE DAMN DOG OUTTA HERE!" (65). The spiritual leaders from the Bardo now appear as characters in the scene; the father is played by Gandalf, sporting the same long beard, and the new maid turns out to be Maryamma. Their visible attendance underscores the presence of spiritual guides upon her life's journey. While practicing her first words, speaking in baby-like babble, Miss Witherspoon unexpectedly pontificates, much to the stunned surprise of her parents: "In order to survive, we must find a way to break through the centuries of stressing tribal differences, and evolve to finding tribal and human similarities." By the play's end, she has learned the first Noble Truth of Buddhism that "suffering and life are mysteries. . . . We can't choose to escape" (67).

The plays in this chapter show how Durang's comedic characters derive or attain personal meaning through spiritual belief systems. They all experience or find in religion a method of evaluating the rightness of their choices, whether it is the Religious Right judging Lulu or whether it is the character orienting himself more communally, as in the case of Man in *Laughing Wild* leading a group meditation. Miss Witherspoon as a later development of Durang's differs markedly in her spiritual practice from his earlier characters, such as Eleanor, who suffered unceasingly as testament to her Catholic faith, or Diane, who was distressed by the universe's silence in the face of her personal tragedies. In this later play, the doctrinal nature of religion is replaced with a view that emphasizes self-sufficiency over blind obedience, and the communal good over individual concerns. In writing *Miss Witherspoon*, Durang is clearing the way—and clearing his aura—to write plays about the painful necessity of interdependence.

CHAPTER 3
ONE-ACT PLAYS

Jon Jory, who launched the practice of the ten-minute play at the Actors Theater in Louisville, Kentucky, once described the short play as "American theatre's haiku." Christopher Durang may be the master of the comedic theatrical haiku. Jory offers further insight into the aesthetic nature of the form: "They must, by nature, imply rather than explain. They often depend on metaphor to extend their reach. They stick like glue in the mind because the viewer remembers the whole play" (Jory 1997, vii). One-act plays, with little exposition and a concentration of effects, can be assimilated whole; their very brevity makes them easy to digest and retain. Originally one-act plays began as "curtain-raisers" for the English theatre—lightweight pieces meant to entertain the theatre audience as they waited for latecomers to be seated. One-act plays later found a place in the variety theatre or "vaudeville," as it was known in Europe and America, where these sketches were part of the evening's entertainment (Clark 1938). Here, they were open invitations to playwrights to create absurd scenarios, as they did not require the explanatory causality of longer plays. As Anton Chekhov wrote to his friend A. S. Souvorin, "I like the 'vaudeville'. . . . In one-act things you must write nonsense—there lies their strength" (qtd. in Mitchell 2003).

The pleasure of releasing oneself from the constraints of logic is what makes the one-act play so appealing to playwrights, as well as the speed of its narrative progression. Moreover, the speed of a one-act play makes it the antithesis to both thinking and emotion. The quick juxtaposition of events has a subversive quality, thus making one-act plays ideal for attacking conservative conventions in society, as well as being an ideal antidote to both logical thought and empathy. Events befall the characters too quickly for anyone to have the time to require explanations or to muster an emotional reaction. Durang admits that his own beginnings as a playwright came from watching TV sitcoms or variety shows which predisposed him to events unfolding at a faster rate than normal. Rather than the typical leisurely exposition of modern drama, he explains, "I want to know—BAM!—what's going to happen" (Hodgins 1996)—an indication of the urgency at the heart of his craft. Moreover, Durang's interest in the one-act play most likely came from participating in the Yale Cabaret as both a playwright and a performer. While a graduate student at the Yale School of Drama, Durang was frequently involved in the cabaret, writing, producing, and performing plays that would move from rehearsal to staging in a matter of weeks. Durang was often cast for small or supporting parts, and he learned stagecraft from his fellow actors, such as how to liven a scene or how to determine character motivation. Performances were planned only a few weeks in advance, incorporating whatever news and events were in the headlines, and this spur-of-the-moment nature encouraged the impromptu quality of the plays that were written. The cabaret's atmosphere of serious playfulness and toss-away irreverence inspired and shaped Durang's playwriting style.

During a hiatus Durang took from the theatre world (1988–93), he designed an evening of sketches and songs reminiscent of the work he did at Yale Cabaret. "Christopher Durang and Dawne" was a nightclub act filled with parodic songs and medleys that he performed a number of times over the years with two good friends, John Augustine and Sherry Anderson. The two singers played the single character Dawne, giving a cheeky nod to the musical group Tony Orlando and Dawn, where the female backup singers comprised the musical group "Dawn," by which they meant the time of day. Durang makes a joke of a common misunderstanding and uses the name "Dawne" to suggest two people who are the same woman, a multiple personality gag on par with Durang's recurrent theme of unstable identities. Durang alludes to his withdrawal from writing plays as he introduces himself: "Hi, I'm Chris Durang. I used to be a playwright, but it was too difficult. I'm hoping that being a lounge singer is easier." The three performers sing songs laughingly inappropriate for a lounge singer's repertory, such as "Bali Hai" from Rodgers and Hammerstein's *South Pacific* and "Aldonza" from Dale Wasserman's musical *Man of La Mancha*, as well as a medley of "rock songs they were forced to learn" to appeal to the younger generation. They offer relatively prim versions of Madonna's "Express Yourself" and Michael Jackson's "Bad," the pop-culture lyrics at odds with their brassy vocalization of musical theatre. Durang twists the song lyrics, rewriting lines in "Over the Wall," from Kander and Ebb's *Kiss of the Spider Woman* ("There are big-busted women over the wall") or mocking the naivety of "Sixteen Going on Seventeen" from Rodgers and Hammerstein's *The Sound of Music* with wry spoken commentary.

Fortunately, Durang did return to playwriting, in part due to Walter Bobbie's decision to direct a series of Durang's one-act plays called *Durang Durang* at the Manhattan Theatre Club during the fall of 1994, which was successful. The evening consisted of six short plays: "Mrs. Sorken", "For Whom the Southern Belle Tolls", "A Stye of the Eye", "Nina in the Morning", "Wanda's Visit", and "Business Lunch at the Russian Tea Room". This production was followed by the South Coast Repertory offering another series of one-act plays, *A Mess of Plays by Chris Durang*, in April 1996. Many of his one-act plays have been produced in a variety of venues; "The Actor's Nightmare," for example, was a one-act paired with *Sister Mary Ignatius*, but its inside jokes about the theatre make it a stand-alone staple. Taken as a whole, Durang's short plays can be considered as falling into three different comedic genres: caricature, parody, and absurd scenario. Although there is overlap among these three categories, the differentiation is helpful for analysis. The first group of plays, caricature, offer depictions of quirky personalities painted in exaggerated strokes. In the second group, Durang offers parodies of well-known works or the artistic styles of other playwrights. And the third type of play, absurd scenario, is so called due to the existentialist underpinnings.

All of Durang's plays—both long and short—showcase portraitures of bizarre and irksome personalities whose eccentricities affect everyone around them. Like Shakespeare's Malvolio from *Twelfth Night* or Monsieur Jourdain from Molière's *The Bourgeois Gentleman*, these exaggerated types amuse us because of the particular idiosyncratic traits each character presents, whether it is Malvolio's self-righteous quips, or Monsieur Jordain's preening self-pleasure. The quirky character study is an ideal fit for the tight frame of a one-act play. "In the short play," an English anthologist once noted, "the author has no time in which to develop character and situations. His character must be flashed on the audience, in the round, so to speak, like figures passing a window; his situation must be apprehended quickly, like a picture hung on a wall" (J. B. 1937). Durang's caricatures are like portraits hung on a fun-house wall, a maddening collection of humanity in all its unpredictable glory. However, unlike Malvolio and Monsieur Jourdain, who either depart from the stage or adapt to new circumstances, Durang's characters are frozen in a particular personality type, and their obnoxious rigidity makes normal interactions with others impossible. In his review of the one-acts comprising *Durang Durang*, Randy Gener saw the collection of various character types as Durang's "sustained satiric attack on affectation and artifice" (Gener 1994). In other words, Durang creates portraits of pure annoyance without explanatory contextualization or comeuppance.

The character of Mrs. Sorken, however, who introduces the evening of one-act plays in her piece entitled "Mrs. Sorken," is not a malicious portrait. A cheery housewife *cum* theatre docent, she helpfully reveals to the audiences which of the evening's one-act plays were parodies and which were not. Her monologue also serves as a useful introduction to any evening of one-act plays as she provides a whimsical overview of drama. Overlooked in her own life, she delights in hosting the show and sharing her knowledge about the theatre with the audience in a lovely digressive fashion. Drawing attention to the etymology of the word *drama* from the Greek word "dran," she mistakenly associates that word with "drain" as well as Dramamine. Therefore, she concludes that the theatre "cures us of the nausea of life," by draining people emotionally, a convoluted but accurate interpretation of Aristotle's classic tragic formula of catharsis. Mrs. Sorken is one of Durang's self-interested characters, whose "high-spirited silliness" (Gener 1994) captivates us through the nonsensical wonderland of her mind. The twists and turns of her fanciful spiel reveal surprising truths amid the nonsense; in her hands, the well-worn saw about theatre encouraging empathy becomes an illuminating testament to a person's thought process: "Evita was a woman, I am a woman," she explains. "Or 'Sweeney Todd was a barber, I go to the hairdresser.' Or 'Fosca in *Passion* should have her moles removed, I know a good dermatologist.' That sort of thing" (Durang 1995, 4). The daffy Mrs. Sorken becomes a prototype for several of Durang's later characters, such as the mother in *Why Torture Is Wrong*, and the eponymous character in *Miss Witherspoon*—characters whose zaniness occasionally yields relevant insights.

Durang enjoys creating characters who break the fourth wall and address the public, so that they might toy with the audience response. Mrs. Sorken, blissfully unaware of her own balderdash and lacking in theatrical expertise, nevertheless charms the audience. The character in the monologue "Woman Stand-up," however, makes the audience uncomfortable. Having chosen to participate in the tough arena of stand-up comedy, she unfortunately lacks the skills to make people laugh, and her self-denigrating comments result not in laughter but in uneasiness. Unlike Joan Rivers, whose tough-as-nails persona invited the audience to laugh along with her as she made fun of her own romantic life, face, or career, the "Woman Stand-up" lacks the stage presence to carry off such self-mockery. She performs her stand-up routine with the typical effervescent rhythm and conventional one-liners, such as "I have such low self-esteem that when my mother told me to get a nose job, I bought a Pit Bull and had it bite my nose off" (Durang 1995, 129), but the painfulness with which she describes her feelings of worthlessness obscures any humorous release. The vignette explores the nature of self-deprecatory humor, which many comedians employ, both men and women, and points to the difference between laughing at a *performance* of low self-esteem versus laughing at low self-esteem. Furthermore, the play's humor comes from the incongruity of the character and context, that is, a woman who by her own choosing places herself into the wrong role. Durang, in reversing the expectations of the stand-up genre, manipulates the audience's own discomfiting laughter; we feel anxiety laughing at a woman who is clearly emotionally battered, yet laughter is the only way to assure the comedian of her success.

Another character who elicits uncomfortable laughter appears in "Nina in the Morning." This short play was inspired by the Victorian artwork of Edward Gorey, as Durang mentions in his Afterword. He was intrigued by Gorey's macabre style depicting "all those thin creatures with long dresses and capes who stand around staring dispassionately while awful tragedies occur one after another around them" (Durang 1995, 55). Nina, the main character, maintains a glacial demeanor, while an onstage narrator voices aloud her internal monologue, the eerie voice-over adding to the gothic tone of the piece. An aging diva whose loss of beauty concerns her more than the well-being of her children, Nina sits in her chaise lounge before her mirror, bemoaning aloud the fact that the pins for her face-lift have fallen out during the night, a calamity worsened by the fact that her plastic surgeon is on vacation in Aruba. Her decadence and unflagging egotism make her a successor to the gothic narcissist Vivien, the mother in Durang's full-length play *Death Comes to Us All, Mary Agnes*. The self-indulgence she manifests regarding maintaining her beauty is disturbed by the fraught relationships she has with her children, who have been trying to attack her. In defense, she instructs her manservant, Foote, to shoot them with sedatives, prompting the deliciously horrible line, "I always liked my children best when they were unconscious" (59). The first son tries to attack her face, the second son tries to shoot her with a pistol, the third child, called "La-La," for the limited "la-la-la" noises she makes, remains "willfully retarded." The incongruity between her glamorous emotional frostiness and the obscene violence that occurs provides a surreal quality, akin to the darkness witnessed in the Gorey pictures. Similarly, because her surgically treated skin is impermeable to pain, she shows no emotional reaction when she accidentally pours hot coffee down her face or after her son shoots her in the shoulder, adding to the dark humor. The catatonic Nina attempts to make a decision at the play's end that results in her stasis: does she accept the fact that her children wish to kill her, or does she decide what to eat for lunch. This caricature of a socialite with her frozen face and mind satirizes perfectly the unfeeling self-centeredness of the economically privileged.

Durang's predilection for psychological abnormality runs the gamut from catatonic to neurotic, as evidenced by another play, "Naomi in the Living Room" (1988). The play was written as part of a "home" series for the Home for Contemporary Theater, where each contributor was asked to write a play about a different room of a home. Durang offered a case study of psychosis played out in the living room. Naomi is a woman who alternates between offering compliments and attacking her guests verbally, without any explanation for her vacillation. Irrational people behave according to their own internal logic and Naomi is a perfect example; Naomi has moments of rationality before shifting to aggressive bouts, creating an off-kilter experience for the home visit. She begins by introducing her guests, John and Johnna, to the various rooms of the house with comments of mundane functionality: "The dining room is where we dine. The bedroom is where we go to bed. The bathroom is where we take a bath. The kitchen is where we . . . collect kitsch" (Durang 1995, 118). After inviting her son and daughter-in-law to make themselves at home, Naomi races to the couch as they move to sit down and berates them for complying with her bequest. Her extreme personality shifts from pleasant and conversational to crass and confrontational make the visit an exercise in social terrorism. She luxuriates on the couch to the point of orgasm and makes callous remarks, responding to Johnna's revelation that all five of their children died in a tragic car accident with: "God, some people can't get over their own little personal tragedies, what a great big crashing bore" (121). The final *coupe de grace*, however, occurs when the focus shifts from Naomi's odd behavior to John's; without any explanation, he changes into Johnna's clothing, shaves his mustache, dons a wig, and gaily enters the room as her look-alike, imitating her speech and feminine gestures. In his inexplicable transformation, John seems to have concluded that "you can't reason with crazy," and has contributed his own eccentricity by means of reply. This final image of a psychotic woman and a cross-dressing man depicts the liberating pattern of insanity that serves as a template for so many Durang plays.

"Naomi in the Living Room" follows the pattern Durang uses in many plays, that is, using characters' normative behavior to offset a central character's deviance; initially, at least John and Johnna seemed normal. Durang's play "Wanda's Visit" is another study in the defining lines between appropriate and bizarre behavior. The lives of Jim and Marsha are cast asunder by a surprise visit from a former girlfriend, Wanda. She enters their home and refuses to leave, unexpectedly relieving them of the doldrums of their married life by her frenetic energy. While the play is predicated upon middle-class phobias toward the unkempt members of the *hoi polloi*, the comedy lies in how Wanda's lust for life points all the more obviously to the couple's lackluster relationship. Her antisocial behaviors, which warrant eviction, trump their polite manners. Her topics of conversation are all cause for alarm, such as her ready-at-hand prescription of Seconal in the event she needs to commit suicide, the herpes she contracted from her second husband, or the face-lift she had to get after working for a criminal lawyer, but it is the contrast to the couple's bland stereo-typicality that provokes hilarity. Not only are her topics of conversation troublesome but also the way she breaks the basic rules of civil discourse. Jim and Marsha are visibly disturbed by her monopolizing the conversation with her windy diatribes or excessive personal information. Upon her decision to sleep over, she keeps the couple up all night with stories of her life, relayed as a series of one-liners while the clock ticks to indicate the passage of time and the one-sidedness of her conversation:

> WANDA: (*Coquettish*) And I said, "Billy, why didn't you tell me you were 16?"
> (*Clock ticks*)
> WANDA: (*Chatty voice, just telling the facts*) And the policeman said, let me see your pussy, and I thought, hey, maybe this way I won't get a ticket.
> (*Clock ticks*)
>   . . .
> WANDA: (*Energized, telling a fascinating story*). And Howard said he wanted me to kill his mother, and I said, "Are you crazy? I've never even met your mother." And he said, "All right, I'll introduce you."
> (Durang 1995, 81)

The following morning, the three go to a restaurant where Wanda is sighted by two hit men who abscond with her. She leaves Marsha and Jim numb with astonishment, but relieved to be rid of her. As their lives return to normalcy, they decide to seek counseling to help their marriage. The craziness of Wanda's visit, with her zestiness and sexual promiscuity, makes their lack of passion all the more painfully obvious.

In most of these caricature pieces, it is the contrast between the reasonable person and the peculiar character that provides the comic incongruity, whether the contrast is provided by other onstage characters or the audience itself. Watching an imminently sane individual confront an irrational force always provides humor—if only because it is all too relatable. Anyone who has ever visited the Department of Motor Vehicles knows the frustration of being at the mercy of an authoritative bureaucracy and welcomes a satirical sketch criticizing this government agency. Durang provides just that in his one-act play "DMV Tyrant", where the character trying to get his driver's license is confronted by so many obstacles from the service agent that he finally decides his only option is to leave the state. Another contrast between the sane and the ridiculous occurs in *Funeral Parlor* (1987), a sketch Durang wrote for a televised Carol Burnett special, in which a grieving widow is disturbed at her husband's wake by an eccentric mourner. Yet, as he persists in teaching her how to keen, he gains her trust and encourages her emotional release and, in so doing, helps her mourn. In this case, the singularity of his character type provides welcome relief to the staid protocol of a funeral. In the televised version starring Carol Burnett and Robin Williams, the animalistic guttural sounds Williams made to suggest grief broke through the artificial facade of Burnett's public façade. These caricature plays, showcasing erratic personality types, are a guide for understanding Durang's longer plays. Sometimes the absurd characters represent circumstances that would be best to avoid; at other times these characters represent freedom from conventionality.

The second category of his one-act plays, his parodies, allows the perfect forum for his wit. Vincent Canby, in a celebratory review of an evening of Durang one-acts, *Durang Durang*, draws attention to the lost art of parody that Durang possesses in spades:

With the help of Mr. Durang, the fine art of parody has returned to the New York theater in a production you can sink teeth and mind into, while also laughing like an idiot for at least half the time. . . . I have no idea why good parody, including Mr. Durang's, can be so insidiously satisfying. In part, I suppose, it appeals to a primal need to burlesque established icons, and an urge to deflate reputations, thereby to force re-examinations of what have become given, if often dusty, truths. (Canby 1994)

Much of Durang's work has a self-referential quality to it, but his parodies directly take on well-known literary or pop-cultural works, sharing with the audience the destruction of esteemed literary pieces or contemporary favorites. An early parody, "The Hardy Boys and the Mystery of Where Babies Come From," spoofed the popular 1970s TV series starring teen heartthrobs Parker Stevenson and Shaun Cassidy. Mocking the preppy, jejune nature of the two teenage detectives, Durang creates a scenario where the two sleuth their way into discovering what the phrase "bun in the oven" means. In so doing, Durang highlights how the pair of men are oddly lacking in romantic or sexual inclinations. With his fellow Yale Drama School classmate, Wendy Wasserstein, he wrote a lampoon on the Greek classical tragedy *Medea* in honor of Juilliard School's Drama Division's twenty-fifth anniversary in 1994. Performed with Harriet Harris as Medea and Kevin Spacey as Jason, the play appealed to the dramatically savvy audience, by making allusions to other well-known plays such as *The Importance of Being Earnest*. The actress playing Medea addresses the inherent problem women face in the theatrical profession in having fewer acting opportunities than men do, referring to such unexciting shows as *Designing Women* and *Little House on the Prairie* that did hire women actors. In addition to such in-group commentary, the play parodies the overly wrought language of classical Greek plays. Medea cries, "Come, flame of the sky, / Pierce through my head! / What do I, Medea, gain from living any longer?" and the chorus deflates her histrionics, chanting, "But tell us how you're really feeling" (199).

The delight of parody is in breaking down formal aesthetic standards or the standard bearers themselves, those timeless classics that everyone assumes to be noteworthy. More than simple mockery, parody is, as Linda Hutcheon reminds us, *repetition with critical difference*. Parody's use of laughter distances us from the traditional interpretations of the piece and allows for a novel point of view. The characters can be reimagined from a humorous perspective; no longer do they exist only as tragic icons, but as emblems of cultural values that should be overturned. In the one-act

"For Whom the Southern Belle Tolls," for example, Durang takes Tennessee Williams's gossamer play *The Glass Menagerie* and holds it up to the harsh light of reality. As a memory play, the main character Tom Wingfield reflects upon a time in his life just before leaving his family when he was asked by his mother, Amanda, to find a potential husband for his sister Laura and ensure her financial security through marriage. The tragedy of William's well-known play relies upon Amanda's holding onto antebellum beliefs and practices that cannot be sustained within a working-class society. Most theatregoers familiar with the play remember the mother's tenacious hold on her debutant code and her insistence that a woman using "gaiety and charm" can seduce a man. They may recall the fragility of a disabled daughter, Laura, both physically and emotionally withdrawn from the world, as well as Tom's desire not to be saddled with caring for his mother and sister. Despite the play being a tragic tale of one man's guilt for abandoning his family, Durang notes his annoyance with Laura in his Afterword, confessing how this "sweet, sensitive" character irritated him after seeing the play too many times (1995, 11). No longer a play about the nostalgic hold memory has over a writer's psyche, Durang's parody turns it into a humorous sketch of learned helplessness.

In "For Whom the Southern Belle Tolls," Durang reverses the male and female roles and thus dismantles the societal code that Amanda Wingfield has lived by, chiefly the model of man as caretaker. In the original version, Amanda Wingfield encourages her daughter to be "charming and vivacious" and to pad her bra with "gay deceivers" to entice her gentleman caller and signal to him her marriageability. Laura's delicate nature, her longing to stay at home and dust her little glass figurines rather than take typing classes to find employment, makes her a perfect match for this gendered dichotomy of active male/passive female roles. In other words, Williams's symbolic trope of fragile, spiritual people suffering within a materialist world depends upon a traditional, dualistic view of gender, which Durang's parody exposes. In Durang's version, the delicate Laura is now Lawrence, a man with a psychosomatic limp who scratches at his eczema, puts on his nightshirt in the presence of company, and suffers from asthma. Instead of fondling the delicate collection of glass animals for which the play is named, Lawrence plays with a collection of cocktail swizzle sticks all evening, reciting the various names he has given them: Q-tip, Blue, Pinocchio, Henry Kissinger. Durang thus eliminates any gendered tolerance we might hold for a "sensitive soul"; Lawrence just seems tiresome and weird. "Now Lawrence," his mother tells him, "if you can't go out the door without getting an upset stomach or an attack of vertigo, then we have got to find some nice girl who's willing to support you" (14). The disillusioned matriarch becomes the acerbic Amanda Wingvalley, skewering the painfully thin skin of her young charge: "Oh, Lawrence, you're so sensitive it makes me want to hit you" (12). In other words, Durang's script makes quite plain the frustration that is normally left unspoken, turning the subtext into text, as Gussow notes (1994), and eliciting laughter. The gentleman caller is now a woman, a butch lesbian, Virginia, or, as she bellows, "CALL ME GINNY," due to her hearing impediment. She works with Tom at the warehouse and is saving up her money to buy a farmhouse and a tractor. Her presence and her speech are boisterous and rough, and she laughs uproariously at her own jokes and mishears everything said to her. Throughout the evening, Amanda Wingvalley maintains a brave facade, covering up the desperate situation with the energetic charm of Southern hospitality even as she realizes Ginny, who has a girlfriend, will not propose marriage to Lawrence. "The disgrace," she bemoans, "The expense of the pigs feet, a new tie for Lawrence" (23). As John M. Clum explains, Durang "shares Williams's penchant for creating damaged people," but he obviates the tendency to romanticize characters, revealing instead through his parodies "the muddled thinking that traps [Williams's] characters" and eviscerating the tragic dimension of the play (Clum 2008, 167).

Moreover, in the parody he humorously brings to the fore the repressed sexual desire inherent in Williams's plays and thus liberates the queer subtext (Clum 2008, 166–7). While Williams kept his gay sexual orientation out of the public eye, many closeted references appear in his plays, and Durang depends upon the audience's knowledge for his double entendres. For example, in the original play, Tom frequently found escape in going to the movies, which serves as a space for male sexual encounters, as suggested by Williams in his short stories. Durang's version of Tom makes his sexual proclivities more explicit by referring to the pornographic titles of the movies *Beaver City* and *Humpy Bus Boys*, as well as sharing his dreams to join the merchant marines or the Ballet Trockadero. He continues his exposé of repressed sexual longings in "Desire, Desire, Desire," a histrionic mash-up of *A Streetcar Named Desire* and *Cat on a Hot Tin Roof*. In Durang's parody, Stanley randomly shrieks the name "Stella," Blanche propositions the visiting Census Taker, and Maggie wanders in from her respective play, asking for Brick to help her conceive a baby. In addition to these heterosexual problems, Durang mocks the tragic tension of closeted homosexual desire. The working-class Stanley from *Streetcar* discusses the nuances of his relationship with his male friend Skipper, taking the speech that was originally Brick's in *Cat on a Hot Tin Roof*:

> Maggie the cat, you make everything dirty. What's between me and Skipper is good and holy and there ain't nothing dirty about it. Oh, sometimes when we wuz on the road together, we'd reach across the bed and shake hands, like men would. Oh, and sometimes if it was hot, we might take showers together. And sometimes, if we had nothin' better to do, we might dress up like lumberjacks and French kiss for an hour, but it was nothin' dirty. (1995, 191)

The original lines expressed by Brick about the nobility of male friendship bespoke a gay subtext wherein Brick was in denial regarding Skipper's feelings for him. The parody, with its obvious depictions of homosexual escapades, turns his disavowal into ludicrous fun. Durang takes Williams's misfit characters and exaggerates them to the point of affectionate ridicule, showing just how disabling their illusions are. For example, when Cora from O'Neill's *The Ice Man Cometh* wanders into the apartment discussing "pipe dreams," Durang draws attention to how frequently American playwrights wrote about the eclipsed dreams of their characters. Tennessee Williams may be Durang's favorite playwright, but that does not stop Durang from mischievously toying with his *chef d'oeuvre* (Durang 2017a). It is no wonder Gussow describes the tone of his sketches as "malicious with a dash of affection" (1994).

Durang has a knack for mocking the stylistic qualities of some of America's best dramatists. The timing of *Durang Durang* could not have been more perspicacious. It opened days before the revival of *Glass Menagerie* at the Roundabout, as well as the premiere of Sam Shepard's new play *Simpatico* at the Public Theater, which gave Durang's high-energy parody of Shepard's writing style, "A Stye of the Eye," immediate relevance. Theatre reviewers attest to the provocative nature of Durang's parody, such as Lloyd Rose (1994), who seized on its usefulness as literary interpretation. He wrote how Durang's parody illustrates how "interior Shepard is as an artist, in spite of his evocation of the wide-open spaces. His plays about life on the spacious frontier are sealed, hermetic." Vincent Canby appreciated the parody's lit-crit approach as well: "As Mr. Durang condenses and rethinks

A Lie of the Mind, he cannily, sometimes meanly and often hilariously, calls attention to Mr. Shepard's familiar obsession with, among other things, the twinship of male characters, speech patterns and the use of symbols (the American flag, blindness, mental retardation), which also become actual cymbals in 'A Stye of the Eye'" (1994). As Durang sends up contemporary theatre, he attacks the pretentious vagueness that writers resort to under the auspice of figurative art, such as Wesley's random gesture of carrying a bloody lamb onto the stage in *Curse of the Starving Class*. He fillets the hyperrealistic style of Shepard and David Mamet that demands audiences accept their simulated reality as truthful. Linda Hutcheon acknowledges that parody can possess "a threatening, even anarchic force, one that puts into question the legitimacy of other texts" (2000, 75), and Rose's review seems to agree, in its conclusion, that "Durang's demolition of Williams and Shepard isn't fair, it's just nastily accurate."

"A Stye of the Eye" consists of the typically odd, working-class characters of Shepard's plays: Maniac Jake, a psychotic redneck with multiple personalities, calls his amnesiac mother to inform her that he has beaten his wife, Beth, to death because he suspected her of adultery; in actuality, she was participating in a community theatre production. Ma isn't surprised or angered by the information, but rather states that he should "settle down and marry your sister." Jake switches back and forth between himself and his "good brother," Frankie, on the phone, a Durangian spoof on Shepard's habit of creating characters who represent dualities. The character of Ma points out the blatant exemplification: "You know, you and Jake sound so much alike that sometimes I think you're both two different aspects of the same personality. That means I gave birth to a symbol and me with no college education" (Durang 1995, 37). The play then provides a flashback to Beth's community theatre performance in *Agnes Is Odd*, a parodic combination of both John Pielmeier's *Agnes of God* (1979) and Peter Shaffer's *Equus* (1973)—plays that use popular psychology to explore aberrant behavior in the characters, a nun who murders her newborn and a young man who blinds horses. In *Agnes Is Odd*, Dr. Martina Dysart provides arbitrary psychoanalytic interpretations for Agnes's cryptic sentences, pompously assuming that psychology can explain the young woman's damaged psyche. Echoing the psychiatrist from Shaffer's play, that is, *Martin* Dysart, she summarizes the character's questionable dilemma of envying his patient's sexual drive: "My life as a psychiatrist is drab and depressing, and even though I think it unappealing that [Agnes] killed her baby and blinded the horses, still I envy her passion" (38). With this one sharp line, she deflates the watered-down, armchair psychology implicit in Shaffer's script.

After the flashback of the performance, Beth appears at her mother's house, because she is not dead, as Jake suspected, only brain-damaged ("No Restoration comedy for you, young lady!" her mother advises [44]). Mae, Jake's sister, arrives and she and Jake arouse passionate desire in each other, represented by their running at each other repeatedly from opposite sides of the stage: "We come together like two cymbals crashing, don't we?" The play continues in this symbolic vein: Beth's mother, Meg, develops a "stye in her eye," yet attempts to fold an American flag that has become infested with maggots while wearing eye patches over both eyes; Ma, who has also gone blind, tries to assist her flawed attempts to maneuver the American symbol. Jake shoots his brother Frankie, but because he has a multiple personality disorder he essentially kills himself, which causes confusion to everyone on the stage; no one can tell who killed whom. ("I didn't follow that visually at all," complains Meg [46].) Nonetheless, Jake rises and announces he will travel out west in a speech that parodies Western masculinity: "I'm sick of women. I'm gonna find me some Mexican whores and some tequila, and I'm gonna drive me down some highway with open spaces on either side of me, and I'm gonna sit in the car with my legs spread open real wide, so my peter can breathe" (48), evoking the "mystique of male aggression and testosterone-driven wanderlust" (Gener 1994) that permeates Shepard's plays. The whole ending is mock portentous, with the heavy-handed use of jazz music and lighting to hide the fact that significance has been drawn from nothing.

Finally, the third kind of one-act play that Durang writes can be categorized as the absurd situation, coming from the world of farce. Durang constructs scenarios of human pettiness, failures, and vices, and then demonstrates the radically logical results of these behaviors. In "Canker Sores and Other Distractions," for example, Durang takes a note from Alexander Pope's line "What mighty contests rise from trivial things." A perfectly innocuous evening's dinner is set off course by the distraction of a canker sore and a dust mote in the eye, preventing a man and his ex-wife from reconciling their differences. In another play, "1-900-Desperate," a telephone chat room for singles illustrates the problem with the dating scene when too many women—and one small boy—call at the same time. The piece "Phyllis & Xenobia" is about two sisters who may or may not have killed their mother. In each of these plays, Durang begins with the preposterous question "what if?" and we watch the random events unfold.

One-Act Plays

An early example of Durang's ability to construct chaos is his play "Diversions," which he wrote at the age of eighteen. The Loeb Experimental Theater at Harvard College presented this self-described "young person's version of Existentialism" in the fall of 1967. True to its existentialist form, the play's opening and closing image is of a man about to jump to his death, recalling Samuel Beckett's "Act without Words." What follows is a type of Rube Goldberg chain of events, where the intervention of a suicide results in several deaths, including an accidental homicide and a wrongful execution of a witness, showing that any small event can have ridiculously large consequences. A Man is prevented from taking a suicidal leap by a Nun, but their resulting fracas necessitates the help of a bystander, Aloysius Kain, and a Policeman. In the ensuing struggle, the Policeman accidentally falls to his death. The bystander to the event, a Hysterical Woman, or "Hysteria," played by Bonnie Raitt in this early production, summons another Policeman to have the whole group arrested for murder. A Kangaroo court is convened, much like the Knave of Heart's trial in *Alice in Wonderland*, and the protocol goes awry. The Judge, continually distracted by the Clerk delivering his dry cleaning, has no control over the proceedings, the Attorney mounts a ridiculous trial wherein Hysteria is the only witness, and Aloysius's wife voices her support for having her husband executed in order that she might marry the Prosecuting Attorney. Aloysius is convicted and executed for murder despite the suicidal Man's protests to the contrary. The Man, having observed this outrageous series of events—and more—assumes his position from the start of the play and once again is about to kill himself, now motivated by the irrationality of the world. The actions of good Samaritans are misinterpreted, the legal system is nefarious and unjust, and relationships are treacherous. Like a shaggy-dog story with a long-awaited punch line, the play teasingly proffers hope that justice will prevail, only to end cynically.

Durang's absurd scenarios not only are humorous but provide an opportunity for pointed satiric commentary. In his self-referential play "Business Lunch at the Russian Tea Room," he takes on the Hollywood film industry, particularly those individuals whose work involves developing scenarios for movie plots or TV series and finding the writers for these ideas. The play recounts Durang's own experience as an up-and-coming playwright approached by Hollywood story developers; the writer in the play is, in fact, named Chris. He is given potential scenarios to transform into screenplays by Melissa, a crass, fast-talking movie producer, while having lunch at the famed Russian Tea Room. The humor rises as the contrast between the two becomes more and more pronounced: her self-absorbed, aggressive personality (she is currently suing six people, including her own mother) in contrast to his slow-thinking, placid responses. She pitches him scenarios, one about a priest and rabbi who fall in love, and each has a sex change without telling the other, in order to have a relationship as a heterosexual couple. Another pitch resembles the movie *Cruising*, where Al Pacino disguises himself as a leather-wearing homosexual in order to track down a serial killer involved in heinous S&M murders of gay men. However, Melissa puts a "twist" on her version, by involving child actors: "It would be like [the movie *Bugsy Malone*], only sick." "I might write that," Chris responds with understated affability, "Wouldn't we all go to jail?" (1995, 101). The play gives vent to any writer's dilemma of wanting to write true art as opposed to a commercial product that will fill Hollywood's greedy maw. Chris bravely tries to envision one of the scenarios Melissa suggests, and two imaginary characters enter to depict the "priest-Rabbi-sex-change-but-it's-touching" story. As Chris considers different possibilities of how they meet, date, go to a disco, or walk in a park, the Priest and Rabbi physicalize each of his suggestions, and humorous scenes ensue. However, Melissa's dictatorial voice keeps interrupting, demanding changes, so that each time Chris's mind probes a possibility, such as the Rabbi saying he wants to "schtupp" the Priest, Melissa interjects a critique, and two characters stand still and stare at Melissa and Chris, unsure of how to proceed. The competing dictates of the commercial movie industry and the contemplative playwright end when Melissa decides she will write the movie herself and Chris returns home to fold laundry, assisted by his imagined Priest and Rabbi. Hollywood assumes it knows the stories that the American populace wants, but this assumption has a price; the sordid scenarios, conveyed as public taste, lowers the quality of popular American culture.

The one-act play "John and Mary Doe" is a satire on the purported ideal of the happy nuclear family. It opens with an ordinary married couple who set up an atmosphere of plausibility until they recount a disturbing list of horrific violence. With an opening monologue that recalls the banality of Ionesco's *Bald Soprano*, John Doe talks about the typicality of his and his wife's names, before he arbitrarily asserts, "My wife and I have never molested our children. Or if we have, we've forgotten it entirely. And we hope they have" (Durang 1995, 209). They discuss bland subjects such as their daughter's drawing of a snowman, interweaving such nurturing familial details with sadistic abuse; not only do they embrace the child lovingly, place the picture on the refrigerator, and sit to play the piano, they also reveal they have tied the child to the piano after force-injecting her with a water enema. Durang's grotesque comedy is at work here. The physical violence underneath the surface depiction of the pleasant familiar life demands that we question the supposed normalcy of all families. Wilhelm Kayser, in his book on the grotesque, provides a similarly twisted tale of familial regard from a novel by Wilhelm Busch. The tale relates, "though not without humorous overtones," how the remains of a child so dearly beloved by his parents are placed by these same parents on a shelf with cheese and pickles in a basement. The grotesque, Kayser explains, lies in the discrepancy between the love felt for the child and the parents' sacrilegious treatment of the remains (1966, 118). Durang's use of the grotesque provides an assault on the nostalgic vision of 1950s family life. The play firmly establishes itself in the 1950s by the names given to the pets: a dog named Sputnik, the cat John F. Kennedy, Jr., and a goldfish named Jason Robards, Jr., as well as references to the atomic bomb and the fear of communism. Each time John relates grotesque behavior, such as how the neighbor murdered and dismembered his wife, he recasts the episode by suggesting it was only a lie, exemplifying the willful numbness of historical revision. He shifts back and forth from mild-mannered details to sickening violence, and it is the intersection of these two matrices—the cozy familiarity and the sadistic harm—that provides the satiric commentary on the glowing vision of the postwar boom.

Another use of the absurd scenario as societal critique appears in "The Book of Leviticus Show." Durang's satirical target is the Religious Right, just as in another of his plays, *Sex and Longing*. The preposterous premise he designs is a public execution done in the name of religious beliefs and televised on cable television. Lettie Lu and her husband Tommy, following the biblical injunction in the Book of Leviticus that states a person should be killed for adultery or homosexuality, have kidnapped and conveyed an adulterous woman and a homosexual man to a hotel room. Lettie Lu proceeds to shoot them, while her husband serves as the camera man, sharing her deed on public access television. As John Morreall reminds us in *Taking Laughter Seriously*, one principle important for comic technique is "to maintain an atmosphere in which the audience's sense of reality is preserved" in order to create a greater disturbance to one's ordinary world frame (1983, 83), which Durang does. As the camera pans backward, the two hostages are discovered taped and tied up, weakly protesting, until

Lettie Lu turns the gun on them and shoots. The humorous shock of this comic one-act comes from Lettie Lu championing her religious convictions on television while causing irreparable damage. The ordinariness of the religious bigot in contrast to her subsequent horrible act is the point of Durang's satire: the American public's tolerance of Christian evangelists' recurrent speeches against homosexuality has the unfortunate result of normalizing their harmful behavior.

One of Durang's best-known short plays, "The Actor's Nightmare," is a perfect example of Theatre of the Absurd. An accountant, George Spelvin, inadvertently walks backstage before a play begins and suddenly finds himself filling in for the lead actor. His protests of disbelief are treated humorously by his fellow actors, and he is pressed into performing. Deferential and eager to please, George gamely tries to improvise his lines from vague memories of the plays. Each time he tries to back out of a scene, the dialogic exchange with the other actor, Sarah Siddons, forces him to continue, either by repeating his cue line until he finds the correct response or by having the stage manager feed him his line, evoking the sense that he is a prisoner within this theatrical space. It is pure comedy to watch, yet there is a certain menace to the inexorable situation; each time he forgets a line, she prompts him with, "I bet you were going to say . . . " (1995, 357). When he doesn't give her the right response, she repeats the question aggressively, "How was China? How was China?" until the stage manager, dressed as a maid, enters to whisper to George the correct response from the Noël Coward play: "Very large, China." When the play turns Shakespearean, the witty dialogue transforms to more abstract phrases; it no longer matters that George offers *non sequiturs* as their lines are not predicated on what George says. When Sarah enters as Gertrude and states, "Oh, speak to me no more," and he responds, "Very well. What do you want to talk about?" she instead exits by repeating, "No more!" When he is suddenly cast in the spotlight for a soliloquy, without the aid of the stage manager or fellow actors, he ad-libs valiantly, stringing together a random series of lines:

> Uh, thrift, thrift, Horatio. Neither a borrower nor a lender be. But to thine own self be true. There is a special providence in the fall of a sparrow. Extraordinary how potent cheap music can be. Out, out, damn spot! I come to wive it wealthily in Padua; if wealthily, then happily in Padua. (*Sings*) Brush up your Shakespeare; start quoting him now; Da da . . . (363)

George epitomizes the comic hero with his attitude of improvisation; even though he gathers that he is not making any sense, he understands the ontological imperative that the show must go on.

"The Actor's Nightmare" is a theatrephile's treat, with humorous moments of theatrical mishaps and allusions to various well-known plays. Noël Coward is quoted and misquoted; his line "some women should be hung regularly, like tapestries" is revised to "some women should be struck regularly, like gongs." George Spelvin's very name is an inside joke, as a common pseudonym of actors. He is pressed into the lead role of Noël Coward's *Private Lives*, about reconnecting with an ex-wife while on a honeymoon with his current wife; he performs in *Hamlet* with Henry Irving playing Horatio; he next plays Willie to Ellen Terry's Winnie in Beckett's *Happy Days*; finally, he finds himself as Sir Thomas More in Robert Bolt's *A Man for All Seasons*, where he is ultimately executed for treason. The parodic fragment Durang constructs from *Happy Days* is a delightful send-up of Beckett's style; Ellen Terry reads not only Winnie's line but also her stage directions: "It's just another happy day, pause, smile, pause, picks nit from head" (365). Durang's parody illustrates how incomprehensible Beckett's stoic vision might seem when played out of context. When Winnie goes blind, she feels panic, then quickly snaps out of it: "Oh what a terrible day. Oh dear. Oh my. (*Suddenly very cheerful again.*) Oh well. Not so bad really. I only used my eyes occasionally. When I wanted to see something. But no more!" (366). When George is about to be executed and frantically tries to change the outcome, Ellen Terry's lines espousing resilience—"Nothing to be done. That's what I find so wonderful"—sound outlandishly out of place when applied to someone else's demise.

His execution in the final moments of the play can be seen as an irony of fate, as well as an intertextual joke. Double-billed with *Sister Mary Ignatius Explains It All for You*, "The Actor's Nightmare" describes a character struggling to discover his purpose in life, which stands in striking contrast to the self-righteous security that religion provides. As Sister Mary Ignatius reads off her list of the damned, the name Georgina Spelvin appears, along with other "sinners" such as Roman Polanski, Zsa Zsa Gabor, and Mick Jagger, which may be Durang's own inside joke.[1] The last role George Spelvin plays is Thomas More, who was killed because he refused to acknowledge King Henry as the Supreme Head of the Church of England. It is suggested that George Spelvin, who had intended to join the monastery but had "stopped believing in all those things," may have been executed because he lost his faith. While the preoccupation of being in front of a live audience and forgetting one's lines is any actor's literal nightmare, the inability to comprehend the larger meaning or purpose of our lives absent religious belief results in existential unease. "The Actor's Nightmare" serves as an allegory for human existence, the belief that we all play roles within a script that we cannot remember, over which we have little control. Albert Camus used a similar theatrical metaphor to capture the feeling of alienation after the Second World War: "This divorce between man and his life, the actor and his setting, truly constitutes the feeling of Absurdity" (1955, 6). George expresses the unease of his insubstantial identity at the play's onset when the other actors call him George: "My name isn't George," he states, "it's . . . well, I don't know what it is, but it isn't George" (354). Evidently for George Spelvin, the danger of not knowing his role or his purpose in life went beyond stage fright or existential misgivings; it resulted in death.

Northrop Frye, in discussing satire, described its riotously destructive nature, noting how it breaks up "the lumber of stereotypes, fossilized beliefs, of superstitious terrors, crank theories, pedantic dogmatisms, oppressive fashions, and all other things that impeded the free movement of society" (1944, 79). Each of Durang's one-act plays mutinies against some fossilized belief or oppressive practice, whether it is egotistical individuals, the tolerance for irrational behavior, the unblinking admiration for a playwright, or misplaced nostalgia for the postwar era. After watching an evening of Durang's one-act plays, Ben Brantley remarked about Durang's novel perspective:

> Like most work by this uneven, prodigiously gifted playwright, *Durang Durang* is both endearing and exasperating. It can seem as juvenile and predictable as a wisecracking college revue, but then it opens up into moments of coruscating comic insight that soars way beyond the material's ostensibly limited nature. Mr. Durang has generally worked better in short, explosive fragments than in sustained narratives. Now in his mid-40's, he shows no signs of growing into a conventional storyteller. But do we really want him to? (1994)

Durang brings into sharp focus the dark undercurrents buffeting the placid surface of American ideals, whether it be contemporary theatre, politics, or the family. His caricatures are never just a simple depiction of a person, but rather a portrait that is packed with ridicule. His parodies are exercises in literary criticism, exposing the play or playwright's style for further interpretation. And his absurd scenarios exuberantly demonstrate the logic causality of the most absurd premises: flawed suicide attempts, bad acting choices, and conservative thinking. As Randy Gener noted about the evening of one-acts, *Durang Durang*, "All the plays share typically Durangian preoccupations: narcissism, fear of engagement with a wide world filled with danger, the strangulating nature of family ties, sexual disorientation and the tenuousness of individual identity" (1994). These plays, ridiculous in their premises, ribald in their comedy, and puerile in their nonsense, are of a style that is quintessentially Durang.

CHAPTER 4
FAMILY DYSFUNCTION

The idealistic vision of the harmonious 1950s nuclear family governs Christopher Durang's plays—that is, this fiction of the family comes under relentless attacks. Durang, born during this postwar period known as the "baby-boomer" generation, was a product of a family-oriented ideology that emphasized the family unit as the most important personal network for individual association, far better than societal, religious, or civic groups. This impetus to create large families came at a time of increased prosperity and security. Couples moved to the suburbs and populated their large houses and yards with children, inspired by the boom in postwar housing and the pastoral imagery these neighborhoods provided. In doing so, they fulfilled a socially constructed vision of the American Dream that was rooted in conservative views of the family. However, inasmuch as people refer to traditional views of the family, Stephanie Coontz argues, the nuclear family was not "traditional" at all and was rather a new phenomenon. In *The Way We Never Were: American Families and the Nostalgia Trap* (1992), Coontz discusses how the cultural myths that Americans have about families were imagined during this postwar period: "Rates of divorce and illegitimacy were half what they are today [i.e., 1984]; marriage was almost universally praised: the family was everywhere hailed as the most basic institution in society." Furthermore, "At the end of the 1940s, all trends characterizing the rest of the twentieth century suddenly reversed themselves," she writes. "For the first time in more than one hundred years, the age for marriage and motherhood fell, fertility increased, divorce rates declined, and women's degree of educational parity with men dropped sharply" (1992, 24–5). Coontz uses historical data to demythologize the value-laden concepts, such as "homemaker" or "breadwinner," and offer a clearer sense of how families actually operated. Americans, Coontz reveals, "consistently told pollsters that home and family were the wellsprings of their happiness and self-esteem" (25). Anyone critical of the family unit at the time would be going against the mainstream or majority viewpoint.

Furthermore, the TV shows of this era contributed to the nation's understanding of the family and promulgated the belief that families were the bedrock of democratic values. Even while the United States was in the midst of urban conflict, the beginnings of the civil rights movement, and the tensions from the Cold War, the networks could reassure the country by touting shows of familial stability and suburban bliss. As Ella Taylor argues in her book *Prime Time Families* (1991), television programming provided uplifting models of social progress, embedded in story lines that exemplified traditional values of "honesty, simplicity, individual freedom within a protective community, and free enterprise" (1991, 39). The major sitcoms of the 1950s showcased happy, middle-class American families living in the suburbs, or aspiring to do so: *Leave It to Beaver*, *Ozzie and Harriet*, *Father Knows Best*, and *I Love Lucy*, followed in the 1960s with similar collaborative families as *My Three Sons*, *The Patty Duke Show*, *The Andy Griffith Show*, and *The Donna Reed Show*. The defining goal of television—to model a beneficent social order for a largely unknown audience—clearly worked. Till today, when people wish to evoke an innocent, wholesome time in the national psyche, "the 1950s" are conjured up along with the attendant black-and-white images from popular TV shows. In all these shows, families were presented as nurturing, trouble-free companions, and if conflicts should arise, they could be easily solved by wise, loving parents. Furthermore, one sensed that these TV celebrities were close friends due to the intimacy of their televised lives, delivered right to the family living room. Consequently, a unique mirroring effect of what it meant to be a family occurred between filmed representations of families and real-life families, where both children and adults saw reason to imitate the characters they saw on television and assume that their families would model similar behavior, too. Television was the most instrumental and subtle propaganda tool America had yet witnessed and the young Durang could not help but be influenced.

Durang came of age at a time when the televised American family resembled a golden-age holdover from a luminous fairy tale that never existed. This chapter explores how Durang anatomizes the damaging rapports within families and close relationships. Writing about the family, Durang joins the tradition of American playwrights whose plays demonstrated that buying wholeheartedly into the American Dream can undermine raising a healthy family. Plays by Eugene O'Neill, Clifford Odets, Lillian Hellman, Tennessee Williams, and Arthur Miller illustrated the internecine battles that marked American family life and were a far cry from the idealistic visions depicted by their folksy contemporary, Norman Rockwell. However, unlike these literary forebears, Durang used the subversive power of comedy to attack the family ideal. This TV world of familial harmony and safety must have struck Durang as decisively at odds with what he knew of his own family, as evidenced by the dark cynicism he injected into the seemingly happy domestic interiors. One such example from *The Vietnamization of New Jersey* occurs when Ozzie, Harry, and their son Et gather complacently around the breakfast table until the moment Et pours cereal down his pants. The alcoholism, fights, and parental neglect he experienced were not only painful but markedly different from the purported reality that appeared nightly on television. The grotesque, as Kayser has noted, is particularly useful at magnifying the discrepancy between the ideal and the actual (1966, 118), and Durang took recourse in this aesthetic mode, capturing the disjuncture between the expected harmonious family and the unsatisfactory reality. His specialty, as Ben Brantley noted, was steering "the suburban domestic comedy into dark and uncharted waters" of the 1970s (1999).

Titanic

The disaster movie genre, popular in the 1970s, provides a perfect substrate for cultivating family dysfunction and the Titanic, with its ill-fated voyage, offers an ideal background. Disaster films typically follow a formulaic plot, and, as Durang parodies these generic conventions, he exposes the hypocrisy behind American ideals. Nick Roddick has argued that 1970s disaster films like *The Poseidon Adventure* effectively focus on the social cohesion that develops in response to the disaster. In a disaster film, a random group of people is brought together for some ostensible purpose such as a journey. They subsequently become caught up in a catastrophe involving great human destruction, while a small group emerges and coalesces in order to survive. The cataclysmic event, while providing the narrative impulse, turns out to be secondary to the survival strategies the small group must put into place despite great odds. The disaster is important, but the film's true focus is on how the group unifies and how individuals transform into better people. The narrative moves toward collective action and selfless values, Roddick explains; feeble relationships are strengthened, weak ties between people become stabilized, and "greed [gives] way to generosity and permissive liberalism to a disciplined hierarchy" (1980, 250). Durang's play, *Titanic*, which he describes as "the most sexual, insane play I've ever written" (2017b, 83), offers none of these socially redemptive values; his characters tie each other up, hit one another, stab each other with hypodermic needles, and the son shoots both of his parents at the play's end. Durang turns the disaster genre on its head and depicts individuals who are wildly self-serving in their pursuit of their sexual proclivities.

Richard and Victoria Tammurai, on board the cruise ship of historic significance, pronounce at the play's onset their plan to divorce upon arriving onshore. The Tammurais, a self-centered, willfully immature couple, are even worse as parents: they have retarded the development of their son Teddy, who accompanies them on the cruise, keeping him in short pants at the age of twenty oblivious to his real age; his mother remarks, "I've never seen a fourteen-year-old with such hairy legs" (320). They proceed to have adulterous affairs, with both the Captain and the Captain's daughter, Lidia, whose initial presentation of pigtails and a tiny skirt belies her sexually predatorial alter egos. Durang also gives a mocking nod to the 1953 film *Titanic* starring Clifton Webb and Barbara Stanwyck, about a woman absconding with her children to America, only to be secretly followed by her estranged husband aboard the doomed ship. When Richard belittles his socially aspiring wife for her family background of Idaho pig farmers, Victoria takes her cue from the Webb-Stanwyck argument about the father's lack of paternal connections to his son and informs Richard that Teddy is not his real son but the result of a traipse with a beach derelict one night. Not to be outdone, Richard informs his wife that her daughter, Annabella, is not really *her* daughter, but is the legitimate offspring of their family friend Harriet, with whom Richard had an affair—perhaps the first time in literary history when anyone has denied a mother's biological connection to her offspring. Even though she claims to have given birth, Richard informs her that it was all an optical illusion done with mirrors. The opening scene exposes the kind of half-truths that can exist between couples, but in Durang's hands this ever-changing construction conveys not mutual dependency but the disturbing idea that even biological connections can be invalidated as only smoke and mirrors.

The play's dominant tone is black comedy, as established from the opening scene; upon hearing the orchestra playing "Nearer My God to Thee," Victoria quips to her husband, "Listen, they're playing our song"

(318), morbidly comparing their relationship to the song the orchestra played at the historical ship's demise. The first-mate Higgins's continual attempts to warn everyone about the impending iceberg are ignored and his pleas become a running gag, just like the sounds of destruction that the Captain's wife plays as a prank by putting a sound effects record over the loudspeaker system: "*Sounds of enormous ripping, water gushing, alarms, sirens, and so forth.*" Her inciting fear among the passengers warrants her execution at sea, and yet the illicit, bad behavior of the rest of the passengers goes unpunished. The Noël Coward witticisms and the bedroom farce antics keep the tone light, despite the play's matter being one of the darkest tragedies in twentieth-century history. No one is invested in collective action to save the group; unlike disaster films that promote the evolution of leadership, the ship's captain would rather have sex with his passengers than heed the warnings given about the fatal iceberg on the horizon. ("Higgins, I've told you to put these comments in the log" [1995, 343]). The characters' sexual licentiousness eclipses any acts of selfless courage or disciplined survival strategies expected from disaster films.

Instead, what Durang's play typifies is the orgiastic mode of the 1970s; the play was well suited for its initial productions at small theatres at eleven o'clock at night.[1] The sexual rebellion of the 1960s and 1970s unleashed an attitude of buoyant hedonism, in conjunction with the era's release of societal strictures on sexuality, living arrangements, and drug use. Joe Orton captured the spirit of the times with his outrageous sexual farce *What the Butler Saw* (1967), and Durang followed in his footsteps with his own character's polymorphous perversity, as well as a parent unknowingly having sex with a child. Although Lidia begins the play as the Captain's young daughter, she is later recognized as Harriet, Victoria's long-lost sister with whom Richard has had an affair. Victoria sexually seduces both her sister Harriet and later the Captain, the latter by tempting him with a loaf of Wonder Bread she has pulled from her skirt. He later appears with a slice of bread stuck to the dildo on his forehead because of his own fetish for frontal lobe penetration, causing a character to remark: "You look like you've been engendering biscuits" (327). In another scene, Teddy loses his own clothing and has to borrow the sailor's clothes, only to be sexually seduced by his father, whose past forays involve sexual intercourse with a transvestite that looks remarkably similar to the sailor whose clothes Teddy now wears. In his confusion, he propositions his own son, and later scenes show him sitting with Teddy on his lap, whom he now calls "Dorothy." The Captain resolves the impropriety of the sexual situations by marrying Victoria to her sister Lidia/Harriet, and marrying Richard to his son Teddy/Dorothy, dissolving any and all prohibitions against adultery, homosexuality, or incest. It does not need to be said that these family liaisons are a far cry from the conservative, hetero sexual relationships Durang saw on television growing up.

Where Orton's play showcased libido liberation, Durang gravitated toward a sexuality of the grotesque. The Captain's daughter, Lidia, a disarmingly ingenuous school-girl, has the bizarre propensity of harboring animals inside her vagina: a hedgehog, hamsters, and later a seagull, as indicated by the telltale signs of molting feathers floating from her skirt. Animals nesting in genitalia would be a striking example of Durang's use of the grotesque; as Geoffrey Harpham has argued, the grotesque is the perception of one thing illegitimately placed inside of something else (2007, 11). Later, when both she and Teddy feed the seagull after-dinner mints while sitting at the Captain's table, Victoria yells at her, worried about social propriety: "Really, a douche is one thing but a vaginal zoo is quite another!" (334). After Teddy has sex with Lidia, he describes how "awful" his first experience was, being tied up and having his penis attacked by Lidia's carnivorous pets, giving new significance to the "vagina dentata" myth. Lidia's lack of sympathy—having been gang-raped herself for two days by twenty-two Portuguese sailors—is indicative of the entire group's social indifference. From the group's behavior, Teddy grows to understand that individual sexual satisfaction surpasses any type of concern for others. In other words, the true disaster is not the iceberg, but the lack of any substantial foundation for compassion or trust in others.

The ending of the play, rather than the unification typical of disaster movies, is one of divisiveness and revenge. Teddy and Lidia arrive dressed in macabre black evening wear, representing a dangerous change in demeanor from Act 1; they have matured and grown-up perverse. Based on the humiliation he has suffered from both parents, Teddy is angry, and after one last public embarrassment by his mother, who rips his long pants into shorts, Teddy shoots both of his parents, egged on by Lidia who cries "GO GET 'EM, HEDGEHOG" (347). But even as Teddy retaliates against Victoria and Richard for being, as Lidia insists, "very bad parents," Durangian plays rarely, if ever, offer moral criticism; rather, the perspective is morbid glee in detailing the destruction egotistical people leave in their wake. The plight of the young Teddy crying at his parents' dinnertime arguments or being used for his father's sexual needs never receives judgmental criticism; his shooting them at the end of the play seems an act of absurdity as much as consequential revenge. In other words, the play does not end with the expected moral code that one finds in disaster films. Durang's disaster play shows no such logical consequences of bad behavior; it does not criticize the moral weakness of self-indulgence nor demonstrate the devastation caused by disunity. "Disasters are a moral affair," explains Roddick about the film genre, "and though the wicked are not the only ones to perish, they rarely survive" (260), but Durang shares less conviction regarding poetic justice. Michael Ryan and Douglas Kellner have also noted that in contemporary disaster films, society attempts to solve its social problems through a depiction of "strong male leadership, the renewal of traditional moral values, and the regeneration of institutions like the patriarchal family" (Ryan 1988), but in *Titanic* no male leadership emerges, the characters lack morals, and the family visibly disintegrates. Rather Durang's play illustrates the mayhem, destruction, and psychic abnormality that exist in place of the purported ideal of the traditional family. As the Captain summarily states during the marriage/funeral ceremony, "We have passed from the rigid law of the Old Testament . . . to the more humane law of love in the New Testament . . . onward finally to the new nonexistent law of today to the deep-think of nothingness" (340). Durang's disaster play signals the hypocrisy between society's wishful self-image and the actuality.

Death Comes to Us All, Mary Agnes

Continuing the pattern of destructive family relationships, Durang's next play *Death Comes to Us All, Mary Agnes* (1975) uses the gothic horror genre to convey the psychological and emotional captivity children suffer from narcissistic parents. As psychopathologies go, narcissism is particularly harmful for the effects it has on others, especially children raised by narcissists. Citing as his inspiration Alice Miller's book *The Drama of the Gifted Child*, originally titled *Prisoners of Childhood*, Durang relies upon the characteristic qualities of a gothic family saga, that is, mystery, melodrama, and family secrets, to emblematize this particular form of relational torture. He sets his one-act "last-will-and-testament" parody inside the drawing room of the Jansen-Hubbell mansion, complete with a dying patriarch who is never seen, but whose substantial estate makes his death eagerly awaited by his children and grandchildren. His mad wife, Mrs. Jansen-Hubbell, is kept tied up in the attic at the family's behest, save for sporadic appearances when a servant escorts her out. The socialite daughter's return to the home, the self-centered Vivien Jansen-Hubbell, initiates the play's action, along with her estranged husband, Herbert Pomme, an obsequious man lacking an arm as well as his masculinity, and her identical twin sons, Tod and Tim Pomme. The daughter whom she abandoned years earlier, Margot Pomme, also arrives at the ancestral home, traumatized from being left by Vivien in an orphanage at the age of five so that Vivien might travel the world unencumbered except for her adoring twin sons. Three servants round out the cast list, offering caustic commentary on the family's negotiations: a secretary, Coral Tyne, simmering with resentment from her unfulfilled life; the distinguished butler, Martin; and the scullery maid, Margaret. The play, in part a "Grande Dame Guignol" and in part a black comedy along the lines of the 1939 film, *The Cat and the Canary*, captures the oppressive weight of narcissistic parenting, except that the villainess is never punished for her crime.

Narcissism breeds familial prisoners. The *Diagnostic and Statistical Manual of Mental Disorders-IV* defines a narcissist as a person with "a grandiose sense of self-importance," "preoccupied with fantasies of unlimited success, power, brilliance, beauty, or ideal love" and as someone who requires "excessive adoration" and who "lacks empathy—that is, is unwilling to recognize or identify with the feelings or needs of others." Vivien Jansen-Hubbell's narcissism is evident from her early sense of herself as a great beauty and her fear of losing the attention of others. She frequently reads aloud the melodramatic bouts of self-pity she has written in her diary: "Dear Diary, I fear I am not loved enough. I fear it" (Durang 1995, 304) and reminisces about how she has been adored lifelong by men: "I was the most beautiful young girl who ever lived. I hope you will not think this is mere hyperbole" (297). She is histrionic in her performance of her narcissism, and the humor comes from the outrageous nature of her self-laudatory comments. She expresses the enormous burden of maintaining her charm and beauty and mourns the artificiality to her existence: "I have been cast to play the role I play, [and regret] that I can't be someone more elevated, more hopeful, even just more human" (297). Vivien tells a story of her first son, Narcissus, whom she adored because the two of them were beautiful together, but how she killed and tossed him in the garbage when he stopped complimenting her beauty: "Because we all need love, you see?" (303).

Her performance would be solely laughable if it were not for the harm she inflicts upon her children. As psychologist and author Elan Golomb describes in her book *Trapped in the Mirror: Adult Children of Narcissists in Their Struggle for Self* (1992), children of narcissists do not exist as independent beings but as extensions of their parents' selves. These children consider themselves valuable only insofar as they fulfill their parents' sense of self-worth. Tod and Tim, Vivien's twenty-six-year-old pretty-boy twins, have learned to pay attention to their mother's needs, painting oil portraits of her as a goddess or writing plays or poems about her to suit her fancy. "The power of the narcissist's influence permeates everything with which the child has contact. It becomes automatic for the child to conform to the parent's viewpoint in order to avoid disapproval," writes Golomb (1992, 35). In Tod and Tim's case, they are not merely avoiding disapproval but, in light of their brother's demise, avoiding *death*. Having accommodated themselves to her needs, they developed superficial, provisional personalities, an "as-if personality" as Alice Miller phrases it, and seem blissfully ignorant of the emptiness behind their facades. Both tan and winsome, affected and blasé in their speech, they manifest their mother's callous behavior and are indifferent to the pain they inflict on others. They insult Margot in tandem; toss hot tea onto the scullery maid; coerce young delivery boys into casual ménage-a-trois; and they are unmoved when their father dies from a stroke. In short, they are mini-narcissists themselves, having been groomed by their mother's behavior. Their incestuous three-way dalliances, what they call their "potluck" game, are emblematic of a narcissist's conceit and rapacious appetite. As mirror images of one another, they represent the self-immolation of narcissism; one can only love the self.

Margot's imprisonment in her mother's narcissist behavior is more painful because of her own need for love and acceptance. In contrast to her brothers, who see themselves as only an extension of their mother, Margot actually perceives her true self and wishes for it to be acknowledged by her mother. Having broken out of the institutional enclosure of the orphanage, she returns to her family, hoping to find resolution for the damage that has been done to her. However, her mother's crime inflicted upon her daughter—that of nonacceptance—cannot be undone because Vivien refuses to recognize her daughter. When Margot greets her, she is only rebuffed:

> MARGOT: Hello, Mother.
> VIVIEN: You must be a new maid of Father's?
> MARGOT: I called you "mother."
> VIVIEN: Did you? Well, I can't be expected to listen to every word people say to me. (291)

Margot's desire to be loved is repudiated by every member of the family. Even her father, who rescued her from the orphanage, feels no attachment to her and remains loyal to his ex-wife. Moreover, the narcissism appears to be endemic, a pattern of learned behavior passed from one generation to the next. In conversation with her grandmother, released momentarily from the attic, Margot reminds her about a time years earlier, when she was fifteen years old and turned to the older woman, seeking affection. She had asked her if she would ever feel the security of unconditional love and, as she recalls, her grandmother's response was "no," she would never be loved, because "there never was [love] for me!" (290). The poignancy of Margot's vulnerability contrasted against the cruelty of a grandmother's retort is funny in its incongruity, but Durang's underlying satire is consistent: the self-centered adult who refuses to nurture her own flesh and blood presents a damaging form of child abuse.

Repeatedly, the play uses the grotesque to demonstrate how narcissism is a violence that intrudes visibly upon daily life. The grandmother, kept hidden and chained in the attic, is a monstrous reminder of the secretive nature of familial harm; during her first appearance she spits out yellow vomit on the stage, from having chewed on a rat in her tower lair. Likewise, when the eponymous character, Mary Agnes, makes a brief appearance, it is to share a tale of how her husband killed her dog in a most gruesome fashion. In a sweet-tempered manner, she describes how the dog was cut into pieces, the eyes gouged out, and the innards removed; however, when Margot touches her gently on the arm, Mary Agnes screams angrily, then suffers an epileptic seizure, evidently not accustomed to kindness. Her uncle confides that Mary Agnes is having trouble adjusting to married life, a banal explanation that compensates poorly for the emotional distress just witnessed. Ionesco once pointed out that peoples' sufferings "can only appear tragic by derision" (Latour 1986, 260). It appears that Durang's attempt to narrate the psychological agony of domestic violence manifests itself in the ludicrous and surreal.

The play is a comical complaint against narcissistic parents, and yet the narcissists receive no comeuppance; rather, they are rewarded through funny twists of fate. The grandfather bequeaths his entire estate to Vivien, much to the dismay of his loyal secretary who provided him care and sexual favors over the years, such as placing and licking egg yolks off his body. Margot naively reprimands the secretary for her self-serving beliefs: "Money is so unimportant, Miss Tyne. It is love and affection, that matters. Comfort yourself with that thought" (302), but the play's action undermines the wholesome sentiments behind these lines. Margot hopes that her own father will advocate for her against the wickedness of her mother's abandonment, but he is unable to see past Vivien's charm before he dies, kneeling at her feet. Desperate for some matriarchal guidance, Margot turns to her grandmother for advice, whose only words to her are "DON'T DEPEND ON PEOPLE!" before she chokes Margot to death (310). The ending of the play, both shocking and ironic, is particularly *grand-guignolesque*. It is reminiscent of such wry twists of fate as *L'Horrible Expérience* (1909), a play in which a grieving doctor is strangled by his own dead daughter whom he has resurrected momentarily by the use of an electric shock. In true Durangian fashion, poetic justice is never served: the narcissistic matriarch treats people cruelly and ends up winning her father's inheritance, while the abandoned daughter, who seeks a sense of familial belonging, is strangled by her grandmother. In this way, the title of the play is fulfilled: death *does* come to everyone.

'dentity Crisis

Parents control to a great extent the material conditions of a child's life, but they also determine the psychosocial environment of the home, establishing a frame of reference that children implicitly trust and use in order to navigate their world. However, these parental constructions are just that—subjective interpretations of the world, which may or may not correspond accurately with reality. Oftentimes, a parental figure establishes such a skewed vision of reality that only by leaving the family fold can the child gain a clearer, more normative sense of his or her existence. In the play *'dentity Crisis* (1978) and its forerunner *Better Dead than Sorry* (1973), Durang incorporates the grotesque and the absurd to represent this warped socialization process and shows the degree to which children can be psychologically damaged by the parents' aberrant construction of reality.

In a play Durang wrote for the Yale Cabaret, "Better Dead than Sorry" (Durang 1971), a fragile but sane individual is harmed by her siblings who have empowered themselves to redefine their biological family relations. Carol, Darryl, Kenny, and Jenny are brothers and sisters, yet this biological truth is withheld until the play's end. Rather, Carol and Darryl perform in televised specials as an upbeat, real-life married couple along the lines of the 1970 entertainment personalities, Sonny and Cher. Kenny and Jenny, the younger siblings, are left at home. Jenny, played by Sigourney Weaver at the Yale Cabaret, exhibits odd behavior; she is catatonic, she cries and screams aloud at odd moments, and her attempts at suicide result in her being institutionalized. Despite the personal tragedy of the situation, the play is a comedy and her madness is treated lightly; Jenny manages to sing the title song while being tied up in a straitjacket and receiving electroshock therapy. As the play evolves, more deranged details transpire, but this time about the seemingly normal characters: Kenny gets arrested for molesting young boys, and Carol, after giving birth to a baby with Down syndrome, instructs her nursemaid to allow it to die. When it is revealed that Carol and Darryl are, in fact, incestuous siblings and not husband and wife, Jenny's insanity is recast as the only normal response to her familial circumstances: her insanity is the logical outcome to repressed memories of the true familial relations and horror at the violation of taboos. Yet despite her accurate moral sensibility, her siblings' control over the family reality renders her the traumatized victim, and she is the one who is institutionalized. The darkly comic humor of this play requires a particular audience sensibility. Such an aggressive manipulation of reality by family members defies all human empathy; all one can do is laugh.

"Better Dead than Sorry" parallels Durang's later published play *'dentity Crisis* (1971), where family members manically refashion biological ties. The first "I" of the word "identity" is amputated to suggest how the *ego* (Latin for "I") can be divorced from the person. The family in this play, through their distortions and prevarications, force the daughter to develop a multiple personality disorder. The play begins with Jane, a depressed young woman, having returned recently from the hospital after having tried to commit suicide by cutting her legs. She lives with her mother, Edith, and her brother, Robert. However, Robert is not a single person, but multiple; at varying times, he becomes a young boy, Dwayne; his father and Edith's husband, Arthur; his grandfather; and a fourth persona, Edith's lover, the count from France. Thus, even while Jane and the audience see only two people, Edith and Robert's crazy game demands that Jane recognize five: Edith, along with Robert's four separate selves. In order to play four different characters, the actor playing Robert modulates his voice and behaviors to depict three different ages and adopts a foreign accent for the count. In the original Yale Repertory Theatre production (1978), the set design included pictures of the two children, Jane and Robert, but

Robert had four identical pictures of him hanging on the wall. In sum, what the play dramatizes is the psychological process known as a "double bind," where a person receives two or more conflicting pieces of information, each one canceling the other out.

Durang drew his inspiration for this play from a book by R. D. Laing and A. Esterson called *Sanity, Madness and the Family* (1964) that consisted of case studies of schizophrenic patients. The book consists of a series of interviews with families, from 1958 to 1963, who each include a member who has spent time in psychiatric hospitals. Working against the typical model of schizophrenia as biologically based, the two psychologists advocated for studying the person in the context of the family cradle where the self is formed. Laing did not fault parents for causing mental illness, as is sometimes assumed, but rather he and his coauthor suggested that the way some families interacted with one another could create psychotic distress in one member, who would bear the brunt of family dysfunction. Laing's psychotherapy involved listening to the patient's words as a guide to how his or her world worked; despite their words being symbolic or surreal, he believed that the language used was a logical index to the experience the child had suffered growing up, that is, an experiencing of distrusting his or own perceptions and instead relying upon the memories and opinions of others. Drawn to their case studies, Durang wished to write a play "about an extreme and blatantly malfunctioning family where the craziness is totally evident and totally denied" (1995, 264), and how this type of psychological harm can affect the individual. The character who has been diagnosed as mentally ill, Jane, in effect sees reality correctly. The audience sees how her accurate perspective on reality is overshadowed by the insane behavior of the people around her.

One way by which groups of people establish the reality of a situation is linguistic, as in agreeing upon such statements as "it is too cold to go outside" or "it's not nice to cheat." Aligning everyone's perspectives together creates a reality that the entire group can perceive as "true"—or as close to "true" as possible. This mutual complicity of perspective is what sociologists refer to as the social construction of reality. When people are not in agreement, confusion and frustration ensue. The mother in *'dentity Crisis*, Edith, encourages her daughter Jane to play the piano even though Jane insists she has never learned and cries in frustration as she tries; Edith imposes a different interpretation on Jane's inability to play, explaining that the strain of her depression inhibits her skill. Edith later makes "banana bread," but rather than produce the bakery item as it is typically known, she skewers six pieces of Wonder Bread with a banana and designates it "banana bread." Humpty Dumpty's oft-quoted phrase from *Through the Looking-Glass* aptly encapsulates Edith's linguistic tyranny: "When I use a word . . . it means just what I choose it to mean—neither more nor less." Later, Edith uses circular rhetoric to negate Jane's comments, "A daughter doesn't contradict her mother" (268), and then lies outright: "Besides, you mustn't make up stories. I don't" (270). Furthermore, the semantic power she has to determine reality comes from Robert corroborating her nonsensical verbal statements, which Jane is defenseless to challenge, as seen in the following conversation where Robert acts as Edith's son, husband, and grandfather:

> ROBERT: Don't act odd, Jane. Tell your father you'll be normal.
> JANE: I'll be normal.
> ROBERT: I'll be normal, comma, Father.
> JANE: I'll be normal, comma, Father.
>   (*Enter Edith*)
> EDITH: Oh there you are, children.
> ROBERT: Mother, don't leave me for that Count. Edith, what is Dwayne talking about?
> EDITH: I'm sure I don't know, Arthur. (*Whispers to Robert*) Don't let your father know about the Count.
> ROBERT: Mother, I love you. Edith, what did you just whisper to Dwayne?
> EDITH: Oh, nothing, dear. Just that Grandad's hearing is getting worse. Look, I've invented banana bread, aren't you proud of me?
> ROBERT: Congratulations, Edith. Gee, Mom. (*Deaf*) What?
> EDITH: (*Shouting*) Banana bread, Grandad!
> ROBERT: It's too early for bed.
> JANE: I only see two people.
> EDITH: I'm sure you see more than that, dear. (274–5)

Since Edith and Robert have "agreed" that Robert really is four different people, their imaginary game becomes the reality despite Jane's logical protestations to the contrary. Every time Jane insists on proof, such as asking for her father's or grandfather's driver's license, she finds herself in conflict with their construed reality: Robert's driver's license shows his age as fifty, and the grandfather does not have a license, for he doesn't drive.

Edith matter-of-factly remarks, "The truth is the truth no matter how you look at it, Jane" (269), which is blatant hypocrisy in light of the fact that the audiences only witness two actors upon the stage. Their manipulation of the truth causes Jane to doubt her own sanity; as she tells her psychologist, "There's a man living in the house and I'm not sure whether he's my brother or my father or my grandfather. I can't be sure of anything anymore" (271).

Another determinant of reality comes from the identities of the people with whom we interact on a daily basis. When people act the way others expect them to act, that is, when people maintain stable identities, then the members of the group can live and work together effectively, but when people consistently lie about their identity, they alter the situational reality for everyone. In addition to Edith and Robert affecting Jane's mental health, Jane receives a visit from her psychologist, Mr. Summers, who purportedly treats her for her depression. Summers at first appears to be a voice of reason, trustworthy and stable, and his presence feels like a welcome relief against the oddity of the Edith-Robert team. He challenges Edith's nonsensical comment of having invented cheese and reassures Jane that she is not irrational, only tired. However, when he returns later in the day, he has transformed himself into a woman. He and his wife, he explains, bored with their marriages, have both had sex-change operations; thus, the Woman (her character name) who arrives insists to Jane that she is really Mr. Summers, and Mr. Summers subsequently insists that he is the wife, Harriet. When the married couple express their discomfort in their new clothing (albeit not their new *bodies*), they decide to change clothes and return attired as each other—that is, the male actor who played Mr. Summers in the first scene, now purports to be Harriet Summers and is dressed in woman's clothing, and the Woman is dressed as a man. The layers of gendered identity representation are more confusing than any of Shakespeare's comic heroines; in Durang's play, the characters have exchanged their sexual selves, but have retained their gendered ones. While Jane knows for certain their sexual reassignment surgery is a ruse, once again she is outnumbered two to one.

Children are particularly vulnerable to the information given to them by grown-ups as they lack any frames of reference by which to challenge such knowledge. Jane shares a childhood memory with her psychiatrist that speaks to the fictions adults create for children, describing a particularly disturbing experience while attending a production of *Peter Pan*. In typical stage productions of *Peter Pan*, Tinker Bell, the fairy that helps Peter, nearly dies when she drinks some poison. In order to bring Tinkerbell back to life, Peter Pan then turns to the audience and requests that they clap to affirm their belief in fairies. This request requires that the children enforce their faith in a fiction. In the twisted version that Jane recounts from her childhood, however, she and the children clapped their hands to revive Tinker Bell, but the actress playing Peter Pan dismissively told the audience, "That wasn't enough. You didn't clap hard enough. Tinkerbell's dead" (272). Here the grotesque rears its fantastic head; it is blatantly offensive to ask children to clap with the assurance of reviving a fairy's life, only to shatter their trust by announcing the fairy's death—and holding them culpable. Yet, this crazy manipulation of reality defines, for Durang, the family environment. The story Jane remembers from childhood, complete with sobbing children in the theatre, relates the power adults have to determine reality and how childhood innocence can be affected through adults' artful or cruel fabrications.

In a final showdown between the count, Dwayne, Arthur, and the grandfather, who all want Edith for themselves, Edith admits she loves all of them equally and embraces the four different men Robert is playing. All seven personalities (although only four people) introduce themselves to one another and encourage Jane to celebrate her birthday, even while she insists it is not her birthday. In a fit of frustration, she takes the cake knife and slices the top off the banana, a gesture that the therapist couple read with stereotypical Freudian nonsense as releasing her libidinal energies. Jane "catches" Mr. Summer in a lexical slip, referring to his wife when he should have used the word "husband," and exposes their game for what it is. At this point, the guests then begin introducing each other to one another as "Jane," and randomly singing French children's songs, like a music box gone awry. The mechanical rhythm of the scene recalls the last scene of Ionesco's play *The Bald Soprano*, where the cartoon characters chant inane phrases and then change roles with one another during a blackout. In Durang's play, when the lights go out, Jane is tied up and her mouth taped, seemingly in retaliation for having challenged their game. Her mother releases her when Jane tells them she is not Jane, but Jane's mother Emily. The play ends as she and her mother make a small child out of baking ingredients, the two therapists offer a psychological reading to the evening's events, and Robert conjugates the word "identity" as if it were a verb: "I dentity, you dentity, he she or it dentities" (282). Jane's decision at the end of *Identity Crisis* to become Emily is not simply playing along, but a forced adaptation to her family's reality so that her life becomes tolerable. As was the case in "Better Dead than Sorry," madness provides a strategy for survival.

The play '*dentity Crisis* has the silliness and symmetrical tightness of a traditional, bedroom farce; however, instead of changing lovers, these characters exchange identities. Like Joe Orton before him who satirized the violence of the psychiatric industry in *What the Butler Saw*, Durang, too, uses farce to examine psychological harm. In fact, *What the Butler Saw* is famous for having transformed the nature of farce from merely an evening's entertainment of disorderly lives to a representation of identity dissolution. As C. W. E. Bigsby noted, in Orton's play, "role playing is not a series of false surfaces concealing a real self; it is the total meaning or unmeaning of protagonists who survive by refusing all substance" (1982, 17). In '*dentity Crisis*, Robert's masterful enactment of four different personalities incites laughter because it defies expectations; the self, seemingly unified, is in actuality fragmented and confused. Likewise, the reversal of expectations— where the insane person is actually sane, and vice versa—also provides an intellectual delight for the viewer. Edith, Robert, and Mr. and Mrs. Summers blatantly flout the cooperative standards that society relies upon, and they are humorous in their rebellion of typical behavioral norms. However, the laughter turns sadistic when one considers Jane's point of view, when the collective aberrations of her family and therapist create a disordered world that puts pressure on Jane's cognitive load and instigates her identity dislocation.

Baby with the Bathwater

Baby with the Bathwater (1983) and *The Marriage of Bette and Boo* (1985) are Durang's two companion pieces about the damaging effects of child neglect. Not since George Bernard Shaw's *You Never Can Tell* (1897) has anyone written a comedy about child abuse; it is, in fact, rare to treat such a painful topic comically. While child abuse is primarily thought of as physical or sexual, Durang's two plays illustrate a form of abuse known as *neglect* and demonstrate the long-term harm it has on children. Neglect, though not as apparent as physical abuse, is defined as an act of omission, such as an adult not adequately fulfilling the child's basic material, educational, or medical needs. Furthermore, neglect is also seen when parents fail to meet a child's emotional needs for affection or solace, also creating irreparable harm. A child needs appropriate affective responses from an adult figure in order to understand and interpret his or her own feelings. When a parent attends to a child's emotional life, children develop a strong sense of identity and personhood; failing that, children grow up without a clear core identity or a sense of competence. The opening lines of Philip Larkin's poem "This Be the Verse," "They fuck you up, your mum and dad. / They may not mean to, but they do," offer the wry perspective that childhood damage is inevitable because of the nature of parenting, but the abused child at the center of *Baby with the Bathwater* offers no such easy forgiveness of his parents: "I suppose my parents aren't actually evil," he states. "They're not evil, they're just disturbed. And they mean well. *But meaning well is not enough*" (2003, 296; emphasis in the original).

Baby with the Bathwater opens with a spotlight illuminating a white wicker basket in the darkness. The image has an ominous quality to it and signifies themes of isolation and abandonment that reoccur throughout the play. Helen and John, projecting the innocence of young newlyweds, stare adoringly at their newborn infant, but their conversation quickly turns sour. Helen tells John she wants a divorce and justifies her request with nonsensical reasons: he has just referred to their baby as "a baked potato" and she does not like men with blond hair. Helen's immediate need for a divorce seems superficial and without motivation; yet worse than that, the insubstantiality of her claims, as Chung-Wee points out in his thesis on Durang, "carry with them a disturbing psychotic undertone" (2003, 55). Helen apparently suffers from radical mood swings; she focuses on irrelevant details or amplifies resulting consequences. She warns the baby to "beware of men" and recites a litany of vices: "Boys and men hit one another constantly. They attack one another on the street, they play football, they wrestle on television, they rape one another in prison, they rape women and children in back alleys" (265). John cannot understand Helen's abrupt change in attitude, remarking, "I don't understand. We were very happy yesterday" (266), but he possesses his own aberrant psychological disposition: his noncommunicative behavior (Chung-Wee 2003, 55). He suffers from depression, as evidenced by the week he spent sitting behind the refrigerator or avoiding reality with his head under a pillow. Neither of them can face the responsibilities of parenthood. Healthy parenting involves coping with the stress related to caring for small children, but when their baby starts to cry, they are both too inept to respond usefully. John cannot remember the correct lyrics to a lullaby, so he sings a flawed version: "Hush little baby, don't you cry, / Mama's gonna give you a big black eye" (266) and yells "shut up" when the song does not work. "How can we love the baby," Helen bemoans, "it won't stop that noise" (267). Nor can either one of them capably comfort the baby because Helen has drunk a cocktail for lunch and John took Nyquil with Quaaludes. Their ultimate cruelty is their choice to avoid giving the baby a gender identity; uncertain of the baby's sexuality, they dress him in girl's clothing and treat him as a girl until the age of eleven when he looks at a medical text book and realizes he is a boy.

The arrival of the Nanny, dressed sensibly in tweeds, would seem to be an antidote to their incompetence because she coos to the baby appropriately and offers folksy wisdom about raising children: "When it cries, you hold it. You should feed it regularly. You should keep it clean. Be consistent with it. Don't coo one minute and shout the next" (280). Yet her wisdom is undercut by her careless stupidities; she pulls out a trick jar with a snake, making the baby scream in terror and later gives the child a toxic toy containing lead, asbestos, and red dye #2, because she imagines that the "the cautionary warning is satiric!" (279). She refuses to get up at night when the baby cries and tosses the baby brusquely into the bassinet, adding her own brand of psychological terror to the chaos. Described as "a sex-starved Mary Poppins in leopard-skin panties" (Richards 1988), she bullies John into having an adulterous affair, then dismisses his scruples with a cavalier disavowal of morality: "Wrong, right, I don't know where you pick up these phrases" (273). The Nanny's self-righteous wackiness is in direct contrast to their self-centeredness, seeming to give sound advice; she states, "It's bad to fuss too much as a parent, your child will grow up afraid," yet in the same breath propositions John, "You want a quick one?" (273). Meanwhile, the seemingly normal next-door neighbor, Cynthia, wanders into their apartment; like Nanny, she at first appears to be a responsible adult. She identifies their inadequacies and rationalizes that she is a better parent than the three of them: "You three are heartless. You don't hold the baby when it cries, you dress it wrong so it can't move in its pajamas, and you're both so inconsistent as people changing from one mood to another that you'll obviously make it crazy. That's why it never smiles" (278). However, she is grieving the death of her own baby who was eaten by her German Shepherd after she left him alone on the floor. Consequently, she kidnaps their baby, only to get killed by running in front of a bus. John and Helen run after her in pursuit, and Daisy is saved by falling between the wheels of the bus; "Baby had never even seen a bus before, let alone been under one" (280), Helen pointedly remarks. The parents' behaviors such as neglecting, belittling, and ridiculing the child, as well the Nanny's actions of terrorizing the child, all constitute forms of psychological maltreatment that impede the young child's cognitive and emotional development.

The humor behind such cruel treatment of a baby is only possible because Daisy is not played by a real baby but by a toy doll. This distancing device of an artificial doll makes it easier to laugh at his harmful treatment, but it also reminds us of how babies are often treated as no more than objects under adult control: "They get tossed around, dressed down, trotted about and left behind," one reviewer notes (Richards 1988). The phrase "to toss the baby out with the bathwater" is an idiomatic expression referring to mistakes people make when they inadvertently remove something good when trying to solve a problem. Durang's use of the phrase implies that the parents treat the baby no better than the bathwater—both are disposable objects. The vulnerability and powerlessness of babies are emphasized by Daisy's toy-like quality: one domestic scene in particular shows their significant abuse of Daisy. He is head down, in a pile of laundry, his two little legs with red sneakers poking out the top of the pile. The image is striking in its polyvalent meaning: as part of the laundry, he is little more than a household accessory, stuck in place for safe-keeping and incapable of movement, a symbol of the couple's own ineptitude. The image signals the messy, mixed-up world that Daisy inhabits, as well as an eternally sad picture of the helplessness and pathos of the young child.

While Helen and John are primarily responsible for Daisy's destructive upbringing, Durang indicts the larger society in this play. He widens the circle of supervisory adults to include not only the Nanny but others who bear witness to the abuse but fail to help Daisy out of his own complacency. In one scene at a park, when Daisy is a toddler, Helen treats him horribly in front of other mothers. Annoyed by his catatonic behavior of lying on the ground and not moving, Helen rudely yells at the offstage Daisy "GET UP, YOU LUMP OF CLAY" and asks a little boy to poke Daisy with a stick or pull his hair. As narrated by the three women, Daisy finally moves, running and hurtling himself in front of a bus, which Helen does not try to stop; she calmly explains it happens all the time, as the two other mothers watch in horror. After she leaves, the two debate calling child protective services, which they would be justified in so doing, having witnessed Helen's verbal spurning of Daisy and her unwillingness to protect her child from danger, but they decide against it. Later, when Daisy enters school, his cries for help are still disregarded. His teacher brings to the attention of the school principal an alarming essay Daisy has written. In this essay, amid expressing wishes to commit suicide and violent images of German Shepherds, Daisy confesses, "How did I even learn to speak, it's amazing. I am a baked potato. I am a summer squash. I am a vegetable. I am an inanimate object who from time to time can run very quickly, but I am not really alive" (290). The childhood trauma he has suffered is evident from these descriptions, but the Woman Principal discounts Daisy's fraught essay as a brilliant literary work rather than evidence of a disturbed psyche. In describing the macabre phrasing as "an intriguing combination of Donald Barthelme and *Sesame Street*," she abdicates any responsibility she has for the child's well-being, as others have done before her.

The play's tone is clearly satirical; Durang sets the degrading pattern of child neglect against a farcical background. The Woman Principal, played by the same actress as the Nanny, represents a waggish version of adult negligence; comically flirting with her male secretary and reading an "Ah Men" underwear catalog, she is a risible example of an educational leader. It is as if Durang's characters reside in a Roy Lichtenstein print—melodramatic, overblown, and tongue-in-cheek. In production, directors emphasize the cartoon nature of the characters: a performance at Penguin Repertory's Barn Playhouse, Stony Point, New York (1987), used a "bold black-and-white comic-strip look" for a setting, while a revival by the Vanguard Theatre Ensemble in Los Angeles (1997) had a set design that established "a satiric tone of false naiveté" by the "trompe l'oeil window painting with real curtains and the music-box chimes of the sound design" (Herman 1997). The farcical quality to his parents' behavior underscores Daisy's chaotic world: Helen shifts from aggressive to passive within minutes, lambasting Daisy for keeping her in a loveless marriage and frustrating her ability to write her book, then lying inertly on the floor and refusing to answer John's requests for dinner. John, in turn, throws a tantrum by breaking Daisy's toys and threatening to leave Helen with the bag of laundry—including Daisy—slung over his shoulder, reinforcing the child's object status. Despite the frightening physical and verbal abuse, the immaturity of the adults is humorous: John smashing Daisy's toys as an effort to get his wife to respond is undercut by his discovering—and *drinking*—the vodka Helen has hidden from him in Daisy's toy duck. Dan Sullivan pointedly acknowledged the plays' cartoon nature in the Public Theater's production (Los Angeles) as intrinsic to his interpretation: "The exaggerations make you laugh, which is why [Durang is] an entertaining writer, and the likenesses make you wince, which is why he's a valuable one. In this play one also sees the beginning of a certain compassion for the figures trapped in his cartoons" (1985).

Moreover, again, in this play, Durang relies upon the humorous grotesque as a shock technique. Durang's use of grotesque details, such as the German Shepard that eats a baby,[2] is as indicative of society's fascination with the gruesome mishaps of others as it is of societal unwillingness to help. James Schevill describes the American grotesque as part of the contradictory values of the nation: "Grotesque is what we become when we seclude ourselves in the suburban community closed to wonder, the mechanical mirage of technological comfort" (Schevill 1977). Suburbanites isolate themselves from the pain of others, yet continue to relish the distressing stories with a voyeuristic glee. For example, the two mothers at the park, Angela and Kate, although appalled by Daisy's psychological abuse, relativize Daisy's mistreatment as just one of many terrible events that occur in contemporary life. Kate discusses a roller-skating fanatic who "skated right under a crosstown bus," while Angela outdoes her with a horror story about a child "found dismembered in the garbage cans outside the 21 Club." As the two exchange horrible stories about chemical explosions in New Jersey, the murder of Karen Silkwood, or David Berkowitz, the infamous Son of Sam killer, they heighten their own sense of helplessness, even while fascinated with morbid delight. They accept the inevitability of painful life circumstances and convince themselves that the harm done to a child loses its significance in light of chemical explosions or celebrity stalkers. The grotesque satisfies a strange perversion of people to dwell on the harm done to others, and here Durang criticizes the women for not only their complacency but also their tendency to glamorize aberrant behavior.

In the second act, Daisy, no longer played by an inert doll but by an adult actor, expresses his side of the story. Having grown up to be a disturbed and depressed young man, he seeks the help of a professional therapist. The sessions take place in abbreviated form, revealing glimpses into the different phases of his ten years of treatment. Daisy steps forward into a spotlight, "Chorus Line" style, appearing particularly foolish in a dress, while the therapist is played as a voice projected from the back of the auditorium, and remains unseen; the effect is such that Daisy, breaking the fourth wall to speak his troubled soul, positions the audience as therapeutic listeners. Daisy, from years of abuse, is neurasthenic. Identified as a girl for the first half of his life, he has no sense of personhood; he is only a projection of his parents' emotional turmoil. After being enrolled in college for thirteen years, he is still unable to complete his essay on *Gulliver's Travels* and get his degree, and his identity confusion leads to his sexual promiscuity, because sexual intercourse frees him from his ill-defined identity: "There's always 10 or 20 seconds during which I forget *who I am* and *where I am*" (295, emphasis in the original), he confesses. Daisy believes it is better to be dead or unborn than to suffer from malignant parents, and his despondency is so dark that he fantasizes about throwing a random child he sees in the neighborhood in front of a car to save him from being raised by insane parents. The therapy works, but only up to a point, and Daisy must take responsibility for his life. His therapist, exhausted by the same stories after almost 400 sessions, yells "You're smart, you have resources, you can't blame them forever. MOVE ON WITH IT!" (297). Part of his therapeutic conversion is to acknowledge his anger with his parents by returning home and viewing John and Helen from an adult perspective, rather than that of a helpless child. Daisy's return to the house for his birthday turns out to be traumatic. His mother has bought him a kilt for a gift, as a demented joke about how she and John used to dress Daisy as a girl. John has become a Christian Scientist, a religion that has come under attack in the United States for encouraging parents to rely upon spiritual healing over medical treatment for their children, the consequential death from natural causes arguably being a form of neglect. Nanny, as a surprise visitor, contributes to the nightmare when she jumps out of a birthday box and scares Daisy. Returning to the scene of his childhood environment, Daisy feels a mixture of hostility and pity toward his parents; John, for example, is particularly pathetic, as his alcoholic hallucinations cause him to duck from imaginary owls. The liberation that results from this difficult home visit is that Daisy sees his parents not as evil monsters, but as morally deformed, and that his psychological disorder is not innately his, but stems from their abuse.

The ending is hopeful, which is a significant change from Durang's earlier plays. Unlike Durang's earlier works, such as *Titanic* or *'dentity Crisis*, the character's ability to escape the psychological damage of his past reveals a change in Durang's own life. In his thirties, Durang discovered that he had control over the kinds of people with whom he interacted; he realized that protecting himself from the harmful behavior of others gave him a sense of self-worth that he did not have growing up. Originally a one-act play that ended on a depressing note with the parents waving a toxic toy before the traumatized baby, Durang added a second act wherein the grown-up child possesses the self-awareness to adjust to the misfortune of bad parenting and the resilience to recover from difficult circumstances. "Such resilience amazes Durang," one critic noted, "almost as much as the perversity of parents and other adults angers him" (Richards 1988). The final scene repeats the first scene of the play, following the circular pattern of much absurdist theatre, but with a difference: Daisy and his new wife Susan care appropriately for their new baby, picking him up and comforting him. Daisy reverses the violent lyrics that John has earlier sung to him; rather than "mama's gonna give you a big black eye," the lyrics he sings advocate reassurance and agency: "And if that big black poodle should attack / Mama's gonna teach you to bite it back," or "And when baby grows up, big and strong / Baby can help mama rewrite this song" (305). The grown-up Daisy is a character who possesses insight: he recognizes how his parents' unpredictable behavior harmed him and thus consciously chooses not to recreate that kind of parenting. Frank Rich observes the new feeling previously absent from Durang's works, "the joy of being sane" (1983), yet the ending is equivocal; one reviewer sees in Daisy's performance "a blend of resignation and limited hope for the future" (Sullivan 1985).

The Marriage of Bette and Boo

Baby with the Bathwater portrays child neglect in a ridiculous fashion, bordering on buffoonery; whereas *The Marriage of Bette and Boo* (1985) offers a more psychologically nuanced view of child neglect based on the parents' own disappointment and lack of family support. However, both plays offer biting commentary about the damage adults can create when they are ill-equipped to be married, let alone start a family. An autobiographical play that situates the family as foe, Durang's piece is akin to Eugene O'Neill's *Long Day's Journey into Night* or Tennessee Williams's *The Glass Menagerie*, although it is more a "tragedy disguised as a mad farce" (Heilpern 2008), as one critic put it. Durang uses the device of the onstage narrator to structure his memory play, similar to the character of Tom Wingfield in *Glass Menagerie*, and played the role himself in the play's premiere. Matt, the narrator, envisions various moments of his family's past life, from his parents' marriage to the day his mother dies, and offers his reflections at the beginning of each scene. Matt's opening comment to the audience, "if one looks hard enough, one can usually see the order that lies beneath the surface" (Durang 2003, 315), attests to his narrative reconstruction of the family's past in order to find an explanation for his parents' flawed marriage and his own tumultuous upbringing. Matt's motivation seems to come from a book that influenced Durang, Alice Miller's *Drama of the Gifted Child*, in which she writes, "For me, making sense of suffering means resolving it. It means seeking and establishing what it is that causes us to suffer today, in order to be able to avoid it in the future" (1987, 6). As the play's narrator, Matt remains detached from his family's suffering. Critically observant of their actions, he provides an analysis of his family and their internal dynamics in order to come to terms with his own psychological distress, and in doing so perhaps be delivered of the pain.

Originally a short play comprised of twenty-four brief scenes, Durang expanded the play twelve years later into a series of thirty-three vignettes detailing the married life of Bette and Boo, particularly Bette's uncompromising struggle to have more than one child and Boo's growing alcoholism. Like a photo album of memories come to life, the episodes reveal the immaturity of the two adults who gave birth to their son Matt, but whose grief regarding the inability to have more children stood in the way of raising him appropriately. The opening tableau of Bette and Boo's wedding, for example, where the family members sing together in unity, illustrates a snapshot of familial wholesomeness and harmony that is belied by the succeeding vignettes' acrimony. Christopher Isherwood describes the cycle of scenes from wedding, to hospital labor, to family gatherings, to divorce and death as a "carousel of horrors masquerading as a bubbly comedy" (2008), while Michael Feingold compares the individual scenes to a collection of *New Yorker* cartoons, tart and taut with their humorous glimpses into an upper-middle-class family, whose urbane facade has no room for the painfulness of life's challenges (2008).

Bette's immaturity is her character's key note. Her daffy cheerfulness defines her; she punctuates the end of each phrase with laughter, she chatters incessantly and at times nonsensically, and her silliness is what has attracted Boo. She confides to the audience on the night of their honeymoon that she does not know Boo very well, as she met him quickly after a failed relationship with a married man, suggesting the couple's fallibility. Beneath her frivolity lies the shame of having been labeled dumb years ago in school, and she shares a grade school anecdote about being publicly humiliated: "The two stupidest in math are Bonnie and Betsy. Bonnie, your grade is eight, and Betsy, your grade is five," she recalls the teacher's saying (319). Even her dream to have a large family is replete with childlike naivete: "My family is going to be like an enormous orphanage. I'll be their mother. Kanga and six hundred Baby Roos" (328). When Bette discovers that she can have no more babies after Matt is born due to Rh incompatibility, she refuses to accept the doctor's diagnosis and subsequently gets pregnant four more times, her bouts of labor all resulting in four stillborn babies. Before a treatment for Rh incompatibility was discovered, if a mother was carrying a fetus whose Rh factor was different than her own, the mother's antibodies would attack the red blood cells of her fetus, recognizing them as foreign, and causing death in the fetus due to severe anemia, or a stillbirth.[3] Bette's extreme pain of wanting children but being unable to have any more is inconsolable and results in her emotionally withdrawing from her one son, Matt. The pain of miscarriage or stillbirth, though spoken about more openly now, was not acknowledged in the 1950s or 1960s. Her mother's platitudes to "think of pleasant things in the world" offer neither compassion nor comfort, and Bette resorts to calling her high school friend Bonnie late one night, even though they haven't spoken in years. In a strangely disconnected monologue, she must prompt her friend's memory about their friendship, and then confesses, out of the blue, "I've lost two babies. No, I don't mean misplaced, stupid, they died. I go through the whole nine month period of carrying them, and then when it's over, they just take them away. I don't even see the bodies. Hello? Oh, I thought you weren't there" (334). Bette never fully expresses her pain to any other character in the play; her reaching out to a distant friend indicates how isolated she is in her grief.

Bette's mild-mannered husband, Boo, is confused and remorseful over her insistence on having children despite the risk to the fetus's life. Boo's own weak nature and his ineffectual skills at helping his wife leads him to take recourse in drink. He complains to Bette that he can no longer tolerate the pain of stillborn babies: "I've had enough babies. They get you up in the middle of the night, dead. They dirty their cribs, dead. They need constant attention, dead. No more babies" (362). Boo turns to drink to assuage these losses and hides in the basement to avoid his wife. Moreover, his parents are insensitive to his plight; after the fourth baby is pronounced dead, Boo, who has been getting intoxicated at a bar, returns to the hospital and asks his father, "Did it live?" to which his father acidly replies, "Not unless they redefined the term" (349). Boo proves to be an emotional coward; he knows he should go into his wife's hospital room to comfort her after the loss of the baby, but he admits, "I don't think I can face her" (349). Bette and Boo illustrate a couple who lack the coping skills for the pressing circumstances placed on their marriage, and their family members only make matters worse.

Unlike the couple in *Baby with the Bathwater*, Bette and Boo's marriage does not occur in isolation but, rather, in the context of a wider family dynamic. Bette's parents, Margaret and Paul, as well as her sisters, Joanie and Emily, are all present for the wedding, as are Boo's parents, Karl and Soot, played by Olympia Dukakis in the original production. Margaret has created a wedge between her three daughters through her pointed comparisons; she mentions at the wedding that Bette was considered "the most beautiful" of her children, while noting how Joanie's own troubled marriage—her husband is notably absent—weighs upon Bette's wedding happiness. Emily has health problems, such as asthma, which are triggered by her bouts of hysterical guilt. Her failure to remember the music for her sister's wedding leads to lifelong apologies and rituals of Catholic self-abasement. After Joanie receives one of Emily's confessional letters, she confronts her sister and hisses, "I *forgive* you, I *forgive* you, I *forgive* you [emphasis in the original]," and threatens to cut her cello strings with scissors. The characters' insensitive comments to one another, so typical of any family interaction, create a type of wry laughter over the darkness of their pain. Bette's mother is described by one reviewer as "a chipper monster who wears her malice and neediness on her well-appointed sleeve" (Anonymous 2008). Margaret plays her maternal role with the forced cheerfulness of keeping up appearances, void of compassion for her children's plights. She offers such platitudes as "marriage is no bed of roses" in response to Bette's complaints about Boo's drinking problem (322) and, later in the play, when all of her children have returned to live in the family home, Margaret expresses her delight in such an elevated, sunny voice that she implies she is anything but. Paul, Bette's father, shows compassion to his children, but his aphasia from his stroke renders his speech unintelligible and thus no one can benefit from his wisdom. Boo's father, Karl, is verbally abusive toward everyone, including Boo, whom he calls "Bore," and especially toward his wife Soot. He speaks in degrading terms to his wife who constantly laughs off his comments as if they were meant as a joke. At one point, Karl remarks that "Soot is the dumbest white woman alive" (321), and she giggles embarrassingly in response, but the sad, searching look in her eyes, as noted by reviewers, indicates the true cost of that laughter. The family dysfunction appears intergenerational, with children adopting the vindictive spitefulness of their parents.

Even more disturbing is the fact that the young Matt is present as a witness to such familial cruelty. Joanie's ability to have several children, albeit without the material means to care for them, causes Bette jealous pain, and the two bicker spitefully, with Matt a silent observer in the background. Bette remarks to Joanie, "You're a neurotic mess. You're going to ruin your children," while Joanie retorts, "Well it's lucky you only have one to ruin, or else the mental ward wouldn't just have Emily in it" (346). Later in the conversation, Joanie comes up with a real ringer regarding their pregnancies: "Well maybe we'll both have a miracle. Maybe yours'll live and mine'll die" (347). Another scene reveals a particularly acerbic fight when Bette chastises both her father-in-law Karl and Boo for drinking too much. As Karl ridicules one of his wife's friends for her body odor, Bette attacks: "HOW CAN YOU SMELL HER WITH ALCOHOL ON YOUR BREATH?" Karl responds by pouring his drink over Bette's pregnant belly and saying, "I think it's time your next stillborn was baptized" (341). Durang acknowledges that he heard such shocking comments coming from his mother's family. He shares in an interview that "her family was so difficult to deal with and crazy [particularly during her trial with cancer]. They were mean, too, but they were more crazy than mean" (Durang 2012b, 58). In a harrowing scene that culminates Act 1, the two families have come together to celebrate Thanksgiving only to have it end prematurely in a climactic shouting match between Bette and Boo, with Matt absorbing the adults' emotional fallout. As the family members arrive, Bette becomes progressively nasty toward her husband and uses the presence of the family to get leverage on Boo and his alcoholism. She asks Boo's mother, Soot, to smell her son's breath for alcohol and publicly belittles Boo's behavior. Shouting angrily in response, Boo accidentally knocks into Emily holding the gravy and spills gravy all over the floor. When Boo proceeds to get a vacuum cleaner, Bette chastises him in front of everyone, "You don't vacuum gravy," at which point Boo begins to bleat hysterically: "WHAT DO YOU DO WITH IT THEN? TELL ME! WHAT DO YOU DO WITH IT?" (337). The holiday scene, at first humorous in its focus on the trivial, reveals family tensions that grow out of hand, where the small accident of spilled gravy represents deep-seated pain in Bette and Boo's relationship. The tension is magnified by the social pressure to appear like a cohesive family unit in the presence of other family members.

Family members must work hard to live together, due to the everyone's differing drives and desires that are frequently at cross purposes. However, the weakest member in this power dynamic finds him or herself in a lose-lose situation, unable to please the other members and locked in a pattern of invalidation because his needs are never met. Matt, as the only son of Bette and Boo's marriage, not only bears witness to the devastating bitterness but suffers from neglect. Bette's broken dreams over not having a large family, compounded by her own sense of inadequacy, cause anger toward her husband and emotional abandonment of her child. Her unavailability to Matt results in inadequate parenting. For example, Emily asks Bette at one point how Matt is doing, and Bette cannot remember to whom her sister is referring. One of the most moving scenes in the play is a young Matt playing by himself on the floor, ignored by the adults as they heatedly argue, unaware of how Matt absorbs their negativity; midway through the scene, Emily intuits he needs attention and sits down to play with him, the only care he gets. Like his onstage character, Durang experienced his own feelings of abandonment at the age of three when his mother underwent a serious depression because of the death of her second baby and his father resorted to alcohol (Durang 2003, 419).

Furthermore, Matt, though a young child, moves into the role of caretaker for his parents. This unexpected maturity, what is now referred to as "parentification," is often the result of conflictual parent-child relationships, where the parents place their children in the position of meeting the parents' needs. During the Thanksgiving catastrophe, Matt adopts the supervisory position, turning off the oven when he smells food burning, or getting the water and sponge to clean up the gravy. In his later years, his parents turn to him for consolation and advice. When Boo is not able to endure the pain of the last stillborn baby, and leaves for the bar instead, it is Matt who removes the dead baby from the hospital floor, addressing what Bette herself cannot face. During one of the play's "flash-forward moments," an older version of Matt visits his father and mother, who are now divorced. The father is feeble and forgetful, emphasizing his loneliness by repeating, "A man needs a woman, son" (342), and pleading with Matt for his friendship. Bette also clings to Matt as a way to give her life meaning, because he is "the only one of [her] children that lived," and making him feel guilty that he does not visit more often (342). The most difficult moment of such role-reversal occurs when Matt is called as a witness for his parents' divorce proceedings, and must testify against his father, Boo, regarding his drinking problems.

Matt is asked to evaluate the severity of his father's alcoholism, but he lacks his mother's righteousness, and merely states his wish to avoid all conflict. The proceedings are harmful to Matt, and they come as the culmination of a childhood of maneuvering through the minefield of his parents' abusive relationship. In trying to act the peacemaker and protect himself from their volatility, he internalized a great deal of his parents' pain.

As with *Sister Mary Ignatius Explains It All for You*, the Catholic Church comes under attack, this time for its failure to provide families with helpful emotional support. While religion and spiritual practice is assumed to provide its adherents with the assurance that a larger power protects and provides, in this play, Catholicism is viewed as promoting Bette's pain, not solving it. Bette relies upon the church as one might utilize the services of a family counselor, even though the Priest is unqualified to provide therapy; not once does he mention some productive steps she might take, such as the possibility of adoption or channeling her love for children into community work. When Emily blithely suggests to Bette that God might grant her a miracle, Bette's own immaturity comes to the fore; she clings to a superstitious belief in miracles despite the doctor's medical diagnosis and visits Father Donnally, who gives half-hearted directives rather than any meaningful advice. Her indoctrination in Catholic stories of miracles obviates his flat-out warning that "miracles rarely happen, Bette" (331); rather, she insists that if she prays, God will enable her to have children and that she "would be a mother as God meant [her] to be" (331). Bette also brings Boo to Father Donnally to sign a promissory pledge to give up drinking, as one would bring a wayward child to be reprimanded by an adult, but once again Father Donnally proves irresponsible and comically inept. During the marriage retreat he organizes, he demonstrates his fundamental lack of understanding married life when he describes the numerous marriages that have "floundered on the rocks of ill-cooked bacon" (352), and then proceeds to demonstrate bacon sizzling in a frying pan, getting down on the floor and twisting and rolling about. Father Donnally is the typical irresponsible authority figure in Durang's plays whose foolishness is in inverse proportion to the power he has over other people's lives.

Further, the restrictions the Catholic Church places on its members work against adults solving problems for themselves, such as the dictate against prophylactics. Soot reflects wryly on Bette's repeated pregnancies, remarking, "Catholics can't use birth control, can they? (*Laughs*). That's a joke on someone" (353). The church's strictures against divorce exacerbate the young couple's grief. Father Donnally reminds Bette and Boo of their marriage vows that "man and wife are joined in holy matrimony to complete each other, to populate the earth and to glorify God" (353), and he expresses his frustration with married people who ask him for a divorce because "the Church does not recognize divorce" and "there is no solution to a problem like that" (353). The "willed denial that keeps couples—particularly Catholic couples—together," as Michael Feingold points out, is the key tension "under the playful surface" of the play. The Church's patriarchal authority requires couples to remain together even while its internal mechanisms are incapable of helping them to maintain their vows.

Only by seeing the play within the context of Theatre of the Absurd can such dire subjects of alcoholism, divorce, and stillborn births be understood as funny. More than quirky character eccentricities, style, or tone, more than "wrapping life's horrors in the primary colors of absurdist comedy" (Rich 1985), the play demonstrates the philosophy of Theatre of the Absurd, particularly the search for meaning in an irrational world. Theatre of the Absurd, as defined by Martin Esslin in 1961, is suffused with rueful laughter, prompted when the reality of existence is in direct contrast to people's expectations. The laughter arises when the characters come face-to-face with the opposite of what they have been led to expect: death instead of life, callousness instead of kindness, neglectful parents instead of supportive ones. The medical establishment, as one example, is expected to be healing and salutary, yet each time Bette gives birth to a baby, the doctor appears before the gathered family members, announces unfeelingly, "The baby's dead," and drops the infant on the floor. The doctor's gesture is grotesque, but it underlies the adamancy of fate; there really is no way to soften the blow, particularly at a time when the imagined outcome is new life. The family members gather gamely during Bette's periods of labor, like vaudevillian characters ready for their song and dance, only to shuffle off after each stillbirth infant is thrown to the ground. The running sight-gag of dropping dead babies on the floor jars noticeably against the upbeat atmosphere of the play: "The dissonance between the ghastliness of the events being depicted and the continually chipper tone in which they are greeted by the characters is the play's signature leit-motif," one reviewer notes, "the chugging generator of its biggest laughs" (Isherwood 2008). The harsh fickleness of fate in the face of the characters' willful expectations results in rueful laughter. The absurd is born when their expectations are met repeatedly with fate's silent refusal.

Matt's search for answers regarding the painful relationships of his family members makes him an absurdist hero. The absurdist hero, as Camus argued in "The Myth of Sisyphus," finds meaning in the process of making meaning, of creating his own reasons why events have occurred. In sifting through the memories of his family's life, as Matt announces at the onset, he seeks explanations for his family's irrational behavior and ultimately discovers there are not any. As a literature student in college, he analyzes the patterns in Thomas Hardy's novels, identifying with Hardy's repeated treatment of the "waste and frustration" of human lives. Drawing a comparison between his own home life and that of Eustacia Vye, a woman in *Return of the Native* who ended her life tragically because of her unhappy marriage, Matt ultimately concludes that marriages are the unhappy pairings of misguided people. Turning to his family, he seeks the same clarity. He asks his grandparents about the destructive patterns of their lives: "I see all of you do the same thing over and over, for years and years, and you never change.... What I mean to say is: did you all intend to live your lives the way you did?" (361). Margaret has dementia and can only respond nonsensically, and Karl shuts down when Matt asks him pointedly why he was so verbally abusive to his wife, Soot. In the last scene, Matt questions his parents while visiting his mother in the hospital, who is dying of cancer: "Why did you drink?" he asks his father, and then turns to his mother: "Why did you keep trying to have babies? Why didn't Soot leave Karl?" (367). Much like the mythological Sisyphus who was doomed for eternity to roll a rock back up a hill, Matt's family members engaged in repetitive behavior; but unlike Albert Camus's version of Sisyphus, none of the characters ever achieve critical self-awareness.

Matt never finds the explanations for why his family members caused each other so much harm; he never determines whether Boo drank excessively on his own or in response to Bette's nagging, nor does he understand why his relatives were incapable of making change for the better, preferring to stay stuck in their own pain while hurting themselves and others. He comes to the ultimate absurdist conclusion about the arbitrary hand of fate in conversation with his mother. As she ponders whether God is punishing her by giving her cancer, he replies, "I don't think God punishes people for specific things. I think he punishes people in general, for no reason" (364). Matt, like Thomas Hardy, understands that there is no teleological direction in life, no causal connection between human behavior and divine providence. And, like Sisyphus, he liberates himself from pain by achieving consciousness over his own choices, and taking responsibility for his life, a phrase that characters in Durang return to frequently. Juli Novick, in reviewing the production, argued that the play offers a transformative vision: "Mr. Durang goes beyond blame . . . into compassion" (1985), which can be seen in the play's final moments when Matt envisions his mother's soul is in heaven, "reunited with the four dead babies" and waiting for her husband and Matt to join her. But the perspective that Matt achieves through this narrative reenactment is more than compassion; the play he offers the audience is a stoic and lucid vision of his life.

Jean-Paul Sartre's oft-quoted phrase "hell is other people" seems the perfect summary for Durang's family plays, particularly because it points so neatly to an inherent contradiction in familial life: the opinion of our family members matters the most to our sense of self because these individuals are so proximal. This awareness of oneself in the eyes of others perpetuates in people a heightened self-consciousness and, in growing up within dysfunctional families, possibly a strong sense of failure. In all of the plays that Durang creates about the family, *Titanic, Death Comes to Us All, Mary Agnes, 'dentity Crisis*, and particularly *Baby with the Bathwater* and *The Marriage of Bette and Boo*, he creates a central character who is sensitive to the forces around him or her, the bare-faced lies, the circumlocutions, and the subtle manipulations caused by another's will. In all of these plays, the family acts as the constraining, judgmental force to which the central character is subjected, but from which he cannot escape. Nor can the individual find strength or solace in religion which, as it turns out, has a constraining influence on family and marriage, as seen in Chapter 2.

Moreover, in these plays, Durang shows the golden image of the traditional family unit as exemplified by the 1950s TV shows to be egregiously flawed. As Stephanie Coontz notes in her work on the family in American television, these conservative shows with clearly defined parental roles—a responsible, financially successful father, a nurturing mother—emphasized how the family provided a secure and stable context for raising young children. Week after week, the foundational values of the family nucleus were emphasized on these shows: group cohesion, collaboration, and a responsibility toward one another. However, the reality behind such representation could not be farther from the truth in many families. Many of the people Coontz interviewed who grew up watching these TV shows experienced feelings of disappointment and guilt that their families did not fulfill the images portrayed on television. "The most common reaction to the discordance between myth and reality is guilt," she writes. "Even as children, my students and colleagues tell me, they felt guilty because their families did not act like those on television. Perhaps the second most common reaction is anger—a sense of betrayal or rage when you and your family cannot live as the myths suggest you should be able to do" (1992, 6). Durang, as the keen satirist, demonstrates the disparity between the nostalgic image of the ideal family and the reality, sometimes exposing the guilt, sometimes the anger, and sometimes the sadness of the central character.

CHAPTER 5
AMERICAN ANOMIE

Society is sick. This remains Durang's take on humanity. Emile Durkheim, contemplating society's ills, coined the term "anomie" to refer to a state of normlessness among social groups, when people are not in agreement about what is right or wrong. Anomie is a condition that is experienced where there is too little social regulation in society, where the values are changing or poorly defined, or where there is a mismatch between what a person believes and what everyone else tends to hold true. Consequently, the lack of a widespread commitment to values, standards, and rules creates feelings of loneliness, normlessness, or meaninglessness. These sensations are articulated by Durang's characters in his 1987 complaint against urban living, *Laughing Wild*. When he returned to the theatre after a ten-year hiatus, his scalpel was sharpened, and he proceeded to attack the dyspeptic nature of society, including inept leadership, outlandish media control, and selfish individualism. He positioned these satires close to home, within the familiar world of rental cottages and suburban neighborhoods, as if to emphasize how far we are from presumed normalcy.

Durang's comedic style is the perfect antidote for this societal incongruity, and the plays in this chapter are all misalliances between personal and wider social standards, set against backdrops of suburban homogeneity. Durang taps into the suburb as an imagined place of wholesome values and demonstrates how far Americans have fallen: family members do not support one another, television determines reality, and torture is an appropriate means to obtain information. In *Life: The Movie: How Entertainment Conquered Reality*, Neal Gabler sums up the ways in which the movie and TV industries have shaped the rhythm and logic of American life: "Karl Marx and Joseph Schumpeter both seem to have been wrong. It is not any '-ism' but entertainment that is arguably the most pervasive, powerful and ineluctable force of our time—a force so overwhelming that it has finally metastasized into life" (2000, 9). While the idealized TV family was a satirical target in his early plays, Durang broadens his sites to encompass television's invasive presence in and its insistent control over American society. Two of Durang's plays, *Media Amok* and *Betty's Summer*

Vacation, illustrate how television transmogrifies what was previously an American form of information and entertainment into something that replaces our reality. In 1996, he expressed his irritation with the TV idiom, whose format of quick sound bites and emotional overlay impeded people's understanding of the world around them:

> Television really is to blame. For an awful lot of [emotional manipulation]. For a news story to be just four sentences on the news, that's very frightening to me. I remember reading that during the Reagan years they supposedly got so good about giving all those visuals that you'd see him eating a hot dog and looking happy. If the story said something negative, all that the people got, supposedly, was that he was eating a hot dog and acting happy. That's very "1984"-ish. (1996)

A century ago, George Bernard Shaw differentiated between his "Plays Unpleasant" and "Plays Pleasant" in an effort to identify those plays whose "dramatic power is used to force the spectator to face unpleasant facts." "Unpleasant plays" is an apt descriptor for Durang's tales about American anomie. The plays in this chapter showcase the uneasy nature of social relationships, and the unpleasantness that can manifest within smaller social units of families and friends. None of these plays have the quintessential "happy ending," but they do end positively, or at least with a promising optimism, which was new for Durang. These later plays provide a sense of balance that the early plays did not possess because Durang introduces a new type of character into his plays: the "reasonable one." Like the *raisonneur* figures of Molière's comedies who point out the folly of the central characters, the reasonable character tempers the irrationality of the crazy ones and offsets their nuttiness by her sensibility. In other words, the absurd and grotesque components of his style remain, but by introducing a sane character's point of view he can present a normalized position against society's deregulation.

Beyond Therapy

Beyond Therapy (1982) remains one of his most performed plays because of its rueful optimism and lighthearted ending.[1] Edith Oliver enjoyed the play, likening it to Durang's version of *Alice in Wonderland* because of the quirkiness of the characters. Most importantly, the audiences found the play funny; critics such as Brendan Gill described how audiences began laughing at the first line and never stopped. In response to critics who felt the characters lacked depth, Gill reminded readers that the conditions of farce do not require the psychological motivation. He explains that we have different expectations of farce:

> Our satisfaction with "Beyond Therapy" springs in large measure from the working out of a symmetrical process of inquiry on the part of a distraught young man and an equally distraught young woman; and the situation that they are distraught about—roughly, the difficulty they find in growing up and forming permanent relationships with their contemporaries—is the excuse for the play rather than the occasion for it. Farce requires only excuse; it is tragedy that requires occasions. (Gill 1982)

The "excuse" or origin for the play came from Durang's friends at the time, particularly women, who worried about their status in life as unmarried and childless at the age of thirty. He acknowledges, "I sort of picked up by osmosis that kind of tension about trying to find a personal relationship." For his friends, the process of dating involved analyzing the interpersonal dynamics of the date afterward with the help of a therapist, which makes the play as much about the misguided feedback of therapists as it is about finding a life partner. Psychology provides the conduit for self-exploration, but also the danger of misdirection if the therapist proves to be an inept professional—a favorite figure of fun for Durang. The play follows two characters, Prudence and Bruce, as they discover who they are through the prismatic reality of dating.

Prudence and Bruce, eccentric and pitiable, meet on a blind date that goes badly. Facing each other at a restaurant table, each character specifies what he or she needs in a romantic partner, rather than explore what the other is like. Prudence admits that she likes her men to be strong, while Bruce insists, "I want you to have my children" (216) and "I want to marry you. I feel ready to make a long-term commitment to you. We'll live in Connecticut. We'll have two cars" (217). The characters' oddities contribute to the scene's humor: Prudence places her foot on the table to show off her toe nail polish, while Bruce cries extravagantly at the restaurant table to show his ability to express emotions. Bruce also challenges Prudence's worldview with his bisexual nature and with his live-in boyfriend, Bob;

he wants to have children with Prudence, but still be with Bob romantically. The market economy of dating dictates the scene: the two of them appear more invested in getting their individual needs met rather than offering a curious receptivity toward another person. And as their respective quirks and requirements continue, their conversation turns argumentative and their date ends in name-calling, hurt feelings, and tossed glasses of water.

Prudence and Bruce, in order to understand or "process" what has occurred on their dates, turn to their respective therapists, hoping their professional perspectives can shed light. Even though Durang concedes he benefited from his therapist as a college student at Harvard, his memories of working with different therapists run the gamut from ridiculous to helpful. He recalls memories of a German therapist while in graduate school who mistakenly assumed Durang was identifying with her, based on her own psychological theories (McGill 1982). In *Beyond Therapy*, the therapists often seem more in need of mental help than their respective patients, resulting in some of the most hysterical therapy scenes ever written. Prudence's therapist, Dr. Stuart Framingham, is a studly playboy, a "tantrummy lecher" (Oliver 1981) who wears boots and jeans. He has previously engaged Prudence in sexual intercourse and treats her disrespectfully. Stuart Framingham is a typical Durangian character whose narcissism makes him oblivious to the ludicrous cruelty of his own comments. In response to his rudeness, Prudence speaks rationally and pointedly, playing, as it were, the "straight man" to his inappropriate overtures:

> PRUDENCE: Dr. Framingham, it is a common belief that it is wrong for therapists and their patients to have sex together.
> STUART: Not in California.
> PRUDENCE: We are not in California.
> STUART: We could move there. Buy a house, get a Jacuzzi. (219)

In addition to his ethical breach in sleeping with his patient and repeatedly calling her "baby," Stuart uses her vulnerability against her. Rather than addressing her concerns regarding her loneliness or her unhappiness with her job, he blames her for seeking perfection.

Bruce fares slightly better than Prudence with his choice of therapist, Charlotte Wallace, as she offers less damaging comments and her heart is in the right place. For example, she encourages her patients "To Risk! To

Risk!" rather than being afraid of rejection. Based in the warm-fuzzy school of positive validation, Charlottes therapy involves animating a stuffed animal on her lap like a puppet, bouncing him up and down, and barking in simulated approval of her patient's success. However, Charlotte suffers from a light form of aphasia, which results in a series of malapropisms: "Did I say porpoise? What word do I want? Porpoise. Pompous. Pom Pom. Paparazzi. Polyester. Pollywog. Olley olley oxen free. Patient. I'm sorry. I mean patient. Now what was I saying?" (222). Her own problems dominate the therapy session, such as her adulterous first husband and her addled brain, but she seems genuinely committed to Bruce's success, encouraging him to be uninhibited in stating his desires. Her form of therapy is more affirming that Stuart Framingham's counsel has been for Prudence; she helps Bruce to write a new dating advertisement by fabricating a new identity for him as a Pulitzer Prize winner. This subterfuge works and the two arrive on a second date because of this misleading ad. Significantly, their conversation differs markedly from their first date; they take the time to listen to one another. Bruce compliments Prudence for being independent minded even while still desiring someone to protect her, and she feels moved by his reassuring comment: "We have to allow for contradictions in ourselves. Nobody is just one thing" (229). In addition, Bruce shares the compassion and reframing techniques he has learned from Charlotte, as well as her tendency to bark "ruff, ruff, ruff!" in congratulatory praise. The second date works because Prudence receives from Bruce the compassion her therapist failed to give her and gives Bruce the pragmatism he failed to get from his. Yet it is clear that both Prudence and Bruce are mentally stuck in their maladaptive schemas and that neither dating nor therapy can help them move forward.

The pragmatic difficulties of Bruce wanting it "both ways," that is, to live romantically with his boyfriend Bob but to date heterosexually, become clear when Bruce invites Prudence for dinner at his apartment. Not only does Bob resent Prudence's intrusion into his relationship but he calls his domineering mother who noisily scolds them over the phone, telling Prudence in particular that she is ruining her son's life. The hurt feelings escalate out of control; Prudence cannot reason with Bob's mother because she insists on singing loudly in lieu of conversation, Bruce runs into the kitchen periodically to check on dinner, and Bob informs everyone he is leaving to commit suicide. Each time Prudence tries to share with Bruce her discomfort with the situation and how he should get his life "in order" before they date, Bob convinces her to make the best of things with a

Pollyannaish optimism wildly out of place for the situation: "Life by its very name is disordered, terrifying. That's why people come together, to face the terrors hand in hand" (240). Bruce finally recognizes the need for therapeutic intervention, and he arranges for Bob to see Charlotte Wallace that evening. However, true to form, Charlotte acts her foolish, silly self and engages Bruce in a wildly inappropriate therapy session. Not only has she not understood that her patient Bob is gay ("He doesn't lisp," she observes), she starts to scream "COCKSUCKER" uncontrollably until she can get her blood sugar levels under control. At his wit's end, Bob takes out a starter gun and shoots her, which she unexpectedly praises because not only is he cognizant of his emotions, he is willing to act upon them. Following this line of thought, she encourages him to find Bruce and Prudence in the restaurant and shoot them as well, and the slapstick and absurdity escalate wildly.

As with most farces, the constraints of the particular predicament reach a breaking point; while at the restaurant, Bruce puts pressure on Prudence to marry him, Stuart Framingham spies on the two from behind potted plants, and Bob walks in, followed by Charlotte, and shoots everyone with the starter gun. The disobliging waiter, unobserved on their first two dates, finally makes an appearance and asks them to leave because of the commotion, but Prudence no longer will be pushed around; she aims the gun at the waiter, and commands that they be served. She then stands up to Stuart and declares she will discontinue therapy because, as she yells, "YOU ARE A PREMATURE EJACULATORY AND A LOUSY THERAPIST" (249). Everyone meekly sits down under her new, imperious personality, yet, in short order, they begin again to advise her on what to do. Both Bruce and Stuart insist that she should marry them, playing on her fears of ending up single, and Charlotte offers her therapy sessions. In response to their pressure, Prudence agrees to marry Bruce, but later, alone with Bruce, she comes to the teary realization that while marrying him would be easy, it doesn't make any sense. Since Prudence does not cry in front of others, her tears are indicative of a transformation. Bruce, too, appreciates the friendship he has with Prudence because it makes him feel special. Earlier, when his therapist Charlotte told him he was unique, he asked in what ways he was unique. Her response, "Oh I don't know, the usual ways," deflated the compliment, but served as a reminder that it is in loving and paying attention to someone that the person becomes unique. Looking around the empty restaurant, Prudence decides she likes the place because it is conducive for their conversation, which corresponds to Bruce's earlier description of the restaurant as "existential"; the waiter's absence provides them unobtrusive time together. By calling it existential, he reinforces the theme of loneliness so indicative of the singles scene set as it is upon life's barren stage. Yet despite the absurdity of their lives, Prudence and Bruce have found comfort in the restaurant and each other, relaxing into the easy give-and-take between friends who have grown to see each other's individuality. They may not be romantic partners, but by the play's end they acknowledge each other as unique individuals.

The aptly named Prudence represents one of Durang's first reasonable characters. Her sensibility and down-to-earth nature contrasts comically with the eccentricities of the people around her. She maintains her equanimity in the face of Stuart's insults and hedonism, but she lacks the courage to leave Stuart, even though their sessions are improper. Prudence is the typical "nice" person; she articulates her opinions, but she does not stand up for herself. The date in Bruce's apartment with his lover Bob belittling their budding relationship is awkward, but she stifles her irritation rather than walking out. By the end of the play, Prudence has learned the courage of her own convictions. When Stuart tells her, metaphorically and pedantically, "You can never go home again," she responds, "Perhaps not. But I can return to my apartment" (220). Charlotte also tries to give Prudence a dose of her cynical philosophy: "We're all alone," she states, "everyone's crazy and you have no choice but to be alone or to be with someone in what will be a highly imperfect and probably eventually unsatisfactory relationship" (255). But Prudence refuses to accept this position: "I believe there's more chance for happiness than that" (255). *Beyond Therapy*, opening as it does with a blind date and its expectations of a love story, gives way instead to questioning whether the attainment of true love can provide meaning in life. Prudence holds onto this belief, despite the cynicism of those around her, and Bruce transforms from wanting to be loved to being loving. Success in this play lies in the characters' ability to move beyond the guidance of others and have confidence in their own point of view.

Media Amok

Durang's 1992 play *Media Amok* voiced frustration with how the media, in the guise of talk show hosts, newscasters, and political pundits, fomented intolerance and hatred under the appearance of news (Durang 1991). Though never published, the play was produced by the America Repertory

Theater, in March 1992, directed by Les Waters. Durang was inspired to write the play while listening to the endless stream of talk shows on cable television. He remembered being bothered watching an episode of *Sally Jesse Raphael* where she interviewed a mother of ten who was incapable of taking care of her children, yet who was pregnant again. Watching the interview and sensing the irreparable damage of her situation, Durang felt "hopeless about life." What troubled him was the way the talk show format focused on the woman's plight as entertainment and how the personal interest story, though insignificant as news, presented itself as authentic and therefore worthy of national attention.[2] Cultural critics often refer to "media culture" or the "mediatization of culture," to describe the sizable impact that media, primarily television, has on public tastes, behaviors, values, and opinions. Journalists, no longer following guidelines of fairmindedness and skepticism, compete with one another to find stories with the most shocking allegations or scandalous details, stoking the fires of hysteria, sensationalism, and fear in order to attract viewers to their TV stations. Media's power shifted considerably in the 1980s and 1990s, when it no longer simply chronicled stories but actually shaped their importance in response to the round-the-clock news cycle. Fringe areas of modern life became dominant as news stations gave these stories inordinate attention, and people became celebrities not based on talent but on savvy self-promotion, using the ubiquitous media outlets to stay in the public consciousness. The term "echo-chamber" was coined to describe this insulating enclave of manufactured news, "a bounded, enclosed media space . . . creating a common frame of reference and positive feedback loops for those who listen to, read, and watch these media outlets" (Jamieson 2010, 76). Inside this echo-chamber, as various media outlets reinforce the same news items and legitimize the same behaviors, a value system is created that purports to be the dominant culture. While it may seem quaint from the vantage of the twenty-first century to look back on media dominance of the 1980s, *Media Amok* dramatizes this new asphyxiating sensation of life in the mediated echo-chamber of twenty-four-hour cable television.

Cecilia and Nigel, the older couple in *Media Amok*, turn on the television as a distraction from the daily stress of neighborhood car alarms and their concerns about the ozone layer. As they sit before the TV set in their living room, the lights go on over the central part of the set to reveal the TV show they are watching. Their TV experience begins innocuously, but they are soon to be besieged by over thirty unbearable, outrageous TV personalities over the course of the play, enacted by twelve actors. Among them are Morton Hell, a dramatic incarnation of Morton Downey Jr., who berates his talk show guests, while his four audience members known as Yahoos heckle and pummel them with objects; Felicia Falana who acts like a real-life Sally Jesse Raphael, asking her guests rude questions under the guise of concern; and Phylicia Butterworth and Chuck Buck who, as early morning talk show hosts, sit on giant coffee cups, exchange pointless banter, and laugh uproariously at their own comments. Even the ostensible reason for TV programming, that is, news and information, is repackaged for entertainment value. The meteorologist Morey Sutter dresses as a rabbit for no apparent reason and gives people the inane weather report that "it's raining." Although dismayed at the pointless programming, Celia and Nigel find that the television will not turn off; they have to hire a technician to come to the house to do so. Furthermore, they are drawn to the TV shows because of the mesmerizing content, and, at a key moment, Cecilia becomes literally absorbed into the TV set and joins the broadcast. Played with gentle bewilderment by a favorite Durang actress, Anne Pitoniak, Celia becomes a guest on the set of the talk show whose politically extreme guests engage in hostile arguments. Celia's experience being trapped in the talk show world is horrifying, which is exactly Durang's point: there is an uncontrollable and illogical encroachment of television into our existence. At the end of the play, Nigel breaks apart the television and enables Cecilia to escape and move to a forest in Vermont, preferring the green world rather than her apartment in Gramercy Park.

Talk show hosts fuel discord in order to generate ratings; they cultivate controversial conversations under the guise of group therapy because such relational conflict is entertaining. For example, Phylicia Butterworth invites onto her talk show Mary Lou Popper, a fifteen-year-old from South Carolina who was raped by her alcoholic father, but who cannot get a legal abortion. Rather than provide a thoughtful deliberation of the social forces resulting in the incest and rape, Phylicia Butterworth instead invites onto her show a "rabid right-to-lifer" to yell at Mary Lou and provoke a debate. Frank Mullaganey enters and pointlessly yells at Mary Lou, "Life is precious! You have that baby, or you'll be a murderess for your entire life!" (31). Moreover, the talk show format, with its ruling ethos of sensationalism, focuses on the margins of society. Extreme lifestyles or abnormal health conditions are emphasized to the extent that human anecdotes of little significance are prioritized over issues of greater worth. Felicia Falana, another talk show host with preternatural cheer, exposes people's pain on her talk show, "All Night News All Night Long." She interviews two "incest survivors who have had sex changes and gone to secretarial school" (16), asking them such invasive questions that one guest starts to cry. Aware of her audience's interest, Felicia asks for a camera close-up of the woman's face and gently suggests that she might consider suicide. Alternative lifestyles are held up for public consumption merely to fill airtime and are scrutinized without ethical qualms. Felicia ebulliently reminds the audience to tune in tomorrow when she will host "transvestites who are talk show hostesses" and ends her show emphasizing the therapeutic power of talk therapy: "Keep the faith, everything can get solved just as long as we talk and talk and talk about it" (19). The satire here is that talking for the sake of filling up air time is not only pointless but damaging. She expresses the need for angry diatribes simply to fill up air time: "Quick, let's have someone say something controversial, and then Morton or Mary Lou can shout at them" (52). The collateral damage is born by the audience members, as the viewing public acquires a dissociative numbness from incendiary stories repeated with increasing degrees of distress.

The tabloid talk show, or "trash TV" as it became known, encouraged verbal screaming matches between guests on the set, which would occasionally result in physical violence. Popular hosts of this type of talk show were Morton Downey Jr. or Geraldo Rivera, who deliberately stoked controversy by inviting polemical guests on their shows, such as neo-Nazi members. Durang parodies these shows with *The Morton Hell Show*, the host played by Lewis Black, a comedian who later became famous for his belligerent tirades on *The Daily Show with John Stewart*. As Morton Hell, he is the most offensive, disgusting bigot one can imagine; he lambastes his characters with ruthless insults and screams full-on diatribes that lack cohesive logic or factual validity. He performs before four Yahoos who cheer, grunt, or express other sounds of outrage whenever he or his guests express opinions, adding to the bullying atmosphere. His screeds are laden with bombast associated with right-wing politics, such as when he introduces a social worker advocating for sexual education in the schools: "Her name is Samantha Hoffman and she's taking our tax money and she's teaching pornography to our kids and calling it sex education." Morton Hell rebuffs another guest, an African American nun, running a hospice for children with AIDS in Greenwich Village, with a string of incoherent judgments, and he redefines Christianity as individualist greed: "Christianity is 'you mind your business, I'll mind mine, but if you step on my property, I'll blow your fuckin' head off with a great big automatic rifle, you shithead piece of fetid garbage, scumbag fuckface.' That's what Christianity is!" (10). The humor in the scene comes from the inexplicably violent reaction to the social worker's or the nun's humanitarian work. At one point, Morton Hell invites four guests who represent the country's extreme racial divide: Morton and the Angry Black Woman argue whether there are any jobs for black people, the King High Pooh Bah mentions how he does not like blacks or Jews, only white people, and Bernie Getz, the last guest, arrives, carrying a gun, a tongue-in-cheek reference to the real-life subway vigilante Bernard Goetz. After the three pundits pull out their guns in response, Morton remarks, "Good, we're all armed. Now we can talk" (64). Only with the threat of physical violence does semi-respectful conversation ensue, suggesting how much trash television has affected civil discourse.

Moreover, the decontextualized way in which horrible events are presented in the news promotes feelings of helplessness in viewers. The news anchor delivers the news on the morning show hosted by Phylicia Butterworth and Chuck Buck; he provides a litany of violent events of horrific magnitude without any societal or historical context, so that the sum result is meaningless. He reports bombs that explode in the Rome airport, killing 40 people, wounding 200, attributed to the Libyan Psychotic Violence Society; another bomb in Ireland at the funeral of a slain Protestant leader, attributed to the IRA; a Skyway 793 jet plane that crashed on a Seattle runway, killing 300 passengers; and that Liza Minelli went on a shooting spree and killed using "an automatic assault rifle that fires 20 rounds at a time," which turns out to be an error: he meant Liza Minulli (25). After he delivers such a horrible litany of events, the talk show hosts are too stunned to make intelligible commentary, although they try:

PHYLICIA: Why aren't there stricter gun laws, Chuck?
CHUCK: I don't know.
PHYLICIA: It makes you think. But not a lot. (26)

Their response to the list of catastrophic events signals an unwillingness to examine issues constructively. By not devoting any time to thoughtful consideration, such as the root causes or potential solutions of domestic terrorism or public shootings, audience members cannot process the information, and their helplessness turns to apathy.

Elevating medical topics to the large scale of media punditry also has its risks; the public at large lacks the ethical capacity to evaluate such issues. Durang makes an allusion to the Karen Ann Quinlan controversy to demonstrate how the media attention exacerbated the standards concerning her medical treatment. Making a regular appearance on the nightly news in 1975 was a complicated case of a young woman in a coma whose parents were prevented from removing her ventilator. As Catholics, they felt morally obliged to remove the apparatus that was keeping her alive by "extraordinary means," but the court-appointed guardian refused, arguing to do so would be homicide. The bioethical questions raised concerning the status of life were aggravated by the inordinate amount of media attention given to the case. One writer noted that of the 137 seats in the courtroom, 100 were taken by reporters, illustrating how the media kept the controversy in the public eye (Lepore 2009). In Durang's play, Cecilia, imprisoned inside the television, attempts to pull out Karen Ann Lutkin's tubes in support of her parents' wishes, saying, "What's the point of keeping her alive this way?" As twisted as it may seem to wheel a comatose body upon the stage, the use of black humor here highlights the way the media cruelly manipulates public attitude regarding sensitive and sacred issues. Frank Mullaganey, for example, has been using her inert body as the cause célèbre for his Life is Precious Party. He yells at Cecilia, as she starts to pull out Karen Ann's tubes, "You are not God!" to which she responds, "Neither are you." Felicia Falana compliments Cecilia's heroism as attractive to the viewing public: "Oh Mrs. Claridge, I think you've gone up the audiences' estimation. This is very exciting. You took a strong stand. It's very good television" (71). Through the grotesquery of this scene, Durang demonstrates how bioethical matters such as health care, the right to die, or abortion are distorted by media hype.

Treating public leadership as a form of entertainment debases governance. The quadrennial political conventions to elect American presidents designed to clarify the candidate's ideological platforms have devolved into pageants staged for the purpose of winning voters. Approval ratings and public surveys are translated into proof of a presidential leader's actual ability to govern. Satirizing the idea of presidential popularity as competency, Felicia Falana conflates the presidential elections with the People's Choice Awards, an American award show in which the general public, instead of the usual board of industry professionals, grants awards for TV shows, movies, and actors. Falana introduces the "nominations for the People's Choice Favorite Candidate for United States President: George Bush for Desert Storm and

Patriotism; Morton Hell for The Morton Hell Show; Some Tired Old Liberal for the Democratic Party; Frank Mullaganey for the Life is Precious Party." While the idea of a "people's choice" for president sounds democratic on the surface, government elections channeled through entertainment outlets turn political leaders into celebrity figures, elected on the basis of their personality rather than knowledge, experience, or expertise. The candidates attempt to sell the public on their electability based on a series of empty slogans and platitudes, in a catalog of nonsensical slogans:

BUSH: Pride in America.
FRANK: No abortion.
MORTON: More cops, more guns, more jails.
LIBERAL: Hot lunches for 5 year olds.
BUSH: Cut the capital gains tax.
FRANK: Christian morality.
MORTON: Legalize hookers on Saturday night.
LIBERAL: Raise taxes just to annoy the Republicans.
BUSH: Cut the capital gains tax, goddam it, how many times do I have to say it?
FRANK: Prayer in the schools. Prayer in the banks. Prayer piped into supermarkets!
MORTON: Public executions on television. (74–5)

The play ends the only way it can: with media destruction. Nigel breaks apart the TV set with a sledgehammer and enables Cecilia to escape the cacophony and pandemonium. The Les Waters production emphasized the intensely grating atmosphere of television through screeching sirens, loud music, and strobe lights (Rendell 1992). In a gesture reminiscent of Henry David Thoreau's escape to Walden Pond to "live deliberately," Cecilia chooses to reside in a forest in Vermont. When Nigel asks if she is frightened by the forest, she says, "No. I like it. I don't find it frightening" (82), implying that the primitivism of nature outweighs the savagery of human beings.

Durang is adept at prompting audiences to see their own responsibility in such tasteless TV programming, a point he will repeat with his next play, *Betty's Summer Vacation*. The relationship between the mass media and viewership operates by a reiterative process of giving audiences what they want, detecting what sells, and then increasingly turning up the degree of violence, flamboyance, or risqué topics programmed into the show. When

Nigel is intrigued by *The Morton Hell Show* despite the host's vicious attacks on his guests, Cecilia questions his interest as well as the kinds of viewers who make such lowbrow media content popular:

> CECILIA: Who is this Mr. Hell, and why is he on television, who's watching him?
> NIGEL: We're watching him, darling.
> CECILIA: Yes, I know, dear, but we're not regular watchers, who else is watching this? Is he popular? (13)

The meanness of the talk show participants is symptomatic of society's malady, and Cecilia remarks about feeling sick: "I feel like I've had toxins put in my blood stream." In *Media Amok*, Durang demonstrates how television infiltrates people's lives with the surreal premise of a woman physically entrapped inside a TV set. As absurd as his scenario seemed, MTV began its experiment of people living within a televised world in 1992, concurrent with Durang's play. *The Real World*, built on the premise of a group of strangers living together while a TV crew films their interactions, was one of the closest interpenetrations of media and reality ever seen. The roommates were selected for their quarrelsome and histrionic natures, in order to increase viewership and feed the viewing public's appetite for controversy. Durang made this ravenous hunger to see humanity at its worst the subject of his next play, *Betty's Summer Vacation*.

Betty's Summer Vacation

Betty's Summer Vacation originated from Durang's lighthearted childhood memories about the summers he spent on the Jersey Shore, but the tale quickly turned dark: "I was just starting [to write the play] when I got distracted by the Menendez trial on Court TV. I watched the whole thing. Then I got hooked on the Bobbitt trial" (Morris 1999). The Menendez brothers, on trial for having murdered their parents after years of alleged abuse, occupied hours of Court TV, as did the Lorena Bobbitt story, a woman on trial for cutting off her husband's penis after he subjected her to domestic violence. Durang was not the only one who was hooked: the live, televised coverage of the trials for the Menendez brothers and Lorena Bobbitt, as well as William Kennedy Smith and Mike Tyson, increased the subscriber base for the Courtroom Television Network from 2.5 million households when it was first launched in 1991 to 14 million (Waters 1994). Durang's self-questioning of his addictive television-viewing behavior turned into a general contemplation of the harm that sensationalized courtroom television inflicted upon the viewing public. He later found himself similarly compelled to watch the 1991 Senate confirmation hearings on the Supreme Court nominee Clarence Thomas, whom Anita Hill accused of sexual harassment. Initially he watched because of their political importance: "But the length of them, the topic of them, and the endless detail of them were sort of inescapably prurient," he acknowledged. "They became a strange kind of entertainment where you started to hope there would be more horrifying details—like [Thomas's alleged comments about] pubic hair on a Coke can" (Horwitz 2000). Reality legal shows, like tabloid talk shows, offered the ideological construct of news and information as entertainment, even if such entertainment consisted of the sordid details of a family murder and created in the American populace a monstrous appetite for such stories. Durang's persistent antipathy toward mediated culture turned into *Betty's Summer Vacation*, a play that Ben Brantley calls "the best satire to date on a nation bent on entertaining itself to death" (2005).

Reality TV shows work by thrusting distinctly incompatible people together into small living quarters, where their idiosyncratic personalities bump up against one another and ignite conflict. Durang turns up the volume on his group's quirkiness. Betty, a lonely young woman looking to get away to the Jersey shore for peace and relaxation, rents a vacation cottage with her friend Trudy, whom Ben Brantley describes as "classic television cutie pie *cum* kook" (1999). The two young women, like Betty and Veronica from 1940s Archie comics, fit perfectly into the 1950s style of the set, with the "bright seashell-kitsch" decor and the "insistent uber-sitcom music" (Hurwitt 1999). The play initially appears to be a cheerful situation comedy about a beach getaway, before Durang reveals the horror behind the façade. Unbeknownst to Betty and Trudy, a group of strangers has also rented the cottage: Trudy's mother, a larger-than-life presence called Mrs. Siezmagraff; a shy serial killer, Keith, who arrives carrying a shovel and a hatbox;[3] a priapic macho stud, Buck, who propositions every woman in sight; and the raincoat clad Mr. Vanislaw, a derelict and exhibitionist invited to dinner by Mrs. Siezmagraff after she found him taking photos of women in a store's dressing room; "I like men who like women," she raves (18). Similar to the behaviors witnessed on MTV's Real World, Durang's characters conduct themselves in eccentric or aberrant ways: Buck shows off photos of his penis and casually asks for flavored condoms when Betty leaves to shop for groceries; Keith, acknowledges his celibacy, then locks himself away in his room to perform surgeries, although remaining vague about the details of his practice; Trudy mentions how her father, Mrs. Siezmagraff's recently deceased husband, used to sexually molest her; and Mrs. Siezmagraff remains remarkably unperturbed about her daughter's trauma. Adding to the oddities are the scenes of violence: after dinner, Mr. Vanislaw enters into Trudy's room and rapes her; Trudy retaliates by castrating Mr. Vanislaw, and then Keith joins forces with her to decapitate him. Recapitulated as a series of events, the play sounds gruesome and demonic, but this quick summary negates the play's wacky tone and slapstick behavior of the characters. The events, directed with the fast pace of farce, make the play resemble the funny loopiness of a sitcom; as a result, the harebrained, shallow characters seem unconnected from the depravity of the actions that occur.

Betty's Summer Vacation is as much a commentary about the public's complicity in its demand for tasteless, sensationalized programming as it is a satiric attack on reality television. "Tabloid America is also democracy in action," Jonathan Alter once noted about the media's responsiveness to its viewing public. "Once a significant portion of the public tires of the story, the media—via overnight Nielsens [ratings], newsstand sales and so forth—will immediately sense it and pull back. In other words, the public as a whole is getting almost exactly what it wants. The channel changer is a kind of ballot box" (1994). Instead of a ballot box, Durang creates three surreal characters that serve as audience surrogates, the Laugh Track People, a device that Robert Combs explores more fully in his essay in Chapter. These are characters who live in the ceiling and provide feedback to the onstage characters regarding the quality of their interactions. Named after the famed laugh track used in TV shows to replace the laughter of live studio audiences, these characters reflect the viewing public's prurient taste and their compulsion for more aggressive programming. At first the Laugh Track People are just voices of laughter emanating from the ceiling; only toward the play's end do they appear full-figure, dropping from the ceiling, attached to TV tubes and wires. Betty hears them for the first time when she discovers that a guest due to arrive has died in a car accident, as darkly predicted by Mrs. Seizmagraff. As she puzzles over Mrs. Seizmagraff's intuition, the Voices above her start laughing, as they find the news of a fatal car crash funny. When Betty walks into Keith's room and screams hysterically upon discovering the decapitated body or finding the severed penis in the freezer, one hears *"Laughter. Applause from ceiling"* (36). The Voices grow more bold and offer the characters directives in order to feed their comic appetite; they compel the characters to do certain activities in order to be amused, grossed out, or entertained. When Buck returns from an unsatisfied sexual outing, the Voices encourage him to violate Keith: "We'd like to see Keith getting fucked by Buck. We're bored" (41); consequently, Buck is castrated and decapitated by Keith and Trudy, adding to the murder and mayhem. The Voices demand greater degrees of cruelty and sexual perversity, representing American audience's appetite for voyeuristic glances into personal trauma. Even when Betty, as the reasonable character in this play, reprimands the Voices for "urging sex and murder," they applaud her speech as a performance and not the true call for human dignity it is.

The laughter of the Laugh Track People provides a means by which Durang captures the audience in his satire. At first, their laughter punctuates appropriate moments, when the characters say a funny line, but as the laughter turns aggressive, the audience becomes uncertain about their own reason for laughing. Ben Brantley attests to his discomfort in reviewing the play when he describes how the audience's laughter tended to blend with the laughter of the Laugh Track People and how this intermingling of the audience's laughter with that of the Laugh Track People seemed "to include us in the play's general spirit of condemnation" (1999). The reasons people laugh are various and often unclear; people laugh in approbation or discomfort, in meanness or in fun, and the Voices even confirm this fact: "We're uncomfortable. And so we laughed. We didn't know what else to do" (20). However, joining in on group laughter is a reflection of one's tastes, as laughing typically implies approval; quite a few audience members angrily left the theatre during previews, discomfited by what they were asked to laugh at. Durang uses laughter's ambiguity and the uncertainty of the audience's response to drive home his satirical message: America's wholesale desire for entertainment inures us to the degradation of media programming, and the audience's complicit laughter proves his point. Durang admits that the play was challenging for some:

> My ability to have two emotions at the same time—to be horrified and amused simultaneously—is something that makes people upset about my work. But it's what comes naturally to me, so I'm surprised each time when audiences are upset. . . . If [these events] were happening in real life, I wouldn't find it funny. But this is fiction. I think, for example,

that most serial killers would not carry a head around in a hat box, so the serial killer in my play isn't very real to me. (Hoffman 1987, n.p.)

The play, as Ed Siegel noted in its Boston production, has "one foot in the exaggeration of camp humor and the other in modernist despair at the way things are—sociologically, politically, cosmically," noting how the play manifests "outrageousness, not just moral outrage" (2001). In other words, the play's grotesque antics are meant to elicit laughter and simultaneously to disturb the audiences by their own laughter at such pathological real-life behavior. Michael Feingold of the *Village Voice* identifies the play's dual nature when he calls it "both a critique of a Chris Durang play and a critique of the sensation-hungry, media-drilled viewers' way of critiquing plays and every other aspect of the culture" (1999).

Rarely does a playwright include rape within a comedy. Rape is an attack on a person's physical and psychological self, as well as a violation of one's sexual and intimate boundaries, and it should not be the source of humor. Durang includes instances of rape in his play to make the larger satirical point that society feeds on stories of rape while disallowing the psychological damage to society that such lurid details create. Keith's quiet admission that he was molested by twenty people in his youth, "we had cousins from the Ozarks living with us," is on the one hand a tasteless joke about inbreeding associated with inhabitants from isolated areas, but moreover, a depressing statement on the lowbrow American predilection for entertainment. American society is criticized for cultivating a rape culture, where people either minimize or trivialize rape of women. Mrs. Siezmagraff clearly does not take her daughter's complaints seriously, and it is her exaggerated nonchalance in the face of such dire accounts that is both humorous and disturbing:

> TRUDY: That horrible man was raping me!
> MRS. SIEZMAGRAFF: I hate all this date rape talk.
> TRUDY: This was not date rape. You brought a maniac degenerate into the house, and he raped me while you did nothing. (33)

Kristine Nielsen played the original role of Mrs. Siezmagraff with a mixture of wildly upbeat energy and Auntie Mame–like insouciance (McKinley 1999); when she makes the dangerous insinuation that her daughter led on Mr. Vanislaw by calling it "date rape," which is blatantly preposterous in light of the facts, her comment is both troubling and ludicrous. She both perpetuates a rape culture attitude by her refusal to acknowledge her daughter's pain and gives Trudy the impetus for retaliation, which the audience cheers on. Trudy, taking a butcher knife, cuts off Mr. Vanislaw's penis while he is sleeping, mimicking the real-life details of Lorraine Bobbitt. The severed penis gets tossed around indecorously when Trudy hands it to her mother, who then tries to hand it to Keith to put on ice; Trudy grabs it and shakes the disconnected member in her face and screams: "He raped me!" (34). The physical business of running around the stage with a cutoff penis is pure farce, while the violation of the body is the realm of the grotesque. And yet the fiction mirrors the reality. Durang describes the ludic quality of the Bobbitt case: "I loved this crazy thing, where she cuts off her husband's penis and throws it into a field, but she's found innocent, and then he's found innocent as well in the other trial. I guess they were just having a bad day" (Hoffman 1987, n.p.).

Mrs. Siezmagraff next puts Trudy and Keith on trial for the murder of Mr. Vanislaw, and Durang's play takes a turn spoofing Courtroom TV. The set transforms into a courtroom, with the rapid-fire music and spotlighting indicative of televised trials. Kristen Nielsen, to whom Durang dedicated the play, gave a tour de force performance as a one-woman trial, performing several roles interchangeably: the defense attorney, the court clerk, and two battling witnesses. The character switches energetically between defending her daughter Trudy and coaching her on how to turn her childhood abuse into a plausible excuse for her behavior. She plays the Irish maid who bears witness against Mrs. Siezmagraff, testifying that Mrs. Siezmagraff knew her husband was abusing her daughter years ago. Finally, she plays herself, protesting the facts until, in a melodramatic confession made for TV exploitation, she cries out, "Don't convict my daughter! It's my fault. I didn't protect her. It's my fault. CONVICT ME, CONVICT ME!" (52). Feingold draws attention to this "bravura feat . . . in which she populates an entire courtroom by herself" because of her talented acting, but what she signals by alternating roles so quickly is the performative nature of all televised courtroom drama. The media circus turns real-life convicted murderers such as Jeffrey Dahmer or the Menendez brothers into celebrities, and Mrs. Siezmagraff's frantic multi-personed acting emphasizes this distortion between the real-life person and the made-for-TV fabrication. Robert Hurwitt's review compliments Durang's play for putting "the seductiveness of evil . . . through a meat grinder of talk TV, Lorena Bobbitt, trials of the century, Jeffrey Dahmer and the national addiction to vicarious thrills" (1999), which is a valid point, but evil can only be seductive if there is a market for it. Through made-for-TV litigation, the media can package human evil into a commercial, consumable item for the daytime and evening news hours.

The final scene of the play shows the only logical end to the entertainment industry: an explosion. Trudy, Keith, and Mrs. Siezmagraff get into a bitter feud, and, at the prompting of the Laugh Track People, decide to blow up the cottage by turning on the gas and lighting a match. Betty tries to stop them, then escapes a safe distance to the beach, where she delivers a monologue alongside the soothing sound of the waves. This conclusion, where the mediated world of televised entertainment is destroyed and the central character escapes into the sanity of nature, mirrors the ending of *Media Amok*. The entertainment industry has insured that the lowest common denominator of unprincipled behavior is elevated to the public's attention, and Durang's play offers only escape and destruction as a solution. Michael Feingold frames the problem helpfully in his review:

> What used to be private horrors have been socialized into public totems; we've gone from the Freudian into the Sadeian Age. The public voice, switching sides with frightening ease, gives every action or assertion an extra queasiness. While the laughter [of the play] lets your inhibitions down, the constant clash of principles induces a kind of moral motion sickness, the cure to which no Dramamine, or drama-meaning, has yet been invented. (1999)

Feingold's last comment is an allusion to an etymological pun made by Mrs. Sorken, another Durangian figure, who believes drama aids catharsis of unwanted emotions. In so doing, Feingold surmises that *Betty's Summer Vacation* is Durang's attempt at purging himself from the toxicity of mediated culture. Betty has been the voice of reason the entire play, interposing such noble beliefs during the trial scene as "we have to agree not to harm one another. That's one of the basic rules of civilization" (50). Her speech is a behest for higher principles, but the dark laughter behind Durang's play aligns the audience with the savage anarchy of mob rule.

Why Torture Is Wrong, and the People Who Love Them

The title of Durang's next play *Why Torture Is Wrong, and the People Who Love Them* (2009) reads like a warped combination between a morality pamphlet and a self-help guide,[4] which perhaps best describes the United States after the tragedy of September 11. This is Durang's 9/11 play, which is not a commemorative play, like Anne Nelson's *The Guys* (2001) or a cynical cast on humanity, like Neil La Bute's *The Mercy Seat* (2002), but a comedy that questions "the new normal" following the terrorist attack on the Twin Towers. The play is anthologized in *American Political Plays in the Age of Terrorism* (Havis 2019). An implausible farce with a hopeful ending, Durang's comedy captures a moment in time when America lost its moral authority and when "torture [served as] a first-resort means of interrogation and raging paranoia [was] an accepted worldview" (Brantley 2009). Debates about the merit of torture in response to September 11 were prevalent; Jonathan Alter's piece in November 2001 *Newsweek*, "Time to Think about Torture," opened up with a surprising admission: "In this autumn of anger, even a liberal can find his thoughts turning to . . . torture. OK, not cattle prods or rubber hoses, at least not here in the United States, but something to jump-start the stalled investigation of the greatest crime in American history," and then proceeded to list the kind of torture that a self-proclaimed liberal would be comfortable with for eliciting information. He acknowledges that physical torture is illegal, but that "we need to keep an open mind about certain measures to fight terrorism, like court-sanctioned psychological interrogation" or even sending our prisoners of war to countries that did not hold ethical qualms about harming people (Alter 2001). His words, disturbing in the cool hindsight of a decade later, are a reminder of the passionate need for retributive violence in the wake of an attack on the United States. In *Why Torture Is Wrong*, Durang questions whether retributive violence is ever a justified response and provokes the audience's allegiance to torture with the morally ambiguous and absurdist nature of the plot.

The play opens with a scene of personal terror: the main character, Felicity, wakes up in a hotel room to discover she is married to a complete stranger. Zamir, a man she has never met before, drugged her drink the night before and married her for financial support. He does not work because "food and electricity and housing should be free" (6), and he hints that the work he occasionally does is a nefarious nighttime activity. Not only does he provide vague details about himself but he proves to be quick-tempered and violent. When Felicity suggests they get their marriage annulled, Zamir speaks to her viciously, announces that all the women in his family are dead, and warns her against provoking his fragile male ego. Furthermore, Zamir's characterization is ambiguous; his dark skin suggests he could be Arab, Indian Greek, or Italian. His name and possible ethnicity as a Middle-Easterner challenges the racial biases of most audiences in the wake of September 11. Durang plays with this ambiguity in order to provoke the audience's own stereotypical associations with terrorism. Zamir's violent nature initially confirms the audience's suspicions that he is the play's villain, as well as the fact that he married Felicity while she was unconscious, but his threats are undercut by humor, which makes him an ambivalent character. When Felicity yells at him, "You married me when I was unconscious!" his humorous response is: "I'm used to arranged marriages" (30). When he tries to intimidate her with violence, saying, "I'll knock you into the middle of next week. I'll tie you to the bed and cover you with honey and release killer bees in the room" (19), the whimsical details of the impending punishment renders the threat—as well as him—ridiculous. Even when he drugs her for a second time, and the audience witnesses him crawling over her unconscious body to molest her, the violence is mitigated by an offstage narrator. A voice-over, known as the Voice, relates the audience's discomfort at witnessing Zamir sexually violate Felicity, and creates a critical distance between the depiction of the harm and the unreal nature of theatrical representation. The sum effect of Zamir's scary but surreal violence is to give the audience the moral desire to label the character as evil, but without the cognitive certitude to do so.

Thus, it is with welcome relief that Felicity visits her parents in their cozy suburban home. Her harebrained mother, Luella, and her conservative father, Leonard, seem a reprieve from her violent entanglement with Zamir. Felicity's father seems the ideal character to protect her from Zamir. A paternal holdover from the Eisenhower days, Leonard demonstrates the stalwart male fortitude embodied by traditional 1950 sitcoms. But he is a creepy protector, with his references to *Father Knows Best* and his patronizing comments: "You need help, Princess? Kitten? What's the problem?" (22–3). He voices his conservative opinions unabashedly: he attacks the United Nations for brokering peace between countries, he insists the family call French toast "Freedom toast" because of France's refusal to join the US coalition invading Iraq, and wishes "the gays" hadn't ruined heterosexual marriage. He is a former Vietnam War veteran whose defining worldview is in conquering the enemy—"There's Hitler and Stalin and Saddam Hussein and then there's Jane Fonda" (15). Furthermore, he is prone to violence, as his daughter reminds him:

> LEONARD: You were happy I had guns when our house was broken into by that group of criminals.

FELICITY: Father, they were children, you shot at children.
LEONARD: They entered without knocking. They were wearing masks.
FELICITY: It was Halloween. (16)

What the conversation makes clear is that violence and violent actions are relative based on circumstances; in light of his daughter being held a marital hostage by Zamir, Leonard's violent nature seems like her only recourse from an unacceptable situation. When he discovers that Zamir has married his daughter without his permission, he pulls out a gun and aims it at Zamir's head. Zamir pulls out his cell phone and counter-threatens, insisting he has wired the house to explode, using his cell phone as the detonator. At this deadlock, Felicity yells: "Stop, stop! This is ESCALATING! Stop escalating. I've made a bad marriage, but let's not have the house blow up because of it" (12). Luella prepares French toast for the family, and they stop fighting long enough to eat, the domestic serenity staving off their mutual destruction.

Felicity needs to be saved from an illegal marriage, and her father's solution is homicide. The plot prompts the question: Is violence ever justified? Durang's comedy entertains this question and offers farcical violence as a calculus toward its solution. He creates a world where the violent actions, though appearing real, have a burlesque quality to them. Leonard, as it turns out, is a member of the Shadow Government and periodically retreats to a secret room in the house where he and others participate in a homegrown militia. As a hardened right-wing fanatic, he is like others in America who believe they are entitled to use whatever violence necessary to save America against potential terrorist operatives. Claiming to his family that he is going to work on his butterfly collection, he instead prepares his network of spies to investigate Zamir, and the set opens up to reveal a gruesome cell filled with guns, swords, grenades, and artillery for his covert operations. The first spy Leonard contacts to help him is Hildegarde, an addle-brained woman, who is an allusion to Harriet Miers, President George W. Bush's personal attorney who would send him greeting cards adorned with puppies. Hildegarde, her underwear repeatedly falling to her ankles, gives Leonard a card attesting to the crush she has on him. Her earnestness coupled with the slapstick device of her malfunctioning underwear erodes any menace she might hold. The second spy Leonard invites is Looney Tunes, so called because of his Tourettes-like condition to shout out cartoon noises uncontrollably. For example, when Leonard decides they will torture Zamir to make him reveal any potential threats against the United States, Looney Tunes exclaims, "Urrrrr, errrr. Beep, beep! Wodents and wabbits! Intewwogating tewwowists! Sewere fewocity! Ex-skew-ciating suffewing in duh cause of duh war on tewwah" (47). He is laughably preposterous and his threats seem without bite, but nevertheless he has access to weaponry. A militant figure whose menace is punctuated with the juvenile absurdity of Bugs Bunny and Elmer Fudd, he is the perfect symbol of flippant immorality in responding to violence.

With this group of torturous spies, Durang makes a satiric point against the way the George W. Bush administration acted during its War on Terror. The loopholes that the Justice Department provided the Bush administration to commit torture and avoid following the Geneva Convention amounted to nothing short of ludicrous logic. Leonard reminds Hildegarde that once they capture Zamir, they will stick to John Yoo's torture definition very closely: "It isn't torture unless it causes organ failure," and even if it does, "as long as the president says the words 'war on terror,' it's A-OK" (35). Later, while spying on a conversation between Zamir and his friend in a restaurant, Hildergarde mistakenly believes she has obtained information about an actual terrorist plot, referred to as *The Big Bang*, when in actuality she has heard details regarding a pornographic film being made about a nationwide sexual orgy: "And they'r goin' be doing it all over, man—in New York, in D.C., in San Francisco," Zamir's friend, the director of the movie, tells him. Having recorded the conversation for Leonard, the two believe they have uncovered a terrorist plot. When Leonard and his group of spies apprehend Zamir and begin to inflict bodily harm to discover more details, Hildegarde squeamishly pleads with Leonard to stop the torture, asking whether they could send Zamir off to Syria where that government would force him to reveal information. Hildegard refers to the practice of rendition of criminals to another country, which is prohibited under the Geneva Convention if there exists the possibility of mistreatment, but which was again refuted by officials advising the Bush administration (Lewis 2005). The hypocrisy and legerdemain necessary to create these kinds of excuses are laughable, but the harm done to the United States' moral reputation—as well as the physical and psychological harm done to its prisoners—was not.

Durang pushes the boundaries of onstage cruelty in his quest to examine the United States' stance on retributive violence. After interrogating Zamir, Leonard walks into the kitchen, covered with blood, and hands two bags to Felicity containing Zamir's three fingers and his ear that he has cut off; Felicity, Luella, and Hildegarde all faint at this sight of physical dismemberment and blood. The director, Nicolas Martin, described the realism as necessary: "I initially thought there should be less blood on the clothes, but that really would have diluted the truth of what was happening to Zamir. And when the father produces a baggie containing three human fingers and an ear, well—we knew we couldn't stint on the blood" (Healy 2009). Mixing a screwball comedy with scenes of a man being tortured may appear unusual to today's audiences, but it was the stuff of Grand Guignol Theater, a form of naturalistic theatrical horror popular in Paris at the turn of the century. An evening's entertainment consisted of four or five plays a night, two plays of violent terror (*théâtre d'épouvante*) alternating with two overblown or ironic farces. John Callahan explains the nature of stage violence: "Comedy further provided a digestible coating to the bitter pill of aggressive amorality" (1991, 165). This concept of comedy as offering a palliative means of absorbing violence elucidates the dynamic behind this scene; it suggests that the goal is not audience's outrage or disgust, but rather a consideration of how such human cruelty could be rationalized or justified. After Leonard has tortured Zamir, the play is hard pressed to return to zany lightheartedness, just as America cannot return to its moral standing after the photographs were revealed of smiling American soldiers next to inmates tortured in the Abu Ghraib prison. It would appear that the Grand Guignol Theater is not without its real-life corollaries.

Farcical plots have a mechanical feel to them, a relational cause and effect, like a Rube Goldberg machine set into motion. Durang capitalizes upon this machine-like characteristic of farce to suggest that the plot might be engineered in reverse. Felicity, after viewing Zamir's dismembered body parts, decides that she can no longer tolerate her present reality. She makes the far-fetched yet theatrically possible request to turn back time and prevent the events from occurring, a wish familiar to anyone who has suffered tragedy. As the character who provides the logical ballast to the play's craziness, she insists the play reverse itself, but the challenge for Felicity is to find the right moment in time to return to. It is not enough to go back to "before Zamir had his fingers and ear cut off," or to the moment when, after introducing him to her parents, Zamir and Leonard entered into a warlike stalemate with Zamir's cell phone and Leonard's gun. As she pursues the correct instant in time, the set, a revolving turntable designed by David Korin, begins to spin backward to show the chronological reversal, and Felicity navigates her way, room by room, through the "spinning zoetrope" as the characters take their places in the respective rooms (Rooney 2009).

In wishing to return to an earlier time, Felicity expresses the wistful desire most Americans possess to turn back the clocks to a period before the country's responsive actions led them astray.

Felicity returns to the scene before the play first began, when she and Zamir met—at Hooters. By locating the final scene in a restaurant that makes the objectification of women's bodies part of family eating fare, the play indicts men's testosterone for behavioral aggression. Ben Brantley comments on the play's depiction of violence as masculine-coded and remarks that "Mr. Durang lets neither American nor Arabic men off the hook for their bone-breaking problem-solving methods and their treatment of their women" (2009). However, Hooters has undergone a renovation from a tawdry eatery to a romantically lit, stylish nightclub. The transformation is a symbolic step toward changing a cultural attitude toward women—and perhaps toward war. Zamir and Felicity meet at the bar and start chatting; when he slips a pill into her drink, she catches him and reprimands him: "I won't have that. We're doing it over so it's pleasant, and that's not pleasant" (62). The characters are encouraged to visualize more positive, affirmative behavior, and the words "pleasant" and "imagine" resonate throughout the final scene's dialogue. Leonard, for example, apologizes to Luella when he steps on her toe while dancing. "Imagine," Luella says, "he wondered how I was feeling. I know it's a small hope, but if he thinks about my crushed toe, maybe we can build on that little bit of empathy?" (63). Every time Zamir says something off-kilter, the music and dancing stops, and everyone looks at him, to show a world acting collectively in reprisal and to remind Zamir to choose to be, as Felicity says, his "better self" (67). "Oddly," she says, "I believe people can change. Just most don't"—a repeated refrain in Durang's later plays, which encourages choosing civility over savagery and compassion over retributive violence.

Living in America in the wake of September 11's tragedy created the surreal experience of perpetual high alert, where existence was defined as a state of vigilance and paranoia. The color-coded threat advisory system was created in 2002 as a Homeland Security measure for protection, but instead of helping people feel safe, it encouraged pervasive feelings of anxiety. Felicity's mother Luella is an anxious character whose heightened sensitivities to the threat of danger make her retreat into an alternative reality. Jean Baudrillard described this "new form of schizophrenia" as caused by the constant state of terror perpetrated by the interconnectedness of all information and communication networks (qtd. in Murray 2004, 61).

Comedic actress Kristen Nielsen performs the ideal neurotic because of her keen ability to make her horrific visions palpably real to those around her. Although she resides in a well-appointed home in a safe suburb, Luella harbors so much anxiety that at times she disassociates from the world around her and her eyes glaze over with a reality only she can see. During a particularly self-absorbed monologue she grows more and more disturbed and her obsessions take on a life of their own. "Your father is pro-life, did you know that?" she tells Felicity. "He loves all those stem-cell things.... Wants to give them the right to vote, just about.... Wants to register them as Republicans.... I said to your father, why do you want to give stem cells the vote, that's complicated, why don't you just steal the election like you did in Ohio in 2004?" (49). Beginning with her husband's pro-life stance, she addresses several politicized bioethical topics, such as whether fetal stem cells constitute human life, which propels her into her next topic, Terri Schiavo, the woman who lived in a persistent vegetative state after a cardiac arrest because her husband could not obtain the legal rights to remove her feeding tubes. Tapping into a political maelstrom among proponents of disability rights, pro-lifers, and groups advocating the right to die, Luella expresses the media scrutiny that kept Schiavo's comatose body in the public's eye and created a wedge between Luella and her husband: "He'd point at her on the television and scream, 'life is precious!' and he wanted her hooked up to tubes and breathing contraptions for ever and ever" (49). Luella, caught in her self-induced frenzy, begins to compare herself to Terry Schiavo in an imaginary argument with her husband: "I don't want your fucking father connecting me up to machines and tubes and respirators and keeping me alive for years and years like I'm some sort of pet rock. PULL THE PLUG, DAMN IT, PULL THE PLUG! (*She weeps*)" (50). As comical as Luella's monologue is in her free-associative hysteria, her speech speaks to an underlying anxiety many people feel in a society whose moral center is awry. The hypocrisy behind Leonard's argument to prioritize one woman's life while torturing others is unfathomable and substantiates Luella's feelings of mania.

Not many playwrights use madcap farce to illustrate the insecurity and fear caused by the perpetual threat of domestic terrorism; in so doing Durang's style is subversively comic. The play exposes fallacious rhetoric, false assumptions, and other misrepresentations, such as the irony behind the Department of Homeland Security making us feel *less* secure. One of the funniest characters in the play is a walking contradiction: Reverend

Mike, the director of the aforementioned pornographic film, *The Big Bang*, describes himself as a "porn-again Christian," who can reconcile Christianity with pornography: "God created sex and it's holy and good and hot and fun, and people can't seem to stop watching it, so somebody's gotta film it" (27). Furthermore, he was the minister who married Felicity to Zamir while she was unconscious. When she recommends to Reverend Mike that he refrain from marrying "someone who's nodding off," he responds with a belief system of radical non-bias: "Sorry, but I don't want to discriminate against heroin addicts. I know a lot of them. They're sweet but troubled" (31). Reverend Mike can defend his ethical failings with warped Christian logic just as easily as the Bush administration can justify torture. Yet, there's something likable in the hippie counselor, who harkens back to a peace broker from the 1970s, with his "make love, not war" philosophy.

It took Durang eight years to write a play that he felt people could feel comfortable laughing not about terrorism, but about the domestic war on terror and the fetishization of violence and hysteria that followed 9/11. But even a decade after the tragedy, critics appreciate the play's relevance, noting how a timely production coincided with the public release of memos issued by the Office of Legal Counsel between 2002 and 2005, detailing techniques used for interrogation of terrorism suspects:

> In a relatively rare confluence of theater and politics, the critically lauded production of "Torture" opened nine days before the Justice Department, on April 15, made public four memos that described brutal interrogation techniques authorized by the Bush administration. The furor over those methods, which included waterboarding, has only intensified during the run of the play, as President Obama, former Vice President Dick Cheney and others in Washington have debated whether it is necessary to hold public hearings and possibly prosecute those involved in the interrogations. (Healy 2009)

Furthermore, when the play was produced at the Sandra Feinstein-Gamm Theatre in Pawtucket, Rhode Island, in 2011 a reviewer in the *Boston Globe* connected the play to the contemporaneous assassination of Osama Bin Laden by US forces and raised the ethical quandary about using inhumane methods to gain important information: "As secret detainee interrogation reportedly helped lead to bin Laden's whereabouts, there's a new currency to questions raised by the play: Do the ends justify the means? Can compassion triumph over fear?" (Brown 2013). Similarly, the Titanic Theatre produced *Why Torture Is Wrong* in 2013 in Boston, shortly after two young men planted and detonated pressure cooker bombs at the Boston Marathon, killing and injuring a large number of people. The director Adam Zahler noted that "recent events [in Boston] have reminded us that [terrorism] is not far away . . . I think [terrorism] hovers over all of us. You can't get away from it. You think you do, and then something occurs like that reminds you, you can't. It's part and parcel of the fabric of our lives" (Brown 2013). While the debates surrounding America's role in international and domestic terrorism can seem a thing of the past decade, the play reminds us of the perennial topicality of terrorism.

The play's erratic structure disturbed John Lahr who, writing in the *New Yorker* (2009), noted that the play seemed a confused mixture between a satire and a sitcom, "a farcical house of cards that can't stand up." However, Michael Feingold appreciated that a world undergoing a seismic shift of values requires a new kind of playwriting:

> Durang's play—loose-jointed, digressive, bearing serious concerns but largely comic in tone—repeatedly breaks and resets its ostensibly realistic framework, sustaining zero pretense of reality. . . . Our crazy world readjusts the framework we live in so constantly that the tidy forms of traditional writing barely seem to match it anymore. (Feingold 2009)

Unlike other realistic plays written about September 11, Durang's play recognizes that normalcy and typicality are hard to find. *Why Torture Is Wrong* demonstrates what would seem obvious to civilly minded people: that torture is immoral. Yet in the wake of September 11, with the desperate search for answers to an unprecedented attack on American soil, Durang's play exposes the unacknowledged belief that torture has a place within a progressive democracy.

Vanya and Sonia and Masha and Spike

Vanya and Sonia and Masha and Spike, Durang's "sunny new play about gloomy people" (Brantley 2012) represents a significant change in tone for Durang; gone from this play are the earlier practices of the grotesque—characters are not cut in half, babies are not dying, and no one's fingers are being chopped off. The change may be due to a number of reasons. First, his early, deep-rooted belief that people never changed, no matter what, resulted in the dark disorder behind many of his plays, but later in his life, he began to see the possibility of personal transformation. His dramaturgical vision had been slowly shifting, too, and he was more invested in ensuring his audience had a positive experience, as noted in the endings to *Miss Witherspoon*, *Why Torture Is Wrong*, and now *Vanya*: "When I was younger," he acknowledged, "my plays were still comedies, but they had dark, nihilistic endings. . . . I found I now had less interest in seeing plays or movies that were despairing and sad. I didn't want the audience or myself to go home depressed" (Iseberg 2014). He felt particular empathy for Chekhov's older characters whom he had studied in college and who were often repentant and unhappy; he identified particularly with a line from the play *Uncle Vanya*, "We'll suffer through a long succession of tedious days, and tedious nights" (Prokosh 2015), which he quotes in his play. As the contemporary expert of making pain funny, Durang turned to an earlier comedic master of regret, Anton Chekhov, and found a way to give Chekhov's characters some relief from their emotions and fears. Commissioned by Princeton University's McCarter Theatre, *Vanya* premiered at Lincoln Center Theater, before transferring to the John Golden Theater on Broadway. Notably, *Vanya* earned Durang his first Tony Award for Best Play (2013), along with several other awards, including the Outer Circle Critics Award for Best Play, The Drama League Award, the Drama Desk Award, and New York Drama Critics Circle Award. The play received eleven regional productions the following year, and during the 2014–15 season, it was produced by twenty-seven theatres around the country, putting it at the head of the annual Top 10 list of most performed plays compiled by *American Theater* magazine. It was clear that audiences loved Durang's newest play, a play in which people can and do make changes to their lives.

The play is set in Bucks County, Pennsylvania, where the playwright currently lives; Durang's country farmhouse, in fact, served as the basis for the set design. It traces a weekend reunion of 50-something siblings who share aloud the "self-delusions and self-pity," as Charles Isherwood notes, of people who "have reached the difficult age when life's path has narrowed uncomfortably" (Isherwood 2013). Vanya and Sonia, having spent their years caring for their deceased parents, have never left their childhood home and spend their days wondering "what could have been." Sonia, who is adopted, is particularly disgruntled to be unmarried at the age of fifty-two; she smashes two coffee cups in the opening scene as evidence of her deep-seated frustration. Vanya is more resigned about their empty lives, although he, too, as a gay man, lacks a romantic partner and gets no recognition for his creative talents as a playwright. Sonia gives exaggerated descriptions of their sadness, "We long for what the world cannot give. We are in our twilight years, and we realize we have never really lived" (19), and dramatizes her unfulfilled existence with well-chosen lines from Chekhov's plays: "My life is empty. And I forget something every day. I can't remember the Italian for window or ceiling" (56). At one point, Vanya remarks to his sister, "I hope you're not going to make Chekhov references all day" (11), which earns a laugh, but underscores the performed nature of Sonia's remorse. Although she cannot be blamed for reciting Chekhov's language— their parents named the children after Chekhov's literary characters—her sadness is reinforced rather than alleviated by internalizing such poetic descriptors of loneliness and futility. The arrival of their cleaning woman, Cassandra, a Caribbean woman prone to prophesying, shakes their morbid remorse. True to her tragic namesake, she launches into an over-the-top visionary tirade: "Beware the Ides of March," she wails, then spews imagistic references to the "Land of Darkness" and "dismal moans arise from Bucks County" (14). At the end of her rant, Vanya wryly remarks, "Cassandra, I have asked you repeatedly to please just say 'good morning.' All right?" humorously undercutting her passion. Once again the exchange garners laughter, but more than ambient levity, Cassandra presents an interruption in their tired lives, a manic burst of energy that intersects the sad resignation of their conversation, in which they analyze their emotional pain without any intention of transforming it.

Their passive funk is further unsettled when their sister Masha, a B-list movie actor, shows up for a visit with an attractive boyfriend, Spike, and announces her plans to sell their family home, leaving Vanya and Sonia with nowhere to live. Decades of sibling rivalry and resentment rise rapidly to a boil, as the two characters express their jealousy of Masha's luxurious lifestyle in comparison to their lost opportunities. Masha, like the Professor Serebryakov in *Uncle Vanya*, arrives with three propositions, or three provocations, as Michael Feingold calls them (Feingold 2013) that disrupt the siblings' inertia; she announces that she intends to sell their only home, the farmhouse; she invites them to join her at a masquerade party hosted in their neighborhood; and she introduces them to her latest flame, Spike, a hunky, muscular actor who is twenty years her junior. In the tradition of

Durang's other narcissistic characters, Masha is self-absorbed to the point of caricature; she is a preening diva who arrives from a world of movement, money, glamorous lunches, and exotic travels, air-kissing (but not touching) her siblings and always turning the conversation to herself. Even her plans for the costume party place her in the spotlight; she plans to dress as Snow White, with Spike as Prince Charming, and to create an entourage with the dwarf costumes she gives to her brother and sister, assigning them the roles of Grumpy and Dopey. Her self-importance gives her license to bully her siblings, going so far as to tell Sonia to refrain from speaking for a set period of time: "Oh darling, sensitive, tedious Sonia. You can't face life can you? No, don't answer. You can talk at 4:30" (26). Her egotism irritates her siblings, who have always played second fiddle to her, and her arrival makes them feel even more inadequate. Sonia openly admits to her jealousy and self-pity:

> Every time I see you, Masha, you make me feel bad. First, you don't notice me in the room somehow, and say hello to me as an afterthought. And now here you are nearing your dotage, and you've hooked up with some young stud. While I am forced to live through a succession of tedious days and tedious nights, and I never have fallen in love with anyone. Nor anyone with me. I'm sorry I was adopted into this family. I wish I had been left in the orphanage and killed myself. Excuse me. (22)

For her part, Masha cannot extend any sympathy because she is too preoccupied appraising her own life. Outwardly more successful than her two siblings with her series of film in which she plays a nymphomaniac serial killer, Masha, too, has regrets; she feels she has compromised her talents by not becoming an actress on the classical stage (Sigourney Weaver as Masha gave the role a delicious irony). But any time she admits to such regrets, she emphatically rejects these thoughts, demonstrating that a career as a Hollywood celebrity has made her unable to admit any flaws or peer behind the mask of her own performance. The play encapsulates the siblings' attempt to ensure that their lives have meaning and, lacking that certitude, they whine and fight with one another over the weekend.

Chekhov is a master craftsman in the sensation of life's futility. In our current culture of triumph narratives and go-getter stories, Chekhov's characters may seem out of place as they analyze problematic relationships or share their unachieved aspirations; however, their clarity in articulating such inner experiences comes close to approximating the human soul. Durang uses his dramatic works as a springboard to consider Chekhov's nuanced emotions in the context of our contemporary moment, in which the climate of self-help directives and speedy, medicated solutions has no patience for suffering or regret. Moreover, the play encapsulates a particular form of regret: nostalgia. Nostalgia, with its original associations of longing for home, is a complex emotional state associated with sadness, but also, a pleasant, wistful recollection of the past. In a play that is more comedy of humors than the typical satire we expect from Durang, this emphasis on nostalgia may be the only point of critique: that feelings of nostalgia are not simply an attribute of old age but an expression of powerlessness created by rapid technological change. David Lowenthal has argued that the constant parade of newer and better ideas in technology, fashion, and mass culture has meant faster cultural turnover, which has meant more frequent feelings of loss; "Obsolescence confers instant bygone status," he writes, and may make us experience a continual and unwarranted feeling of grief regarding items lost over a lifetime, or even just a few years ago. The play's setting of a historic farmhouse heightens the contrast between a piece of untouched Americana and the frenzied pace of contemporary life. Vanya and Sonia use their house as a sanctuary from active engagement with life, much like Chekhov's landed aristocrats. Their farmhouse home is what Gaston Bachelard would call a "eulogized space," as a place that has been infused with the subjective imagination of their memories over a lifetime. Its exposed wooden beams, stone facing, old-fashioned hooked rugs, and wicker furniture is imbued with a traditional way of living whose values seemed more substantial than today's. The play's theme of nostalgia in the face of technological upheaval is similar to the fear of industrialization that bewildered the aristocratic characters in *The Cherry Orchard*; the breaking of the string and the sale of the orchard symbolized the inevitable ending of an era, despite the wishes of the property owners to remain in the past. Durang's characters of Vanya and Sonia willfully cling to their regrets over their past lives because to do so slows down the turbulent pace of contemporary life, even while it keeps them from growing or developing.

Vanya's monologue in Act 2 is an emotional polemic against such rapid changes. It is a tour de force speech railing against the seismic cultural changes that have left him feeling unmoored. Reminiscent of the tirade in Chekhov's *Uncle Vanya* where the lead character Vanya unleashes years of pent-up frustration against Professor Serebryakov, Durang's character attacks the current generation's use of social media that has resulted in the loss of deep human interconnectedness. Prompted by Spike rudely text messaging while the characters gather to read Vanya's experimental play, Vanya launches into a paean to bygone days of focused attention instead of multitasking; he celebrates handwritten letters, typewriters instead of computers, and telephones with rotary dials, contending that the time spent to accomplish these activities attested to the appreciation of the personal relationships behind each task. Vanya regrets that stamps and envelopes now have adhesive strips because the time it took to "lick the mail" reinforced the value of human communication, but Spike finds the sexual double entendre ("lick the male") impossible to resist and laughs sardonically, further irritating Vanya and goading him on. Vanya vents about a loss of shared culture, such as how families played Monopoly and Scrabble rather than video games, or how he watched wholesome TV shows such as *I Love Lucy* or *The Mickey Mouse Show* that provided soothing perspectives: "You didn't feel it was stirring people up and creating serial killers" (81), he cries. Moreover, television in his childhood was an affiliative experience; as the entire country watched the same shows, people could engage in conversations about similar topics, providing a momentary bond. With the later proliferation of cable television programming and atomized internet use, these shared viewing experiences are no longer possible. Vanya complains about feeling profoundly cut off from other people because of the proliferation of individualized technological experience that the digital age promotes: "Now there's Twitter and e-mail and Facebook and cable and satellite, and the movies and TV shows are all worthless and we don't even watch the same worthless things together, it's all separate. And our lives are . . . disconnected." Vanya's operatic lament of cultural decline appeals to the audience members; the speech earns hearty applause in performance as the public shares his frustration over the technological transformation of society and its resulting shift in values and attitudes. Vanya may appear foolish for wallowing in yesterday's memories; Spike in fact rebuffs Vanya's complaint against all things digital with a succinct "Time marches on, dude." But the release of his frustration has been validating to Vanya. The typically low-keyed character has for once taken center stage to articulate memories of life-affirming habits that promoted societal unity. He restores a sense of his own well-being by identifying what he once had, and afterward acts with more confidence and engagement.

The generational conflict between youth and old age is the perennial stuff of comedy, and feelings of loss time and regret are aroused by the presence of Spike and Nina. First, Spike awakens Vanya's latent sexual desire by frequently walking around the stage half-naked, exhibiting his muscular and attractive physique, and prompting Vanya to ask out loud, "Why does he take his clothes off so much?" (Sonia shoots back, "Because he can.") When Masha tells Spike to "do the opposite of a strip tease, and put your clothes back on" (36), Spike proceeds to get himself dressed seductively, by gyrating his body and stroking himself with his clothing. No one enjoys the spectacle more than Vanya, who unabashedly sits down on the floor to watch the performance. Although Masha has written Vanya off as "asexual from so many years of abstinence" (24), Spike's acknowledgment of Vanya's desire validates Vanya as a sexual being and quickens his energy. Second, the arrival of the next-door neighbors' young niece, Nina, with her blossoming air of youth causes Masha to become jealous for Spike's attention. Masha, as an actress surrounded by fresh-looking TV and film stars, feels pressure to look attractive and calls attention to Nina's youth: "You're so very pretty and luminous, and full of youthful hope and enthusiasm. I wonder if it makes it hard for older people to be around you," she ends ironically (33). At one point, Nina, unfamiliar with the 1937 Disney version of *Snow White*, mistakes Masha's Snow White costume for Norma Desmond in Sunset Boulevard, accidentally but aptly comparing her to a faded film star, and Masha explodes in rage. These feelings of bitterness are unbeknownst to Nina, who, as an aspiring actress, is simply elated to be around someone as famous as Masha, and expresses her adulation of her, as well as the rest of the family, whom she happily misreads as eccentric, creative types. For example, when Cassandra offers another prophetic tirade, Nina naively assumes her to be one more actress in the house and compliments her on her monologue. She willingly dons the Dopey costume Masha assigns her to wear to the costume party, even though she has arrived at the house dressed as a fairy princess. Her willingness to "go with the flow" marks her as different from the other characters, but it is this very accommodating spirit that infuses the play, especially when she joins in the staged reading of Vanya's play about climate change. When Vanya casts her in the central role of a molecule, Nina has a moment's pause, but her positive perspective assists her choice:

> I feel this may be a crossroads for me. At this moment I can choose to be one of those actors who argues and frets and challenges endlessly, and who makes rehearsals an enormous trial. Or I can be one of those who listens and says, "All right," and just tries to make it work. I think I'll choose to become the second kind. And take a leap of faith. (69)

As wisdom for any of life's challenges, Nina's speech stands as a touchstone to this play. In her willingness to say "yes" to life, she articulates a basic rule of improvisational comedy, of staying open to suggestions and opportunities. By using the word "choose," she shows that anyone, given a particular destiny or predetermined script, can make choices about one's fate, to either fight against life circumstances or will oneself to make things work. She gratefully speaks about her opportunities to Vanya and Sonia, summarizing how "this morning I woke up with no hopes for my artistic endeavors, and by this evening I have the chance of an agent through Spike, and I'm going to a party with a world-class actress and movie star" (50). Even though a minor character, Nina spreads the invaluable quality of youth: hope.

The central event of the play, the costume party, provides the transformative catalyst for the characters, specifically for Sonia and Masha. Donning a disguise implies a transformation of identity and can serve as a useful analogue to any kind of personal change requiring a new outlook or new way of being. Masha has planned to dress as Snow White, with everyone else serving as her entourage, costuming Spike as Prince Charming, and Sonia and Vanya as two of the seven dwarves, but Sonia will have none of it; rather than dressing as a dowdy dwarf, she instead acquires a starlet dress at a secondhand shop and bills herself as the Evil Queen, as performed by Diana Barrie, the character played by Maggie Smith from the movie *California Suite*. Performing an actress who played a character nominated for an Academy Award yet who didn't receive it, Sonia can identify all too well the feelings of disappointment and shame. Yet the layers of dramatic representation in this scene are noteworthy for calling attention to acting and performance, particularly the performance of one's self. Sonia runs through her monologue, adroitly impersonating Maggie Smith's mercurial riff of Diana Barrie's speech, shifting between hope, alarm, and despair; in so doing, she shows how emotions, too, can be constructed, rearranged, and altered, and do not need to define a person. The moment she tells Vanya in the voice of Maggie Smith, "Let's go to the party, Sidney" (50), she seems to "channel" the actress and gain the courage Smith's character mustered in the face of an anxious situation. In performance this scene receives booming applause because of the talent of impersonation required, but more importantly, the scene shows the resilience and spunk of a woman who, although depressed, achieves self-confidence by adopting another persona, from the shimmering tiara on her head to her slinky, sequined evening gown. Later, when Vanya compliments her for being so outgoing at the party, he encourages her to see this personality as another part of herself, and she is rewarded for this transformation when a man from the party calls to ask her out on a date. While the costume party designates a moment of poetic justice as the dowdy sister upstages the glamorous one, it also emphasizes that Sonia's melodramatic grief for her uneventful life as a single woman has likewise been a costume. She has internalized a belief in pain so great that she no longer sees her emotional state for what it is: a spinster stereotype. Her path to becoming a happier self, as she discovers in the telephone conversation with her potential date, is about choosing another role.

For her part, Masha is able to drop her mask after the costume party and reveal her inner self. As a Hollywood actress living up to certain expectations of success, Masha must continually "keep face" and maintain an image of ease, attractiveness, and desirability, which does not allow her to be herself. After the party, Masha, accustomed to being famous, is devastated because partygoers did not recognize her costume, and instead assumed her to be Norma Desmond or a Hummel figurine. The thematic metaphor of a costume designating identity is repeated here, this time reinforcing Masha's existential predicament: she is no one, because no one can identify her. Moreover, she feels jealous panic when Spike drives Nina home and tells her "Don't wait up"; in retaliation she lashes out at Sonia for refusing to act as a dwarf to her Snow White. The conversation between the two sisters escalates into a fight, as each one accuses the other for her current state of sadness: Sasha resents Masha for abandoning the care of their parents to her and Vanya, while Masha resents the financial burden of having to support them and the house. Much to Sonia's surprise, Masha divulges her fears of aging, her dismay over her five unsuccessful marriages, and her worry that Spike lusts after other women. This exchange of emotional honesty with each other turns into an evaluation over a wasted life; Sonia wails, "My life is pointless. I haven't lived! I haven't lived!" and Masha cries, "Well I have lived and made my money and messed up all my relationships, and now I have nothing! No one loves me, I have no future, my life is over!" (56); the two devolve into a cathartic crying fit over their thwarted affections and disappointments. The unhappiness that plagues these two sisters brings them together momentarily as they are comforted by Vanya, who serves them tea. The scene is perfectly Chekhovian in the contrast between the sister's hysteria and Vanya's resigned presence; he bears witness to their pain as one would a passing storm. John Lahr notes the actor, David Hyde-Pierce, sitting cross-legged on the floor between the two sisters, swishing tea from one cheek to the other as he waits for their crying to abate: "His stoic slow-take anchors the comedy and gives a terrific lift to the manic melodrama around him" (2012, 85). The failure of the party has forced Masha to remove her accustomed mask of self-assured glamour, but it is the familial space of home and sibling relationships that permitted her self-honesty. It is in the rupturing of false postures that characters are able to see their lives in a new light.

For most theatregoers, the ending is hopeful. Masha decides against the sale of the homestead when she discovers that Spike has been having an affair with her personal assistant, Hootie Pie, as this assistant was the one who suggested the sale, among other bad ideas. No longer clinging to Spike to achieve her status as a desired woman, she appears calmer and more assured. Vanya for his part realizes that he and Sonia must find jobs and stop relying upon Masha to send them money, and Nina's parting message, "You must always get your hopes up" (88), feels earned, as does the play's final image of the three siblings listening to the Beatle's "Here Comes the Sun" as they wait for the blue heron to come visit their pond. Grafting his work onto Chekhov's, Durang is able to comically play with his characters' dissolution of purpose, where lines about suffering through "a long succession of tedious days, and tedious nights" can make sense. Michael Feingold, wondering whether Durang's play could stand on its own "without leaning on its [Chekhovian] references?" appears at first to credit Chekhov for the soulful resonances at the core of Durang's play, yet ultimately decides that the play's "crazy mixed-up spirit . . . feels distinctively its own, and very much of our time" (2013). Another longtime fan of Durang's work, Linda Winer lauded the play's cartoon style for sustaining "serious, cosmic purpose without sacrificing trust in the transcendent pleasure of the wicked and silly" (2012). In other words, Durang's belief in the comic spirit lifts his characters above the wackiness and pain that constitutes their lives.

The conditions of anomie run through all of Durang's plays, but particularly in the plays in this chapter, where a logical or sane character questions the practices of those around her. Whether it is Prudence in *Beyond Therapy*, Cecilia in *Media Amok*, Felicity in *Why Torture Is Wrong*, or the characters of Betty or Miss Witherspoon in plays that bear their names, these characters offer the calm, sensible disposition in the face of others' insanity. They provide the audience with a point of reference for appropriate behavior or what can be generally considered "normal." The prying eyes of journalism, the damage from irresponsible public leadership, and the fear of harmful personal relationships are all valid worries that can cause one to wish to escape from society, as Cecilia did, abandoning New York City in favor of living in a forest tree house. *Vanya* was the first play about typical people hiding away from an abnormal world; Sonia and Vanya sought refuge in their family home, the same home where Masha finds comfort in fleeing the superficial, hyped-up world of Hollywood. However, avoiding the craziness of the world is not the answer, and Vanya and Sonia must engage actively with life if they are to thrive. As Durang mentions in his Author's Note to *Why Torture Is Wrong*, "I think I'm just acknowledging my desire for the human race to improve, to emotionally evolve" (82). The question is always there: How does one maintain integrity and beliefs in a larger society that seems crazy, unstable, insane? How does one accept this society and still participate without falling victim to its influences and abuse? How does one work together with people—friends, lovers, family members, colleagues—in ways that are conciliatory and productive? Although these questions will perhaps never yield satisfying answers, Durang successfully explores them and gives the best advice he can: continue to hope, learn from the past, and persevere.

CHAPTER 6
CRITICAL PERSPECTIVES

WE LAUGH TRACK PEOPLE: CHRISTOPHER DURANG'S DRAMA OF AUDIENCE PARTICIPATION

Robert Combs

Like all good satirists, Christopher Durang uses humor, irony, and exaggeration to create plays that are deadly serious in their comic intensity and political in their implications. And sometimes, in order to make his audience realize that they are participants in an absurd world, not simply voyeuristic observers of a theatrical one, he positions an audience within the theatrical frame itself. He breaks the fourth wall not by having actors go into the audience's space, but by bringing the audience, or rather its surrogate, into the actors' space. How an audience behaves is, after all, crucial to a successful performance. But Durang has also realized that showing an audience how they are—as an *audience*—complicit in the follies of their society is an effective theatrical maneuver. I will examine *Betty's Summer Vacation* (1999) according to Viktor Shklovsky's ideas of defamiliarization to demonstrate how Durang explores the role of audience: as participant, enabler, and partner in crime.

In these plays, Durang is working in a tradition of self-aware drama established by Edward Albee in his black comedy *Who's Afraid of Virginia Woolf?* (1962), in which two of the four characters can be seen, at least initially, in an audience role and the other two as performers. A nice young couple, Nick and Honey, new in their university town, are invited into the home of George and Martha, where an evening of "Fun and Games" ensues. They seem spellbound by the increasingly bizarre "performances" of their hosts and are drawn into entanglements with them they later regret. They are finally able to leave at dawn after they learn that the child George and Martha seem obsessed with does not actually exist, but is only a fiction used as a diversion from their deeply troubled marriage.

Nick and Honey are audience surrogates, so the theatre audience observes itself being challenged in its comfortable illusions about polite, bourgeois life, marriage, and much more besides. They understand that George and Martha's savage form of survival through role-playing has its heroic and deeply loving dimensions, especially when compared to the pretensions of their normal-appearing younger guests. Albee uses the device of character-as-audience surrogate in another influential work, his two-hander *The Zoo Story* (1959), in which two very different individuals attempt, but tragically fail, to communicate, leading to violence and death. Typically, one character is relatively conventional (Peter in *The Zoo Story*) and stands in for the audience onstage, while the other is a fringe character (Jerry) who is threatening in his bizarrely obstructive speech and behavior. We find the same meta-theatrical pattern in other plays, such as *Dutchman* (1964), by Leroi Jones, *Night, Mother* (1983), by Marsha Norman, and *Oleanna* (1992), by David Mamet, all of which use the audience surrogate model to explore specific social problems.

Sister Mary Ignatius Explains It All for You, Durang's breakthrough play, follows the pattern of Albee's comedy by assigning an onstage character to the role of audience and bending a familiar, seemingly benign situation toward an ultimate horror. The impact of Durang's play lies not in debunking the original situation, but in exposing a troubling mixture of helplessness and anger in the audience-performer relationship or, in terms of this play, the relationship between congregation and clergy. At first, *Sister Mary Ignatius* seems to be a fairly narcissistic talking-out-of-school play, a nostalgically anti-nostalgic revisiting of the audience's presumed early Catholic school education. The play's setup is a lecture being given by a strict, yet sentimental nun of a certain age explaining for the thousandth time the same religious doctrines she was taught as a child. The audience in the theatre is thus cast in the role of audience of Sister's lecture, and as she speaks, with her seven-year-old student Thomas sitting on her lap, the audience experiences a double consciousness of then and now, of audience and participant, witnessing the disparity between a child's and an adult's view of dogmas such as the Immaculate Conception, the Virgin Birth, and mortal versus venial sin. What this doubled audience (of Durang's play and of Sister's lecture) is also witnessing is the unbridgeable gap between the late 1950s, when the theatre audience were Catholic school children, and the 1980s, when they have become all sorts of things. In addition to the secular social changes that occurred between the two time periods, another set of changes has been equally cataclysmic for Catholics, those brought about by The Ecumenical Council of Pope John XXIII, convened in 1962. Some of the play's best jokes come from the disparities between these time periods, stated in literal terms such as these: unbaptized children who died before the council went to Limbo, but those born afterward have a chance at heaven. Catholics went to hell for eating meat on Fridays before the council, but have nothing to fear at a later date. Durang accomplishes two demystifications in this way. He reveals that certain church teachings are historically contingent, not transcendent. And he suggests that there is something glaringly strange about someone like Sister Mary Ignatius who seems to have no problem with such disparities. Rationalizing all inconsistencies to suit herself, she is simple-minded or crazy or somewhat sinister, perhaps all three.

A useful concept to explain this dramatic technique of treating the audience as character, and vice versa, comes from Russian formalist Viktor Shklovsky's 1917 essay, "Art as Technique." Durang is practicing a farcical/satirical version of what Shklovsky calls "defamiliarization." For Shklovsky, the true purpose of art is to resist the numbing of sensation that occurs as experience becomes automatic or habitual. Making his point, he invokes Tolstoy's *Diary*:

> Habitualization devours works, clothes, furniture, one's wife, and the fear of war. "If the whole complex lives of many people go on unconsciously, then such lives are as if they had never been." And art exists that one may recover the sensation of life; it exists to make one feel things, to make the stone stony. The purpose of art is to impart the sensation of things as they are perceived and not as they are known. The technique of art is to make objects "unfamiliar," to make forms difficult, to increase the difficulty and length of perception because the process of perception is an aesthetic end in itself and must be prolonged. *Art is a way of experiencing the artfulness of an object; the object is not important.* (12; Scholovsky's emphasis)

That last assertion is particularly interesting in light of the outrage *Sister Mary Ignatius* inspired in some Catholic circles, as they accused Durang of being a bigoted "anti-Catholic." In saying that "the object is not important," Shklovsky is suggesting that it is not *what* is being experienced through art that matters but, rather, how *consciously* or *unconsciously* it is being experienced. One could extrapolate his insight in this way: it is not Catholic teaching as such that is wrong (or right), but the habitual way that such teaching, or any teaching, is taught. Any attempt at institutionalizing human experience would have the same liability; indeed, Shklovsky suggests that all human experience tends to become automatic almost immediately, and is thus *known* rather than *felt*, known in the limited sense of merely being identified conceptually. For Shklovsky, Tolstoy is the consummate defamiliarizer, making a flogging, for example, seem "strange" in his fiction by not naming it, yet still describing it in detail. Clearly, for Tolstoy, losing the ability to experience a stone as stony is one step nearer to losing the capacity to see war (or any human barbarity) as something that rightly should be feared, and another step nearer to making people's lives "as if they had never been."

Durang begins his comic defamiliarization with the setup of the play, forcing the *doubled* audience to see what they were not able to see as children, that the cosmology of theology (earth, heaven, hell, etc.) does not really fit with the cosmology of astronomy (earth, sun, moon, etc.), in spite of Sister's naively conflating these two world views on a single large cardboard tablet on her easel. She then explains several esoteric Catholic concepts for the benefit of any non-Catholics in the audience. Such refocusing requires her audience to look at distinctions between purgatory and hell, the Immaculate Conception and the Virgin Birth, and time measured on Earth and in eternity, as if they were simply facts, not metaphors, thus creating in her audience not sympathetic understanding, but intellectual dismay. They are also forced to see that the distinction between Catholics and non-Catholics may not be as hard and fast as they had been taught. Next, she explains why she bows her head every time she utters the words "Our Lord Jesus Christ." It is simply out of respect. But she then proceeds to utter and bow three times in succession. The simple repetition of this gesture out of its normal (unconscious) religious context in church makes it seem ridiculous. All this strange behavior defamiliarizes Sister, encouraging the audience to see, in addition to a rather abstract, cartoonish, habitual nun, how the authoritative powers of the Catholic Church control her as much as she controls the audience.

Perhaps all institutions, not just Catholicism, have the capacity to control their audiences' responses to a worrisome degree. Shklovsky's belief that we need art as a means of defamiliarization suggests as much. In *Betty's Summer Vacation*, Durang finds a corollary to the magisterial

Catholic Church in the vulgar, ubiquitous presence of current media. Tabloid or mediatized culture can devour its audience just as well as any formal religion. The play relies upon a well-known comic setup when a character's seemingly innocent desire for a "vacation"—a temporary escape from the hectic routines of life—leads only to far worse trouble. One thinks of National Lampoon's *Vacation* movies, starring Chevy Chase, or Lucille Ball and Desi Arnaz's classic *The Long, Long Trailer*, or even horror movies in which a nice, young couple leaves New York seeking peace and quiet in Connecticut, only to learn that the old house they are restoring is demonically possessed. While madcap comedy rules in *Betty's Summer Vacation*, it is the horrors discovered in the rental cottage that increasingly up the ante of the play's dramatic action. The audience sees itself here in two onstage manifestations, first in the eponymous Betty, who has come to the vacation cottage much as the audience has come to the theatre, seeking a respite from the "real world." And second, the audience is treated to a vision of itself that is much more shocking: the vacation cottage harbors a personified version of the manufactured laughter played for sitcoms: we meet the Laugh Track People.

In his satire of reality television, Durang introduces a group of characters who are radical in themselves and strangers to each other, cast in the mold of participants from MTV's *Real World* series which began in 1992. Betty, the play's relatively normal protagonist, has rented a beach house in order to hear the "sound of the ocean" instead of city traffic. Her friend Trudy accompanies her, but destroys all peace from the beginning with her compulsive talking, a result of having been molested by her father, she believes. Trudy's mother, Mrs. Siezmagraff, a larger-than-life Auntie Mame figure who touts that she is all for "life, life, life," owns the beach house and is dangerously indiscriminate about the guests she welcomes into their space. She has adopted Mr. Vanislaw, naked except for his raincoat and sneakers, an equal-opportunity sex offender with a touch of Harpo Marx, and another libido-driven visitor named Buck, described by Durang as a Beach Guy out of *Baywatch*. Far more sinister, though, is Keith, well known to us, unfortunately, from the Evening News—that shy, quiet young man who harbors inner destructive madness beneath a seemingly harmless exterior. Betty and Trudy begin to worry that Keith may be carrying a severed head in a hatbox he carries. He tops Trudy's childhood trauma, having been molested in his childhood by *twenty* different people, some of them inbred family members from the Ozarks. When the play turns nasty—and it is just getting started—Trudy cuts off Mr. Vanislaw's penis after he rapes her, jogging the audience's memories of the much reported Lorena Bobbitt case, and Keith cuts off Mr. Vanislaw's head, to add to his "collection." The only stabilizing character in this violent, black comedy is Betty. In her role as observer of the others' outrageous actions, she represents the audience and serves as a touchstone for normalcy.

The Laugh Track People serve as the other conduit for audience identification; Durang labels them as such: "Two men, one woman. They laugh, they applaud. They live in the ceiling" (xvii). Renegades from the world of televised experiences, they are first noticed by Betty, Trudy, and the others as an invisible, unidentifiable source of occasional, mostly inappropriate, laughter coming from *somewhere*. Soon they are identified as the beach house's "laugh track," the nearly ubiquitous accompaniment to the gags of sitcoms—as familiar as Muzak on elevators, or watered-down classical music we hear when placed on hold. In fact, Durang's characters having grown up themselves hearing this device are remarkably tolerant of the laughter. When Buck first hears it, he asks Betty, "What was that?" Betty replies, "I don't know. There seems to be a laugh track in the house." He replies, "Cool," then changes the subject: "Do you like flavored condoms?" (9).

In order to appreciate the implications of these grotesque characters, we need to look at the history of the laugh track, which plays a significant role in the history of television. It is generally agreed that the laugh track was first used in the *Hank McClure Show* in 1950, but it really took off with *I Love Lucy* in 1953. Historians describe it as an extension of radio and television's culture of liveness and intimacy, a sense of copresence with events occurring at a distance, whether the audience is witnessing a news event, a conversation, or a performance (J. Smith 2005, 23). Events are believed to be "live," though, interestingly, they are not experienced in a public space like a theatre, but in a private space, a living room where the viewer is alone or in the company of only a few others. From the beginning, the laugh track was a source of mystery, intrigue, and controversy. Only Charley Douglass, inventor of the "Laff Box," an instrument that looked like an organ with keyboard and pedals, knew how it worked; only he and his immediate family were allowed to touch it. It could deliver any combination of titters, guffaws, and belly laughs, though very few knew exactly how, and as shows became increasingly prerecorded, it could completely replace, not just "augment" the responses of a "live theatre audience" (J. Smith 2005, 40). Some of its harshest critics included Jack Benny, Fred Allen, and Jack Gould, TV critic for the *New York Times*, who, because of the Laff Box's use of recorded laughter from times past—a mix of laughs from the living and the dead—thought of it, along with lip-syncing, as "phony TV with performing half-breeds, the zombies of show business" (1956, 27). Larry Gelbart felt pressured to use the Laff Box on *M*A*S*H*, but when he had more clout he omitted the canned laughter from his next program, "United States." His logic speaks directly to the absurdity being pictured in *Betty's Summer Vacation*.

> We did away with the laugh track, rejecting outright the suggestion to the viewer that there were three hundred people living in the same house as our couple, going from room to room with them and laughing their heads off at their intimate and/or hilarious exchanges. (94)

In addition to artistic objections, there have been deeper worries about the implications of recorded or simulated laughter in the context of what it means to be human. Jacob Smith has discussed the laugh track in the more general context of "laughing records," going back to the 1890s. Smith argues that laughing is the ultimate expression of the human—an irrepressible spasm of life itself, "man's defense against the gods and against himself" (Shayton 1959, 44). Laughter, usually social and interpersonal, is one means by which humans, as humans, connect to one another. However, following the thinking of both Henri Bergson and Freud, Smith also locates laughter in the purely personal domain of bodily reaction. At the intersection of the natural and the mechanical, the body revolts from social control. He speculates that the laughing record may have been part of the recording industry's attempt to reassure the public that the recording machine could, if not *be* human, at least *transmit* the human; that is, if listeners were nervous about being talked to by a machine, hearing human laughter, no matter if it was recorded, would quell their worries (31). Thus the Laugh Track People in Durang's comedy serve this defamiliarizing function of sounding both human and mechanical. In fact, when they finally do break through the ceiling, they appear as a deformed robot, joined at the hip or, if the director prefers, three actors inside black stretch fabric, an obese, unholy Trinity, often speaking in unison. Durang describes them in all their surreal glory:

> Coming out of the tops or sides of their heads are pieces of tubing with bits of wiring coming out of them, as if they had been living somehow inside the ceiling of the cottage, connected to wire and tubing and God knows what else. (60)

They disturb the audience with their random laughter and their annoying presence, defamiliarizing this vacation experience by suggesting that it may have something in common with a scripted sitcom.

Whether laughter is essentially an expression of individual humanity or a way people connect with each other, recent scholarship about television argues that the laugh track functions to make individual viewers *believe* they are part of a "we," a collective audience, and thus encourages a kind of group think. People access their laughter more easily within a group dynamic and are less discriminating about the object of their laughter. Recorded group laughter, strategically positioned, makes the comedy feel safe to laugh at, even if it portrays people's misfortunes and transgressions (Bore 2011, 24). In the process, individuals may stop thinking for themselves, and alternative readings of the show's content are closed down (Neale and Krutnik 1990, 69). Durang taps into such "group think" behavior for his Orwellian critique of televised culture. At one point, for example, the Laugh Track People share with Betty their own mindless reactions, explaining why they laugh at things that are not funny: "We're uncomfortable," they say. "And so we laugh. We don't know what else to do" (20). Increasingly, they pass judgment on what the vacationers say and do in terms of its entertainment value. They represent the public's insatiable appetite for dark, voyeuristic pleasures involving sex, violence, insults, humiliations, and ultimately mass death, reinforcing all appetites with laughter and applause. By incorporating the laugh track, a seemingly benign reinforcement of spectator pleasure, Durang demonstrates how television shapes societal tastes and increases the insensate demand for violent and sexualized TV fare.

Durang does not let the audience off the hook in his critique. Disturbingly, he suggests a kind of affinity between the onstage audience, the Laugh Track People, and the audience watching the play. Their disturbing tendency to revel in lugubrious characters or degrading behavior is magnified with the arrival of a derelict, Mr. Vanislav. A house guest of Mrs. Siezmagraff, he exposes himself, he rapes, yet he amuses the Laugh Track People. Durang thus suggests that unconscious television viewers, just like Mrs. Siezmagraff, may well be letting anything and everything into their homes, since everything they let in is, for them, simply something to be watched. Keith, a sweet serial killer resembling a character from the movie *Night Must Fall*, intrigues them. Buck, a dumb, sex-obsessed oaf, is attractive. They relish the childish arguments between Trudy and her mother, Mrs. Siezmagraff, about the horror of her being molested by her father and are bored when certain characters go to sleep. At one point, after they have crashed through the ceiling and made their presence known, they whine: "Make us laugh. Gross us out. Tell us the latest news of Gwyneth Paltrow. Show us naked pictures of Brad Pitt! Vomit in the sink! Entertain us! Waaaaa-aaaaaaaaa! [*The Voices start to cry—I Love Lucy-'Waaaaa' style—at their frustration at not being entertained.*]" (61). By providing an onstage audience consisting of Laugh Track People, Durang destabilizes the relationship of audience to spectacle, making theatregoers question their own appetite for entertainment. It is as if the audience, finally shocked enough by the murder, rape, and mutilation going on, has been forced to see itself as mindlessly, pruriently curious. The vacation cottage has become a metaphor for any media-driven escapism—the desire to be entertained by the harmful behavior and experiences of others.

The Laugh Track People in *Betty's Summer Vacation* are Durang's stroke of genius, correlating to the audience's most venal wishes to witness sex and mayhem simply because they are bored. Yet this comic device did not begin with this play. Durang had used an onstage laugh track in his 1988 one-act, "Woman Stand-Up," a one-character play about an insecure comedienne who carries her own portable laugh track onstage at the comedy club where she performs. When she calls attention to this intrusive audience surrogate, which she only imperfectly controls, the laugh track defamiliarizes what may be the innately absurd situation of trying to make an audience laugh; it also makes us witness the full pathos of this woman's struggle to endure being herself, who—as audience to herself throughout—sees herself as "hideous and worthless" (131). This sketch captures perfectly a painful experience, seen from both sides of the audience-performer binary, when someone tries to be funny in order to relieve their own insecurity and simply cannot bring it off. It suggests what might have caught Durang's attention about the televised laugh track in the first place: that it encourages people to use laughter to cover up their inadequacies, whether artistic, personal, or moral.

Durang's Laugh Track People represent his indictment of what TV audiences have become in their hunger for predictable entertainment, and, even more frighteningly, what people whose expectations about life reflect the pervasive influence of television have become. It is as if technology had created a life style, a way of playing a role in society, that consists almost entirely of being an audience. Playing this role of TV audience does not even seem to depend upon any particular televised content. Students of television like Paddy Scannell notice that prior to *what* people might be watching on television is simply *the fact that* they are watching, sometimes for long periods of time.

> But what *is* it that people listen to and watch? Is it particular programmes—the news, favoured soaps, sitcoms, Saturday afternoon sport—or is it that people just watch television and listen to the radio irrespective of what is actually being transmitted? (7; emphasis mine)

In other words, playing the role of audience seems to be an addictive activity in itself.

Furthermore, in their addictions viewers become pleasurably aware of their powers as analysts and connoisseurs of media representations of life. To borrow the language of Erving Goffman, every news, performance, or entertainment program is carefully "framed," so that the audience can immediately know what they are watching (Elam 2002, 78). As Scannell says,

> What radio and television do—in a very pervasive way—is to render transparent that social life (at least as displayed in all their programmes) is a performance of one sort or another. The more we get used to radio and television as one essential, seen but unnoticed part of our everyday existence, the more we become connoisseurs of performances. (1996, 57)

Durang clearly suggests, though, that this knife, in sharpening consciousness, cuts two ways. It defamiliarizes illusions as we realize that everything anyone says or does is, in a way, a "performance," but it can also lead to radical uncertainty about what anything means. As Goffman explains at the beginning of his monumental work *Frame Analysis: An Essay on the Organization of Experience* (1974), studying "scrips" of behavior in their framed aspects does not uncover a continuous reality below the surface, but a potentially infinite array of ways to analyze the world of human experience (1). Seeing life as performance defamiliarizes both. Durang dramatizes being caught between living and performing in "The Actor's Nightmare," sometimes done in tandem with *Sister Mary Ignatius Explains It All for You*, by elaborating upon the common dream of finding oneself a performer onstage without benefit of script or rehearsal, called by psychologists "the good student's dream" (352). Just as one is often impressed how "real" good acting can look, one also marvels at how perplexingly "unreal" life can become. And Durang explores the comic terrors of absolute cognitive instability—anything can mean anything—in two scenes from *Betty's Summer Vacation*, the charades scene and Mrs. Siezmagraff's courtroom drama.

The parlor game of charades that the characters play in Act 1, Scene 4 dramatizes the performative aspect of social interaction as well as the process of socialization implied by being an audience. Players give out information *about* themselves while giving *off* information at the same time. Social interaction is, as Goffman says in his highly entertaining *The Presentation of the Self in Everyday Life* (1959), "a kind of information game—a potentially infinite cycle of concealment, discovery, false revelation, and rediscovery" (8). The double meaning of "charade" here comes into play: "A kind of parlor game in which players guess a word or phrase from pantomimed clues," and "an absurd pretense intended to create a pleasant or respectable appearance" (Oxford Dictionaries). This view of society as spectacle and stagecraft puts everyone in this play on the same level: vacationer, vacationer's friend, vacation cottage owner, sex addict, serial killer, and derelict, all play the same way and while playing are only visible in limited ways. Everyone continually alternates between performer and audience. Thus, charades, a metaphor for how people play social roles, suggests that people never really know who or what anyone really is.

Mrs. Seizmagraff's courtroom drama, a command performance for the Laugh Track People, further explores the consequences of seeing life as a stage where people occupy the role of audience-as-participant-to-be-enter tained-by-the-behavior-of-others. In *Sister Mary Ignatius Explains It All for You*, Durang defamiliarized orthodox religion; now he shows how television has defamiliarized the justice system, making it fodder for entertainment. Philip Auslander, in his investigation of the status of performance in a culture dominated by mass media, concludes that law courts are the last bastion of meaningful liveness (1999, 113). In other words, live trials still claim to embody honest investigation and the pursuit of truth for its own sake through live performances given by the accused, lawyers, and their witnesses. Not so in the courtroom of Mrs. Siezmagraff, who alternately plays all three of these roles. Just as in a game of charades, Mrs. Siezmagraff's courtroom is a space where anyone can be anything, depending on how they are "read." She has already concocted the frames that she hopes will save "[her] darling daughter, Trudy, who's been wronged" and "her interesting, disturbed friend Keith" (65). Mrs. Siezmagraff's legal tour de force is her final effort to vindicate Vacation-as-a-Way-of-Life, Auntie Mame style. In this scene, Mrs. Siezmagraff, like Sister Mary Ignatius, "explains it all." She tells the Laugh Track People (her audience and jury) what to believe and they believe it, as long as she can control their attention. When Betty objects to various atrocities going unpunished, the scene becomes a roller-coaster ride, veering between sympathy and condemnation. Eventually, so much moral rumination bores the Laugh Track People. Hungry for more pornographic entertainment, they urge Buck to enter the bedroom with Trudy and Keith, where what was done to Mr. Vanislav is now done to him. It is no longer possible to ignore the fiasco this "vacation" has become, and so the Laugh Track People urge Keith to strike the match that blows up the house. Keith, tired of living, is glad to comply.

The vacation cottage (life as entertainment) is now burning to the ground. The sets, the props, and all the characters except Betty herself are in the process of being reduced to debris. The theatre audience witnesses the final consequences of mediatized culture: everything and everyone are trashed. "Pushed by the demand that it should entertain" (Ellis 2000, 126), televised experience and experience in a televised world become façades that are only temporarily meaningful. This is essentially Durang's critique of mediatized culture, that it encourages a depiction of human experience as contemptible and disposable—simply because it makes for good entertainment. Durang's characters not only trash each other, always confusing the frame for the person, but also trash themselves, characterizing themselves as clichéd snapshots, flickering images from channel surfing. Mrs. Siezmagraff is an "Auntie Mame," Trudy an adult child damaged by abuse, Buck a horny dude, Mr. Vanislaw and Keith tabloid afterimages, remnants of reported horror. Durang "screams and laughs" (Stein 1995, vii) as he finds little evidence of the human in a world consisting of popular culture and consumers consumed by it. Only at the end of *Betty's Summer Vacation* does one feel the stillness of human presence in Betty's final monologue, when, solitary, she finally "begins to feel better" on the beach, as the vacation cottage burns behind her.

As a satiric playwright, Durang can only defamiliarize and criticize the world his audience inhabits; only they can change it. In *A History of the American Film* (1978), which will serve as a conclusion for this essay, Durang gives us an explicit representation of the public's complacency. Entering the theatre, the audience sees onstage a mirror image of itself: rows of occupied theatre seats facing out toward them. In a setup reminiscent of Plato's parable of the cave, the onstage audience stares out over the heads of the theatre audience, presumably at a screen on which movie images are projected from a projection booth located behind the onstage audience. The theatre audience sees itself in the onstage audience watching movies that span the history of American cinema. Cast members onstage act out key moments from the movies, shifting aside their onstage seating as needed, sitting back down when not performing in a scene. They enact parodies of various well-known genres such as shanty-town romance, gangster film, screwball comedy, and Second World War drama. The actors find themselves cast in stereotypical roles across time, in a variety of genres, acting out the same roles over and over again. The onstage actors repeat their scripted identities, unable to escape their conventional parts, incapable of change. When the projector temporarily breaks down, a cast member named Loretta experiences a longing to walk off the stage and embark upon "real life." Unfortunately, before she can lead the actors offstage, away from their roles, the projector starts up again, and they all sit down, mesmerized by the next movie. Durang directly asks his audience to take a hard look in his theatrical mirror and ask if they are capable of change. Paradoxically, at the moment he asks the question, his audience is busy watching his play.

The Theatre of Christopher Durang

THE MARRIAGE OF PARODY AND SATIRE: THE ALL-AMERICAN COMEDY OF CHRISTOPHER DURANG

Jay Malarcher

The idea of parody in performed comedy may be said to date from *The Frogs*, where the works of Æschylus and Euripides suffered the jaundiced glance of master satirist Aristophanes. Parody in American humor dates back at least to Mark Twain's scathing take on "[James] Fenimore Cooper's Literary Offenses" (1895). On the stage, George S. Kaufman and Morrie Ryskind famously parodied Eugene O'Neill's experimental but popular *Strange Interlude* in their Marx Brothers romp *Animal Crackers*.[1] In more recent times, parody held a revered place in Sid Caesar's television work, both on *Your Show of Shows* and on *Caesar's Hour*. One may argue that many of his writers, born into immigrant Jewish households, learned America not from classic novels or poetry, but from the easy popular culture of the movies and television, or the growing suburban culture of the 1950s. Frequently, the writers would convene on a Monday morning and talk up the films they had seen that weekend, which resulted in satires of such things as Kurosawa films or works like *Rebecca*. It is no wonder that Caesar's stable of writers—including Mel Brooks, Larry Gelbart, Neil Simon, and Woody Allen—have gone on to produce scripts that parody common genres.[2] Even the sophomoric *MAD Magazine* featured a monthly film parody of (often R rated) popular movies such as *The Planet of the Apes*, *The Godfather*, and even *A Clockwork Orange*. Iconoclastic television and film parodies were thus in the air as a young Christopher Durang developed his own writing style in the 1960s and early 1970s.

One might consider "American comedy" to be squarely in this parodic tradition, since from the earliest days of colonial America, the literary language and stylistic model were thoroughly British; thus, it may be said that all American literature ultimately follows the British forms and even continental interest in regional or national storytelling, and as such constitute a kind of parody without any satirical angle. Ernest Hemingway famously pronounced that "all modern American literature comes from one book by Mark Twain called *Huckleberry Finn*." As a humorist, Twain's American character cannot be disputed, and by the time Eugene O'Neill emerged in the early decades of the twentieth century, an American literature seemed fixed and identifiable. Comedy, as a performed genre, took more time to find its American voice, but when it did speak up, it very often used parody as a device of choice.

In examining the plays of Durang, one is immediately struck by the sheer amount of parody in his works, whether as a frame for the plot and characters or as a shorthand that allows the author to dive directly into familiar, shared material. In the latter case, it is the literary equivalent of *When Harry Met Sally*'s "let's meet at that place we did that thing that time"—Durang can count on a critical mass of audience members starting the trip with him. A newspaper feature writer touting one of his local productions wrote that "playwright Christopher Durang is a master of parody who is known for producing works that are original, absurd and funny" (McClaran 2007). The sentiment raises a quirky paradox regarding parody: the extent to which any parody can be considered "original." Durang claims that his recent play *Vanya and Sonya and Masha and Spike* (2012) is not a strict parody—at least not in terms of the styles described thus far. A looser definition of parody, one espoused by Linda Hutcheon in *A Theory of Parody*, for example, holds that any work that embodies the form of another work of art (similar containers, different contents) qualifies as parody, regardless of any satirical objective toward the original. Hutcheon includes discussion of more contemporary jargon related to the scope of parody—words like "intertextuality," "transtextuality," and "hypertextuality" (2000, 21 ff.). She sometimes offers a helpful simple definition, calling parody "a formal or structural relation between two texts" (22).

In this way, Durang's appropriation of a Chekhovian milieu for his contemporary story would count as a parody. It may be enough, however, that *Vanya and Sonya and Masha and Spike* carries through an understanding with the audience based on familiar cultural territory and allusions. Every reviewer, it seems, found Durang's play intimately connected to Chekhov's dramaturgy, but with the obvious updated and geographically shifted details. The title, which evokes a bit of *Bob & Carol & Ted & Alice*, may seem at first flippant with the unexpected Spike added to the list of Russian names, but the title, as with Mazursky's 1969 film, actually tells the story in a nutshell. While Spike may seem the most out of place, the function of Spike parallels Chekhov's own use of outsiders such as *Seagull*'s Trigorin. Apart from the strict modeling of Chekhov, Durang brings into the picture the housekeeper Cassandra, who bears more of a resemblance to the disbelieved Greek prophetess than to, say, Dunyasha in the Russian originals. The use of Cassandra, therefore, represents a favorite Durang device in his parodies: the incongruous intersection of several strains of Western civilization. More examples of this mixing of sources will follow later.

Durang's own definition of parody has not ventured into the postmodern mindset of inter-, hyper-, meta-, but remains steadfastly in the entertaining and sly use of familiar territory to land comic points more easily (albeit with more complexity, for what astute audience can wring from it). Most telling is that Durang does not consider *Vanya and Sonia and Masha and Spike* a parody. It is not much of an overstatement, though, to say that parody is the natural mode of Durang's comedy, and so the debt to those comedians that came before him looms that much larger. *Vanya and Sonya and Masha and Spike* may therefore be seen as a significant outlier in Durang's oeuvre: it conforms to parody as Hutcheon frames it, but does not follow the style of parody at the center of Durang's other important works.

In Durang's narrower definition—apart from Hutcheon's broadly formalistic open-ended definition of parody—satire without a sufficient bite squanders the adoption of the parodic posture. The choice of what to parody, and how, lies at the heart of the satirist's operation. Among Durang's works, *A History of the American Film* focuses on a certain type of recurring character, even recurring studio actor in that character type. His *The Idiots Karamazov* stays fairly close to Dostoyevsky's novel *The Brothers Karamazov*, unlike Woody Allen's 1975 film *Love and Death*.[3] "The Actor's Nightmare" does not parody every playwright, instead focusing on three distinct and identifiable authors: Shakespeare, Beckett, and Coward (with a bit of Bolt's *A Man for All Seasons* at the end).

Another consideration regarding parody has to do with the resultant piece: most parodies embody the original's genre and are thus additional examples of the genre. A parody of romantic comedies is often itself a romantic comedy, and a parody of westerns, such as Mel Brooks's *Blazing Saddles*, is itself a western, however sickly twisted. Some parodies, though, leave behind the original genre and simply mock with a larger purpose (again, this is the ideal!). Examples of this might be a Weird Al Yankovic song, or Durang's own parody of *The Glass Menagerie*, "For Whom the Southern Belle Tolls," or his parody of Greek tragedy called, innocently enough, "Medea." Written with Wendy Wasserstein, this "Medea" is more concerned with who is playing the title role and with what acting credits to give her credibility. It is unapologetically full of anachronistic references to *Thelma & Louise, Men Are from Mars, Women Are from Venus*, even

Designing Women. The piece ends happily, sort of, and is typical of Durang's starting point in parody that quickly devolves into absurdism. It lacks the vigorous detail and commitment to the original that something like A. E. Houseman's "Fragment of a Greek Tragedy" possessed.[4] Thus, while parodies often themselves become an example of the genre they parody, no one would argue that *The Idiots Karamazov* is a piece of Russian literature, or "Medea" another Greek tragedy. To ask these pieces to exhibit the integrity of a classical work moves beyond the capabilities of parody as a literary tool, and reduces our ability to see parody as a most useful critical lens.

Parody works from an established oeuvre or stylistic convention. Thus, the contract with the audience assumes a familiarity with the original works that the comedy exploits, and subsequently makes it difficult for the author to talk down to the audience: parody survives through an informed, cultured audience. While a parody may be funny in and of itself, on its own terms, the relation to the antecedents amplifies the comedy and the force of the satire. Thus, a useful rule of thumb regarding parody is, "If the more you know the funnier it is, then it's a parody," a kind of ἀρετη (*arete*) for the device. Parody is not mere allusion, but a strategy. Allusion may be employed, to be sure, but it can only exist outside the established scope of the parody, otherwise it would be subsumed into the core material. For instance, in Durang's "The Actor's Nightmare,"[5] George Spelvin, in the Beckett phase of the dream, is told that they are not waiting for Godot, but for Lefty, whom Ellen relates is "a political organizer. He's always coming around saying get involved, get off your behinds and organize, fight the system, do this, do that, uh, he's exhausting, he's worse than Jane Fonda" (1995, 365). Interestingly, Lefty in this world actually shows up, unlike the character in the Odets original and most certainly unlike Godot! So here, the author employs a double allusion, first back in time to Odets's play for the Group Theatre, and forward to Jane Fonda (one would assume in her then-current incarnation as workout guru, and not as anti–Vietnam War activist). Both references are outside the field of play (Shakespeare, Coward, and Beckett) and so add little to the parody, excepting that Shakespeare especially fills his poetry with allusions to all sorts of cultural referents, but this is likely not the reason Durang employs them. They seem merely to be stream-of-consciousness riffs on ideas floating around in the playwright/dreamer's head, for a suitably comic effect, of course.

Closer to parody itself is the pastiche, which merely seeks to capture the technique and tone of the original work, with usually as little irony as possible. In Durang's *A History of the American Film*, he produces a Depression-era movie musical lyric that goes, in part,

> Hear the pitter patter on the roof,
> The raindrops say that nothing's wrong,
> Pennies fall from heaven up above,
> Inside, we're sleepy and in love. (1997, 135)

This particular pastiche echoes songs such as "Pennies from Heaven" (introduced in 1936 in the eponymous film), itself appropriated for a Steve Martin vehicle by that same name in 1981. The song also echoes the Stephen Sondheim song "Rain on the Roof" from *Follies*, an entire musical that lives and breathes its pastiche. The forty or so years between the Great Depression and both *Follies* and *A History of the American Film* may have given some artistic distance to the generation of the new works, but even in the throes of that difficult period, Ira Gershwin mocked the lack of inventiveness in songs of his day with "Blah, Blah, Blah" from 1931:

> Blah blah blah blah moon
> Blah blah blah above
> Blah blah blah blah croon
> Blah blah blah love. (Gershwin 1959, 151)

The result of such usages in *A History of the American Film* is to cement in the audience's mind several important elements at play: to mark the point in history where the survey has reached; to represent the relative optimism or pessimism of the period, since much of the larger meaning of the piece lies in the evolution of the general American frame of mind throughout the twentieth century; to illustrate the acknowledged vapidness of such lyrics ("above"/"love"), and thus the evolution of the artistic/cultural quality of the productions of the periods covered in the course of the cinematic history. Moreover, Durang sets the scene in shantytown, which comically reduces the Depression to overtly depressed place names as if Hooverville were actually on a map—recall Blitzstein's Steel Town, USA, in *And the Cradle Will Rock* (1937), or the recent *Urinetown* (2001). Ultimately, the parodic use of pastiche may lead a critic to characterize a work as "formulaic," which is the point, or "derivative," again, the point. Writers of parody escape these major criticisms, leaving the choice of referents and the degree of satire as the greatest challenges.

Parody, in the sense that Durang (not Hutcheon) employs it, usually sits firmly within the comedic subcategory of satire, and uses the forked tongue of original and burlesque to speak a larger and (one would hope) more relevant message to its audience. Hutcheon makes the broader point that parody can etymologically be rendered as a work placed "beside" another earlier and known work, not merely a trampling of the reputation of the original. As she points out with Fowles's *The French Lieutenant's Woman*, that author's desire was "to recontextualize, to synthesize, to rework conventions—in a respectful manner" (2000, 33). The extent to which Durang's works move from wicked satire and lampoon to "respectful" becomes a point for debate. Suffice to say, his tongue *seems* more often than not planted firmly in his cheek, with the accompanying twinkle in his eye.

As any literary semiotician might note, all words on a page are simply symbols or signs pointing to other words. The ultimate goal of parody may be the existential understanding that one version of these signs may be interchangeable with any mixture of those signs for purposes of genre identification or other meaning, and that the comic version is superior for its increased entertainment value. In other words, generic elements stirred into a parodic recipe never would amount to anything tasty without the added comic juxtapositions and identifications that a "new" parody affords. In many examples from the history of parody, the genre or style parodied often has reached the end of its useful artistic career, and all of the concomitant clichés and ornaments are firmly established and ripe for ridicule. This is a corollary to the artistic movement rule of thumb that states that "if you can group them into an –ism, the –ism isn't vital anymore." A perfect example of this critical distance when parody considers threadbare and discarded styles resides in *A History of the American Film*, since the only breath the classic Hollywood film productions still possesses may be found on film-buff sites like Turner Classic Movies.

Durang's relationship to the material he parodies, including the theatre itself, is mostly fond, but critic Suzanne Burgoyne Dieckman considers "The Actor's Nightmare" to be not only meta-theatre but anti-theatre. The mirror reflecting not nature, but the reflectors of nature gives credence to this reading. Similarly, Durang uses theatre to manhandle American cinema's tropes in *A History of the American Film*, and the author's affection for (certain) movies is tempered by the unrelenting stabs at them. For example, a running gag involves Jimmy pushing a grapefruit into his wife's face at every opportunity, and a short while later, he tells the onstage piano player, "I thought I told you never to play that!" when he hears the earlier song "Shanty Town Romance." Lest anyone miss the allusion to *Casablanca*, the wife asks the Piano Man whether he knows "La Marseillaise." As Kenneth Turan wrote in his review of the Washington, DC, premiere,

> Once you get past the undeniably entertaining surface, past the deft parodies, the feeling is inescapable that Durang is not telling us that this was all good clean fun, but just the opposite. The play almost seems an act of exorcism, a way to get all of those movies out of your system. This is not a valentine to film, this is the theater's revenge. (1977)

With Durang's "A Stye of the Eye," we find a parody of playwright Sam Shepard's characteristic style and characters, and Durang himself confesses in the introduction to the published version that *A Lie of the Mind* in 1985 "really irritated" him and that "the critical kudos it received at the time baffled and discouraged" him (32). He also manages a few Mamet moments in "A Stye of the Eye," a dash of *Equus*, and some excursions into *Agnes of God* territory (in case one was wondering whether his obsession with the Catholic Church had run its course). Nevertheless, Durang admits near the end of the play's introduction that he actually likes many of Shepard's plays, so the animus seems focused on this one title more than on Shepard's entire body of work, despite having some passing references to *Curse of the Starving Class* and one or two more.[6]

On the other hand, writers of parody usually have an affection for their subjects, a relationship that springs from an abiding respect for the works and their creators. Consider Mel Brooks's *High Anxiety*, which Brooks actually screened for Hitchcock, who pronounced it wonderful (and sent a case of wine to Brooks the following week);[7] or *This Is Spinal Tap*, by Rob Reiner, Christopher Guest, and Michael McKeon, among others, whose depiction of heavy metal music stands as a monumental all-out parody beloved by musicians everywhere.[8] A more affectionate relationship to Tennessee Williams's *The Glass Menagerie* may be inferred from Durang's "For Whom the Southern Belle Tolls." The parody necessitates that the resultant memory play becomes a comedy, and not remain a bittersweet drama. The whole of this short play reads like a kind of "what if?" exercise—what if Laura were replaced by a male, named Lawrence? Durang admitted in his introduction that he did indeed have affection for the original, but that "there is something about sweet, sensitive Laura that seems to have gotten on my nerves" (11). The genesis of the parody idea, according to

Durang, dates from his time at Yale, when he and his fellow playwright Albert Innaurato teamed up to perform Laura and Amanda, respectively, not as women, but as priests with no explanation for the substitution. Perhaps the most meta-theatrical moment comes when Amanda asks Tom, "I hear you out on the porch talking. Who are you talking to?" (25). Here, in a winking line to the audience, Durang gently mocks the contrivance of the memory play and its narrator breaking the fourth wall. Tom's answer, "No one, mother," might easily be played as a wry slight of the audience, in keeping with Durang's love-hate relationship with the objects of his parody and theatre in general.

While a graduate playwriting student at Yale, Durang appeared in the updated version of Aristophanes's *The Frogs*, with a libretto by Burt Shevelove and music/lyrics by Stephen Sondheim. The agon of the Yale production pitted George Bernard Shaw against William Shakespeare, instead of Euripides versus Æschylus.[9] Durang in these formative years experienced not only one of Western culture's earliest celebration of parodies, *The Frogs*, but also a bit of a meta-parody in the updated references. Coming out of his experience at Yale with that *Menagerie* sketch and *The Frogs*, Durang wrote (with Innaurato) *The Idiots Karamazov* in 1974, a send-up not only of Russian literature—specifically Dostoyevsky's—but also of bad English translations—specifically Constance Garnett's. Any attempt at a plot summary would be convoluted and nonsensical, but suffice to say it roughly follows the plot of *The Brothers Karamazov*, with some cultural embellishments such as Alyosha's pop song, "Everything's Permitted."[10] Besides the Dostoyevsky characters, there are also a few Modernists wandering in and out for good measure, most notably an Anaïs Nin knockoff named Anaïs Pnin (after the Nabokov title character). There are Leather Girls—just because—who assist in keeping the spectacle interesting and moving along. Father Zossima becomes a spiritual (if not literal) pedophile with a foot fetish.[11] Alyosha is repulsed: "How can there be a God if there are feet?" (1997, 40).

The use of the Constance Garnett character onstage (played in the original productions by a young Meryl Streep) connects the Great Russian literature to the American consumers who do not know any better when handed an imperfect translation. Thus, despite the very Russian names, the whole of *The Idiots Karamazov* pokes its satire toward American culture—or lack thereof. Far from being a crutch to kick-start his creative impulses, Durang uses parody as a means of expressing the American relationship with culture, perhaps an oxymoron, but undeniably the stuff of comedy.

Many of his original, non-parodies explore American culture more directly. The parodies mentioned in this paper certainly call into question the worldliness of Americans, their educations and values, even the place of America in the lineage of Western civilization. His comedies become recognizable successors to the meta-theatrical works of genius by the likes of Luigi Pirandello and Eugène Ionesco. He has made a career of dovetailing familiar literary tropes with an absurdist point of view. The synthesis of these two sources—American culture and modernist meta-theatricality—creates a style of parody that provides insight into a particularly American sensibility in the later twentieth century.[12] The ultimate lessons to be drawn from Durang's plays, and his parodies in particular, may be for the audience to be more critical in accepting ideas at face value, even if they are wrapped in familiar packaging like "entertainment" and "family." Like many American playwrights, Durang's most common petri dish is the family drama, and his own life reflected its share of domestic drama.

The playwright's childhood and upbringing included a disintegrated marriage between his parents (covered somewhat autobiographically in 1985's *The Marriage of Bette and Boo*) and other moments that Durang frankly admits affected him, but not in a brutal way:

> Strangely, rarely was anyone mean to me. I was just this quiet bystander, watching other people be harsh with one another; or watch them address a problem by banging their heads against the wall, over and over and over. My world view actually improved in my early 30s, when I experienced the adult freedom not to repeat the patterns I saw. (Durang 2002)

Perhaps in Durang's dramaturgy—his choice of subject and his parodic mode—he used many of his sendups of famous works as a way of breaking out of patterns (the Catholic Church, to cite one example), of not repeating them fully. Parody is the literary equivalent of making fun of one's predecessors, of taking potshots at authority figures who purport to know better, but who are blind to their own imperfections. Durang attests to having witnessed his relatives acting in ignorance, unwilling or unable to extricate themselves from destructive patterns of behavior. Durang turns to parody, it might seem, to expose the works and their narrative motifs that have been established for so long they remain unquestioned; or that have been deified so long no one dares criticize them. His own maturation as an artist, and indeed, as an adult, may have used the comfortable familiarity of parody as a reminder of the unspoiled yet imperfect past and his own growth through it, a kind of therapy. Such a psychological reading of an author's intention is fraught with dangerous assumptions, but the foundation of parody is in the revisioning of the original works and their excesses, traits, and through lines. Durang's indulgence in parody may simply be a shorthand for the author-audience communication; going any deeper into the playwright's psyche runs the risk of going *beyond therapy*.

CONCLUSION

No matter how "pleasant" such later plays as *Vanya and Sonia and Masha and Spike* may be, to use G. B. Shaw's categorical distinction, Durang considers himself still an iconoclast, bent on breaking household gods (Durang 2017a). His works will always peddle in black humor, because this form of humor is often the strongest way to address society's ills, short of destroying humanity. If we had to boil down Durang's theatre to a single point of attack, it would be chaos of daily living, irrespective of whether that chaos comes from nature, fate, or other human beings. Diane, in *Sister Mary Ignatius Explains It All for You*, refers to the "utter randomness" regarding the terrible events of her mother's death and her rape; she laments how "*the randomness seemed intolerable* [emphasis in the original]." In a world where people believe they should be able to exert a certain degree of control, they are struck with their own inefficacy in the face of quotidian randomness, as found in sickness, dysfunctional leadership, unreliable relationships, and the irrational behavior of others. This quality of a world out of control is one that Michael Booth sees in farce, both structurally, in the plotting of events, and in the atmosphere of the play. He notes how the very atmosphere places extreme pressure upon the characters: "The actual sanity and existence of the individual are at stake in a world of accumulating disorder and disaster, a world that goes so far as to refuse to recognize him as a person and denies his identity" (Booth 1988, 150). Whether it is the domestic violence Eleanor suffers in *Nature and Purpose of the Universe* or Masha's threat to leave Vanya and Sonia homeless by selling their house, Durang's plays are replete with inconsistent behavior and unstable human connections, creating paranoia and fear of losing one's sense of self. Only by using black humor, as Frank Durrenmatt noted in "Comedy and the Modern World," can such theatre express tangibly and make audiences perceive physically what he referred to as "the face of a world without a face" (1958).

In concluding this book on Durang, I encourage other scholars to continue studying and writing about his plays. My objective was to detail the wide range of the playwright's work over forty years of writing for the theatre, but much is still left to be considered. Further theorizing on Durang's work could consider feminist applications because of the number of strong female characters his plays include as narcissists, fascists, and *raisonneurs*. Black comedy as a dramatic field is under-theorized, and Durang's use of the grotesque to handle challenging topics is an area worth examining. His theatre could be explored from a Bakhtinian analysis both of form and of subject matter, as so many of his sketch-like comedies subvert Aristotelian narration and his satirical plays attack the official, authoritative classes. Durang, as a gay playwright, includes several gay characters in his plays who address their contention with religion and government policies regulating same-sex relations. Durang's sexuality as an identifier in his texts is an area other scholars could explore.

Very little scholarship exists about Durang's theatrical oeuvre, considering the vast amount of plays he has contributed to the American theatre repertory. Durang, labeled by critics over and over as the finest satirist on the American stage, is oddly overlooked. Admittedly, it is hard to write critically about comedy, as much of the significance of the piece involves a dynamic between the actors and the audience. Additionally, drama scholars disagree on how to classify or analyze Durang's work. Anthologies do not know how to include him in their conversations about American drama. Dennis Carroll includes a sizable discussion of Durang's work in Bruce King's *Contemporary American Theatre* (1991), placing him among other "Not-Quite Mainstream Playwrights" as his chapter title states, examining Durang's subversion of social rituals, attack on the nuclear family, and satire against "larger institutional systems" that impose restrictions on individual liberties. The chapter compares Durang's work to the plays of John Guare and David Rabe, based solely on how their plays "protest on the meaningless and random patterning of life." This description seems apt, but lacks a focus on the comedic nature of Durang's plays. Fifteen years later, David Krasner's impressive and thorough survey of the American stage, *American Drama 1945-2000* (2006), treats Durang's work within the course of a single paragraph. He includes him in a summary detailing other comic writers of the period: George C. Wolfe, Neil Simon, A. R. Gurney, and Charles Ludlam's campy *The Mystery of Irma Vep*. Krassner describes Durang's plays of this period as representing "anger-fueled comedy targeting pretension and life's petty injustice" (140), but his seems more of an afterthought in a chapter devoted primarily to David Mamet and Sam Shepard. In Krasner's edited volume *A Companion to Twentieth-Century American Drama*, Durang's work is again briefly mentioned in an essay that summarizes American theatre from 1970 to 1990. The writer, Mark

Conclusion

Fearnow, focuses mostly on the protests surrounding the play *Sister Mary Ignatius Explains It All for You* and briefly alludes to Durang's plays from the 1980s as satirical of marriage and parenthood.

In terms of works devoted solely to Christopher Durang's art, there is a Master's thesis by Robert Spivak, *Christopher Durang: Satire and Beyond* (1991), a dissertation by Christopher Chung-Wee, *The Metanoia of Metacomedy in Contemporary Theatre of the Absurd: The Film, Sitcom, Drama and More* (2003), and a helpful comparison between Beckett's work and Durang's play *Laughing Wild* in Jennifer Beth Philips 2008 dissertation, *Traces of Beckett*. More easily available is Alexis Greene's helpful introduction to Durang's work in Smith and Kraus' *Playwright in an Hour Series* (2011). Suzanne Burgoyne Dieckman wrote an article about the self-referential elements in Durang's play, "Metatheatre as Antitheatre: Durang's *Actor's Nightmare*" (1992), and Miriam Hardin illustrates how Sister Mary portrays the same fascist depiction of education as the Professor did in Ionesco's play: "Lessons from *The Lesson*: Four Post-Ionescan Education Plays" (Hardin 1999). Scholars find connections between Durang's works and the American dramatic canon: John Clum contributed an article, "'Period of Adjustment': Marriage in Williams and Christopher Durang" to an edited collection demonstrating Tennessee Williams's influence on American playwrights (2008), while Troy Appling considers how Durang's plays compare to those of Arthur Miller in "Liturgical Legacies of Arthur Miller: Uses of Religion as Ideological (De)Construction in the Plays of Christopher Durang" (2009). Finally, Naomi Nkealah addresses how a South African audience perceives the homosexual relationships in her article "'Self-Fashioning through Queer Sex': A Case Study of Two Student Theatre Performances" (2012). In total, this academic response seems surprisingly thin for a playwright who has contributed more than twenty works to the American stage.

People repeatedly comment about how Durang the playwright is markedly different from the arch dialogue and the cruel grotesqueries of his plays. Brustein's epithet—"an angelic choirboy with poison leeching through his fingertips"—is the most widely quoted because it seems to mark the paradox between the kindhearted playwright and the vitriolic vision of his plays. Durang acknowledged that the darkness in his plays is a projection, a displacement, a way of releasing the frustration and fear and hopelessness he internalized as a child. His role in the family was to be the "peacemaker," moving between his father's alcoholic behavior and his mother's belittling comments and aggression. As a child of the 1950s and the post–Second World War baby-boomer surge, Durang came of age during the turbulent 1960s and began writing his plays in its disappointing aftermath. He began writing during a time of massive political upheaval in America and of countercultural movements. The spirit of rebellion in his plays might have also been a reaction against the conservative, staid values of the 1950s Eisenhower era, or the conformist groupthink fostered by the social uniformity of the expanding suburbs, as much as against his own family turmoil, where every confrontation "seemed to escalate into a nuclear affair" (Arkatov 1989). The use of his dark comedy, whether it is located is satire, parody, farce, or the comic grotesque, is both personal and political. It is a critique against the idealized notion of family, as well as a fight against middle-class uniformity. Finally, as someone who grew up Catholic but came to witness the harmful authoritarian stance of the Catholic Church, Durang experienced a personal sense of betrayal from religion. Religion often provides human beings a rational explanation of evil in the world so that the world does not seem so chaotic; it provides the much needed structure or stay against the random events of life. Durang, having grown up with family dysfunction, disappointment in political leadership, distrust in the media, and the loss of faith, knows all too well that human beings depend upon some bulwark or supportive stay against the world's chaos. But as the mischievous imp of the dramatic world, in his many plays of life's randomness, Durang deliberately removes that stay.

NOTES

Chapter 1

1 The first production was at the Yale University Cabaret in 1973 before it was produced at the Yale Repertory Theater, New Haven, in November 1974; Christopher Durang played Alyosha in both productions.
2 The world's leading energy trader, Enron Corporation, became at this point in time the largest corporation to declare bankruptcy in America, because of fraudulent accounting practices.

Chapter 2

1 The play has been presented as Readers Theater, where the actors pretend to be students doing a radio version of the script.
2 The play's title comes from a pamphlet that Harvard distributed to undergraduates during the Vietnam War to cope with the student protests and sit-ins: "The Nature and Purpose of the University." Durang misread "University" as "Universe" thus mistaking a university's public relations gesture an existential query.
3 This line, as well as others, is almost identical to that found in the Baltimore Catechism (1885), which reads: "The ninth Commandment forbids unchaste thoughts, desires of another's wife or husband, and all other unlawful impure thoughts and desires." Project Gutenberg.
4 In his letter to the *New York Times*, Reverend Robert E. Lauder, of the Cathedral College of the Immaculate Conception, mentioned Bill Davis's *Mass Appeal*, Edward Sheehan's *Kingdoms*, John Pielmeier's *Agnes of God*, Casey Kurtti's *Catholic School Girls*, Brother Jonathan's *Bella Figura*, and John Powers, *Do Black Patent Leather Shoes Really Reflect Up?* Lauder disliked Durang's play because it did not dramatize a polemic but offered only an atheist harangue against the Catholic Church (Lauder 1982).
5 Organizations of the Christian Right are national groups, such as Focus on the Family, a media-ministry founded by psychologist Dr. James Dobson; the Family Research Council—an educational organization in Washington, DC; and Concerned Women for America, a conservative alternative to the National Organization for Women (NOW).

Notes

6   All references to the play are from the video recording held at New York Public Library, Theater on Film and Tape Archives (Durang 1996).

Chapter 3

1   Stuart Hirschberg points out Durang's repeated use of the name in "Who Is George Spelvin in Christopher Durang's *The Actor's Nightmare*?" (2002).

Chapter 4

1   The play opened in February 1976, with Kate McGregor-Stewart as Victoria Tammurai and Sigourney Weaver playing Lidia, actresses from the Yale Drama School familiar with Durang and his comedic style. When the play transferred to the Vandam Theater, Off-Broadway, it was produced as a one-act play, with an opening medley of songs performed by Christopher Durang and Sigourney Weaver entitled "Das Lusitania Song-spiel," with parodies of Brechtian songs such as "Moon over Alabama," "Mack the Knife," and "Maha Gunney," as well as the purportedly famous "Swiss Family Trapp" number from Mother Courage; in addition the two shared other fabricated stories about Brecht and Helen Wiegel.

2   As much as the details of this story seem fabricated, Durang could have read about such an event. An incident remarkably similar to this one happened in New York City in September 1976 when a pet dog ate a six-day-old baby. A young mother left her newborn alone with her dog in order to return to the hospital and retrieve possessions left the night before, after her discharge. Similar to Cynthia, she had only a folding chair and a rug in her apartment, and she and the baby slept on the floor. She had left the dog alone, without food, during her stay at the hospital to deliver her baby, thus the dog grew emaciated and starving. *The Geneva Times*, September 7, 1976 (AP).

3   The treatment for Rh incompatibility came about shortly after Bette gave up her struggle; the *New York Times* reported in 1968 the preparation of a vaccine that prevents the maternal immune reaction in babies, an irony which Matt discusses with his mother later in the play.

Chapter 5

1   A 1987 film version directed and re-scripted by Robert Altman was a critical and box-office failure; Durang was unhappy with the resulting film because Altman changed it too much without consulting him, removing the humor and eliminating its psychological motivation.

Notes

2 *Media Amok* Program is held at the American Repertory Theatre 1991–92 Collection, Harvard University Library. Folder (363) 4 folders.

3 This hatbox that Keith carries prompts several characters to allude to the movie about a serial murderer who kept his victim's head in a hotbox, *Night Must Fall* (1937). The play *Night Must Fall* (1935), upon which the movie was based, had a revival at the Lyceum Theatre, starring Matthew Broderick, at exactly the same time *Betty's Summer Vacation* premiered at Playwrights Horizon in 1999, a coincidence not missed by some critics.

4 The title may also be an allusion to tabloid talk shows, as an early episode on *Geraldo* was titled "Man in Lace Panties and the Women Who Love Them." See Cadwalladr (2008).

Chapter 6

1 "This would be a better world for children if the parents had to eat the spinach" (60).

2 Neil Simon contributed *Murder by Death* (Agatha Christie) and *The Cheap Detective* (Bogart film noir); Larry Gelbart *Movie Movie* (1930s double features); Carl Reiner *Dead Men Don't Wear Plaid* (film noir); Woody Allen *Love & Death* (Russian literature); and Mel Brooks *Blazing Saddles* (westerns), *Young Frankenstein* (Universal horror), *High Anxiety* (Hitchcock), and *Space Balls* (the *Star Wars* franchise).

3 In Allen's send-up of Tolstoy's *War and Peace* (1869), the hero, Boris Grushenko, falls into several (mis-)adventures that follow the original novel, but add many other elements, in keeping with Allen's interest in such things as philosophy and the films of Ingmar Bergman. *Love and Death* moved from Tolstoy to Dostoyevsky, with some Pushkin and even some Eisenstein thrown in for good measure. One may argue that one of Allen's achievements with this parody is that the film is stylistically unified, if one forgives Allen's Bob Hope-style delivery in many of the scenes, essentially reducing one of the great works of Western literature to a "road picture" starring Allen and Diane Keaton.

4 It may also be pointed out here how natural it seems in a discussion of parody to bring in parodies by others to illustrate more fully the degree to which parody inhabits Western—indeed all—art traditions; Durang certainly does not stand alone in his use of (dependence on?) parody: the sheer number of parodies point to Durang's place in the lineage of American comedy writers.

5 This piece is as anarchic as a Marx Brothers film, and as hard to summarize. The protagonist, George Spelvin (the name professional actors traditionally use in the program when performing in an unsanctioned/non-Equity production), finds himself backstage and called to go on for Edwin, who

Notes

cannot perform that evening. Other actors include Henry, Ellen, and Sarah, who variously help and perplex Spelvin. The fellow actors are also an inside joke: Edwin (Booth), Sarah (Siddons), Henry (Irving), and Ellen (Terry) are all stars of yesteryear and attest to Durang's theatre degree. Spelvin is ushered in and out of scenes that parody the three iconic playwrights—Shakespeare, Beckett, and Coward—always dressed and prepped for one of the other scenarios, hence the nightmare.

6   An interesting but overlooked point of these sorts of parodies arises here, as to how deeply immersed a parodist must be in the works of another author or tradition, and the commitment of time and attention to something ostensibly used as the whipping boy for a comedy. Surely this argues for at least some sympathies and even affection for the originals and their creator.

7   See http://www.imdb.com/title/tt0076141/trivia

8   *This Is Spinal Tap* may seem more vicious in its bite than Guest's gentler and more respectful *A Mighty Wind*'s handling of folk music, reinforcing Hutcheon's point about parody laying the new work "beside" the original as perhaps simply the next in line of these kinds of art.

9   Shaw himself created a similar showdown in his marionette play, "Shakes versus Shaw" (1949).

10 A fascinating article detailing the extent to which one of the most famous lines in *The Brothers Karamazov*, "without God, everything is permitted," is mistranslated by Constance Garnett and as such foments an internet war of words about it, may be found in Andrei I. Volkov's "Dostoevsky Did Say It: A Response to David E. Cortesi" (2011).

11 Might this obsession be a pun on *pedes* and *paidos*?

12 Durang's sizable career output might mischievously prompt the question of what exactly a parody of Durang's works would look like. A carnivalesque House of Mirrors, no doubt?

WORKS CITED

Als, Hilton. 2008. "Fantasy Suite: Sam Shepard and Christopher Durang on Dashed Dreams." *New Yorker*, July 28.
Alter, Jonathan. 1994. "America Goes Tabloid." *Newsweek*, 124/125 (26/1):34+.
Alter, Jonathan. 2001. "Time to Think about Torture." *Newsweek*, Nov. 4.
Anonymous. 2008. "Baby Doom: The Marriage of Bette and Boo." *The New York Sun*, July 14: 11.
Appling, L. Troy. 2009. "Liturgical Legacies of Arthur Miller: Uses of Religion as Ideological (De)Construction in the Plays of Christopher Durang." *Arthur Miller Journal* 4 (1):1–7.
Arkatov, Janice. 1989. "Durang Turns Savage Wit on His Own Family in 'Boo.'" *Los Angeles Times*, Aug. 11, 8.
Auslander, Philip. 1999. *Liveness: Performance in a Mediatized Culture*. New York; London: Routledge.
Bakhtin, Mikhael. 1984. *Rabelais and His World*. Translated by Helene Iswolsky. Bloomington: Indiana University Press.
Barnes, Clive. 1972. "Stage: 'A Play for Peace.'" *New York Times*, Feb. 14.
Barnes, Clive. 1977. "'History of American Film' Proves A Tour de Force of the Theater." *New York Times*, Mar. 21, 41.
Beer, John. 2007. "Delirious New York." *Village Voice*, Jan. 3, 42.
Beerbohm, Max. 1970. *Selected Prose*. Boston: Little, Brown and Company.
Bellow, Saul. 2003. "Wit Irony Fun Games." In *The Public Intellectual: Between Philosophy and Politics*, edited by Jerry Weinberger, Arthur M. Melzer, and Richard M. Zinman, 234–47. Lanham, MD: Rowman and Littlefield Publishers, Inc.
Bigsby, C. W. E. 1982. *Joe Orton, Contemporary Writers*. London: Routledge.
Bloom, Harold. 1997. *The Anxiety of Influence: A Theory of Poetry*. 2nd ed. Oxford: Oxford University Press. Original edition, 1973.
Boddy, William. 1990. *Fifties Television: The Industry and Its Critics*. Urbana: University of Illinois Press.
Booth, Michael R. 1988. "Feydeau and the farcical imperative." In *Themes in Drama: Farce*, edited by James Redmond, 145–52. Cambridge: Cambridge University Press.
Bore, Inger-Lise Kalviknes. 2011. "Laughing Together? TV Comedy Audiences and the Laugh Track." *Velvet Light Trap: A Critical Journal of Film & Television* 68, Fall: 24–34.
Brantley, Ben. 1994. "Durang Durang; Plays That Cast an Irreverent Eye Over Two Revered Playwrights." *New York Times*, Nov. 14, C11.
Brantley, Ben. 1999. "Unraveling, Not Relaxing, at This Beach House." *New York Times*, Mar. 15, E1–E5.

Works Cited

Brantley, Ben. 2005. "Life: Does It Get Any Better after Death?" *New York Times*, Nov. 30, E.1.

Brantley, Ben. 2009. "Panties, Squirrels and Lots of Ammo." *New York Times*, Apr. 7, C1–C5.

Brantley, Ben. 2012. "Insecure Namesakes with a Gloomy Worldview." *New York Times*, Nov. 13.

Breton, André. 1997. *Anthology of Black Humor*. Translated by Mark Polizziotti. San Francisco, CA: City Lights Books. Original edition, 1924.

Brown, Joel. 2013. "Comedy in a Charged Environment." *Boston Globe*, July 26, G.8, Lifestyle.

Brustein, Robert. 1997. "Introduction." In *Complete Full-Length Plays 1975–1995: By Christopher Durang*, vii–x. Hanover: Smith and Kraus.

Brustein, Robert. 2012. "Christopher Durang, Cherubic Gadfly." *Lincoln Center Theater Review*, Fall:58.

Brustein, Robert. 2015. *Winter Passages: Reflections on Theatre and Society*. London: Routledge.

Brustein, Robert. 2019. "Forward." In *American Political Plays in the Age of Terrorism*, edited by Allan Havis. London: Methuen.

Cadwalladr, Carole. "Behind the Scenes at Jeremy Kyle: When Reality Bites, It Leaves Deep Scars." *The Guardian*, Sep. 6.

Callahan, John M. 1991. "The Ultimate in Theatre Violence." In *Violence in Drama*, edited by James Redmond, 165–76. Cambridge and New York: Cambridge University Press.

Camus, Albert. 1955. "The Myth of Sisyphus." In *The Myth of Sisyphus and Other Essays*. New York: Alfred A. Knopf.

Canby, Vincent. 1994. "SUNDAY VIEW; For Limping Parody, Durang to the Rescue." *New York Times*, Dec. 4, H5.

Canby, Vincent. 1996. "Shining a Light on the Mind of a Genius." *New York Times*, Oct. 27, H5.

Chung-Wee, Christopher G. 2003. *The Metanoia of Metacomedy in Contemporary Theatre of the Absurd: The Film, Sitcom, Drama, and More*. Indiana University of Pennsylvania. Unpublished dissertation.

Clark, Barrett H. 1938. "Where Does the One-Act Play Belong?" In *The One-Act Play Today: A Discussion of the Technique, Scope & History of the Contemporary Short Drama*, edited by William Kozlenko, 186–93. New York: Harcourt, Brace and Company.

Clum, John M. 2008. "'Period of Adjustment': Marriage in Williams and Christopher Durang." In *The Influence of Tennessee Williams: Essays on Fifteen American Playwrights*, edited by Philip C. Kolin, 162–74. Jefferson, NC: McFarland.

Coates, James. 1979. "Skylab Danger Isn't as Small as NASA Hints." *Boca Raton News*, July 1.

Coontz, Stephanie. 1992. *The Way We Never Were: American Families and the Nostalgia Trap*. New York: Basic Books.

Davis, Paul. 1990. "Retelling a Christmas Carol: Text and Culture-Text." *The American Scholar* 59 (1): 109–15.

Deffaa, Chip. 1997. "'Early Play Durang's Bad Habit." *New York Post*, Oct. 27, 4.

Works Cited

Dezell, Maureen. 2001. "Durang Looks at the Dark Side of the Sun in His Newest Play." *Boston Globe*, Oct. 21, C.3, Arts.

Dezell, Maureen. 2005. "Cracking Up; 'Laughing Wild' Costars Explore Comedy on the Edge of Sanity." *Boston Globe*, June 3, D21, Arts.

Dieckman, Suzanne Burgoyne. 1992. "Metatheatre as Antitheatre: Durang's Actor's Nightmare." *American Drama* 1 (2): 26–41.

DiRenzo, Anthony. 1993. *Flannery O'Connor and the Medieval Grotesque*. Carbondale: Southern Illinois University Press.

Dryden, John. 1956. "Preface to an Evening's Love." In *The Works of John Dryden*, edited by H. T. Swedenberg Jr. et al. Berkeley, CA: University of California Press. Original edition, 1671.

Durang, Christopher. 1971. "Better Dead than Sorry." In *Plays from the Yale Cabaret, the Beginnings of an Anthology*, edited by Steven Oxman. New Haven, CT: Yale University, 1991.

Durang, Christopher. 1983. "Introduction." In *Christopher Durang Explains It All for You: Six Plays*. New York: Grove Press.

Durang, Christopher. 1985. "'How Do You Feel about Our Career?' 'Go Away,' He Said." *New York Times*, Nov. 17, H1, H14.

Durang, Christopher. 1991. "Media amok: prompt book. Typescript, 84 pages. Folder (363)." American Repertory Theatre 1991-92 Collection. Houghton Library, Harvard.

Durang, Christopher. 1994. *Christopher Durang Explains It All for You: 6 Plays*. Reprint ed. New York: Grove Press.

Durang, Christopher. 1995. *Twenty-Seven Short Plays*. Hanover, NH: Smith and Kraus.

Durang, Christopher. 1996. *Sex and Longing* [video recording]. Lincoln Center Theater. Dir. Betty L. Corwin. The New York Public Library's Theatre on Film and Tape Archive at the Cort Theatre, New York, Nov. 7.

Durang, Christopher. 1997. *Christopher Durang: Complete Full-Length Plays: 1975–1995*. Lyme, NH: Smith and Kraus, 2003.

Durang, Christopher. 1999. *Betty's Summer Vacation*. New York: Grove Press.

Durang, Christopher, 1999a. "Suspending Disbelief: An Interview with the Playwright by Himself." *American Theatre*. Dec. 16:10, p. 38

Durang, Christopher. 2002. "Q&A 2." Available online: http://www.christopherdurang.com

Durang, Christopher. 2006. *Miss Witherspoon and Mrs. Bob Cratchit's Wild Christmas Binge*. New York: Grove Press.

Durang, Christopher. 2009a. *Adrift in Macao*. New York: Samuel French.

Durang, Christopher. 2009b. "The Incipient Existentialist and the Broadway Musical." In *The Play That Changed My Life: American's Foremost Playwrights on the Plays That Influenced Them*, edited by Ben Hodges. New York: Applause Theater & Cinema Books.

Durang, Christopher. 2012a. "My Life with Chekhov." *Lincoln Center Theater Review* (58), Fall.

Durang, Christopher. 2012b. *The Playwright at Work: Conversations*. Edited by Rosemarie Tichler and Barry Jay Kaplan. Evanston, IL: Northwestern University Press.

Durang, Christopher. 2013. *Vanya and Sonia and Masha and Spike*. New York: Grove Press.

Works Cited

Durang, Christopher. 2016. Personal conversation with playwright. Mar. 23.
Durang, Christopher. 2017a. "Information for High School and College Students: Frequently Asked Questions." Available online: http://www.christopherdurang.com. Accessed July 25, 2020.
Durang, Christopher. 2017b. *What Playwrights Talk about When They Talk about Writing*. Edited by Jeffrey Sweet. New Haven, CT: Yale University Press.
Durang, Christopher and Wendy Wasserstein. 1996. "Of Plays about Politics and Politicians at Play." *New York Times*, Oct. 6, H5.
Durrenmatt, Frank. 1958. "Comedy and the Modern World." *Tulane Drama Review* 3:3–26.
Eder, Richard. 1979. "Durang's 'Nature & Purpose' at the Direct." *New York Times*, Feb. 24, 15.
Elam, Keir. 2002. *The Semiotics of Theatre and Drama*, 2nd ed. London: Routledge.
Ellis, John. 2000. *Seeing Things: Television in the Age of Uncertainty*. London: I. B. Tauris.
Evans, Greg. 1996. "Sex and Longing (Review)." *Variety*. New York Public Library, Billy Rose Theatre Division. Clippings. np. nd.
Fearnow, Mark. 2005. "1970–1990: Disillusionment, Identity, and Discovery." In *A Companion to Twentieth-Century American Drama*, edited by David Krasner. Malden, MA: Blackwell Publishing.
Feingold, Michael. 1999. "Betty's Summer Vacation, Night Must Fall, Macbeth (Review)." *Village Voice*, March 23: 147.
Feingold, Michael. 2008. "Deathville, USA." *Village Voice*, July 23.
Feingold, Michael. 2009. "Welcome to Puzzling Days." *Village Voice*, April 15–21.
Feingold, Michael. 2013. "Puzzle Pieces." *Village Voice*, March 20.
France, Peter. 2000. *The Oxford Guide to Literature in English Translations*. Oxford: Oxford University Press.
Freud, Sigmund. 1961. "Humor." In *The Standard Edition of the Complete Psychological Works of Sigmund Freud*, translated by James Strachey, vol. XXI, 159–72. London: Hogarth Press.
Frye, Northrop. 1944. "The Nature of Satire." *University of Toronto Quarterly* 14 (1):75–89.
Gabler, Neal. 2000. *Life: The Movie: How Entertainment Conquered Reality*. New York: Vintage Books.
Garvin, Mark. 2007. "Adrift in Macao." *Time Out New York*, Feb. 15–21.
Gener, Randy. 1994. "Durang Durang (Review)." *Village Voice*, Nov. 22: 78–80.
Gershwin, Ira. 1959. *Lyrics on Several Occasions*. New York: Knopf.
Gill, Brendan. 1982. "Growing Up." *The New Yorker*, June 7, 112.
Gluck, Victor. 1997. "Review of *The Nature and Purpose of The Universe*." *Backstage*, Oct. 24, 40.
Goffman, Erving, 1959. *The Presentation of Self in Everyday Life*. Garden City: Doubleday Anchor.
Goffman, Erving. 1974. *Frame Analysis: An Essay on the Organization of Experience*. Cambridge: Harvard University Press.
Golomb, Elan. 1992. *Trapped in the Mirror: Adult Children of Narcissists in Their Struggle for Self*. New York: William Morrow & Co.

Works Cited

Gould, Jack. 1956. "Live TV vs. Canned." *New York Magazine*, Feb. 5, 27.

Greene, Alexis. 2011. "Durang in an Hour." In *Playwrights in an Hour Series*. Hanover: Smith and Kraus.

Grode, Eric. 2005. "The Winding Road to Nirvana." *The New York Sun*, Nov. 30.

Gussow, Mel. 1977a. "The Daring Visions of Four New, Young Playwrights." *New York Times*, Feb. 13, D1, D9, D13–14.

Gussow, Mel. 1977b. "Durang, at Yale, Overindulges in Satire." *New York Times*, Jan. 27, 30.

Gussow, Mel. 1977c. "'History of American Film,' a Play, Is Glorious Montage of U.S. Myth." *New York Times*, May 23, 22.

Gussow, Mel. 1985. "Less May Be More for Christopher Durang." *New York Times*, May 26, H3.

Gussow, Mel. 1994. "Christopher Durang, a Parodist, Finds Very Little That Is Sacred." *New York Times*, June 27, C13.

Gussow, Mel. 1997. "Helen Merrill, Theatrical Agent, Dies at 79." *New York Times*, Aug. 20, D20.

Gutwirth, Marcel. 1993. *Laughing Matter: An Essay on the Comic*. New York: Cornell University Press.

Hardin, Miriam. 1999. "Lessons from the The Lesson: Four Post-Ionescan Education Plays." *CEA Magazine: A Journal of the College English Association* 12 (1):30–46.

Harpham, Geoffrey Galt. 2007. *On the Grotesque: Strategies of Contradiction in Art and Literature*. Princeton, NJ: Princeton University Press. Orig. published 1982.

Havis, Allan, ed. 2019. *American Political Plays in the Age of Terrorism*. London: Methuen.

Hayes, John. 2000. "Durang Exorcises Demons through Play's Characters." *Pittsburgh Post-Gazette*, Apr. 25, D-2.

Healy, Patrick. 2009. "A Tale of Torture Grows More Timely by the Day." *New York Times*, May 2, C1, C6.

Heilpern, John. 1996. "Sex and Longing for Laughs, in Toothless Political Satires." *The New York Observer*, Oct. 21.

Heilpern, John. 2008. "Durang's Dysfunctional Life." *New York Observer*, July 28: C19.

Herman. 1997. "Lukewarm 'Bathwater'; Theater Review: Nanny Takes Charge in Vanguard Production, Which Does What It Can with Durang's Droll, Skewed Satire." *Los Angeles Times*, Jan. 15, 1.

Hodgins, Paul. 1996. "A 'Mess' of Laughs // STAGE: Who Else but Christopher Durang Would List Lucille Ball and Carol Burnett along with Ionesco and Albee as His Most Important Influences?" *Orange County Register*, Apr. 23, F4, Show.

Hirschberg, Stuart. 2002. "Who Is George Spelvin in Christopher Durang's 'The Actor's Nightmare'?" *Notes on Contemporary Literature* 32(2): 11–12.

Hoffman, Wayne. 1987. "Laughing Wild: Playwright Christopher Durang Takes a Light-hearted Look at Rape, Incest, and Murder in His New Comedy." Unknown newspaper. New York Public Library, Billy Rose Theatre Division. Clippings.

Horwitz, Jane. 2000. "Serial Killers, Sex Addicts and Flashers, Oh My!; Durang's 'Summer Vacation' Is No Picnic." *The Washington Post*, June 13, C05.

Works Cited

Hurwitt, Robert. 1999. "Mystery Souffles: One Fluffy, One Flat." *San Francisco Examiner*, April 5.

Hutcheon, Linda. 2000. *A Theory of Parody: The Teachings of Twentieth-Century Art Forms*. Reprint ed. Champaign, IL: University of Illinois Press. Original edition, 1985.

Iseberg, Barbara. 2014. "Review of Vanya." *Los Angeles Times*, Feb. 2.

Isherwood, Charles. 1999. "Betty's Summer Vacation (Review)." *Variety*, Mar. 22: 46.

Isherwood, Charles. 2005. "The Tuna Fish Can Incident and Other Injustices of Life." *New York Times*, June 16, E5, Theater Review.

Isherwood, Charles. 2007. "Here's Looking at You, Beloved Movie Cliches." *New York Times*, Feb. 14.

Isherwood, Charles. 2008. "Do You, Bette, Take Boo for a Life of Misery That We'll Laugh At?" *New York Times*, July 14, E1, E7.

Isherwood, Charles. 2013. "Underneath Pajamas, Naked Depression." *New York Times*, Mar. 15, C.1.

J.B. 1937. "Introduction." In *Seven Famous One-Act Plays*. Harmondsworth: Penguin Books Limited.

Jacobs, Leonard. 2005. "Does Durang's Latest Boomerang—Or Fly True?" *New York Press*, Dec. 14.

Jamieson, Kathleen Hall and Joseph N. Cappella. 2010. *Echo Chamber: Rush Limbaugh and the Conservative Media Establishment*. New York: Oxford University Press.

Johann, Susan. 2016. *Christopher Durang, Focus on Playwrights: Portraits and Interviews*. Columbia: University of South Caroline Press.

Jory, Jon. 1997. "Introduction." In *Take Ten: New 10-Minutes Plays*, edited by Eric Lane and Nina Shengold. New York: Vintage Books/Random House.

Kaufman, George S. and Morrie Ryskind. 1984. *Animal Crackers*. New York: Samuel French.

Kauffmann, Stanley. 1978. "Rev. of a History of the American Film." *New Republic*, April 22, 25.

Kayser, Wolfgang. 1966. *The Grotesque in Art and Literature Paperback*. Translated by Ulrich Weisstein. New York: McGraw-Hill Book Company.

Keating, Douglas J. 1988. "Durang, Well-Behaved Onstage, His Scripts Sting: But How Does The Playwright, Whose Newest Work Opens Here This Week, Play Offstage? Politely." *Philadelphia Inquirer*, Mar. 21, E.1.

Kennerley, David. 2008. "The Play about the Dead Babies." *Gay City News*, July 21: 29.

King, Bruce. 1991. *Contemporary American Theatre*. New York: St. Martin's Press.

King, Susan. 1990. "Christopher Durang: Writing 'Words on Fire.'" *Los Angeles Times*, Aug. 5.

Krasner, David. 2006. *American Drama 1945-2000*. Malden, MA: Blackwell.

Kroll, Jack. 1981. "With Malice Toward Nun." *Newsweek*, Nov. 9, 101.

Lahr, John. 2012. "Unhappy Families." *The New Yorker*, Nov. 26: 84–5.

Latour, Geneviève, ed. 1986. *Petites scènes, grand théâtre. Le théâtre de création de1944 à 1960*. Paris: Action culturelle de la Ville de Paris.

Works Cited

Lauder, Robert E. 1982. "What Is a Catholic Play?" *New York Times*, Aug. 1, H5–H10.

Lawson, Carol. 1981. "Durang Explains It All for You--Satirically." *New York Times*, Dec. 8, C7.

Lepidus, D. L. 1999. "Review (Betty's Summer Vacation)." *The Westsider*, 8.

Lepore, Jill. 2009. "The Politics of Death: From Abortion to Health Care—How the Hysterical Style Overtook the National Debate." *New Yorker*, Nov. 30.

Lewis, Neil et al. 2005. "A Guide to the Memos on Torture." *The New York Times*.

Maugham, W. Somerset. 1952. *Complete Short Stories of W. Somerset Maugham*. Garden City, NY: Doubleday.

McClaran, Tamara. 2007. "Wednesday 'Durang' is Like 'Saturday Night Live.'" *Florida Times-Union (Jacksonville)*, Mar. 7.

McGill, Douglas C. 1982. "The Warming of Christopher Durang." *New York Times*, May 23, 64.

McKinley, Jesse. 1999. "On Stage and Off." *New York Times*, March 19: E2.

McLuhan, Marshall. 1964. *Understanding Media: The Extensions of Man*. New York, NY: McGraw-Hill.

Miller, Alice. 1987. *The Drama of the Gifted Child and the Search for the True Self (Prisoners of Childhood)*. New York: Basic Books.

Mitchell, Rick. 2003. "Simple Pleasures: The Ten-Minute Play, Overnight Theatre, and the Decline of the Art of Storytelling." *New Theatre Quarterly* 19 (1): 67–81.

Mitgang, Herbert. 1983. "Dispute on Durang Play Is Eased in Missouri." *New York Times*, June 9, C17.

Morreall, John. 1983. *Taking Laughter Seriously*. New York: SUNY University Press.

Morris, Bob. 1999. "In a Tabloid Comedy, the Serial Killer Is Sensitive." *New York Times*, Mar. 14, AR7.

Murray, Christopher John. 2004. *Encyclopedia of Modern French Thought*. New York, NY: Routledge.

Murray, Matthew. 2005. "Miss Witherspoon (Theatre Review)." *Off Broadway: Not Your Grandma's Theater*, Nov. 29.

Neale, Stephen and Frank Krutnik. 1990. *Popular Film and Television Comedy*. London: Routledge.

Neuhaus, Richard John. 2006. *Catholic Matters: Confusion, Controversy, and the Splendor of Truth*. New York: Basic Books.

Nkealah, Naomi. 2012. "'Self-Fashioning through Queer Sex': A Case Study of Two Student Theatre Performances." *South African Theatre Journal* 26 (3): 259–69.

Novick, Julius. 1985. "Review." *The Village Voice*.

Oliver, Edith. 1981. "Rev. of Beyond Therapy." *The New Yorker*, Jan. 19, 91.

Oliver, Edith. 1987. "The Theatre: Bully!" *The New Yorker*, Nov. 23: 153.

Philips, Jennifer Beth. 2008. *Traces of Beckett: Gestures of Emptiness and Impotence in the Theater of Koltès, Kane, de la Parra and Durang*. Unpublished dissertation. University of Texas, Austin.

Works Cited

Prokosh, Kevin. 2015. "American Playwright's Tony Award-winning Comedy Owes Everything to Russian Dramatist." *Winnipeg Free Press*, Feb. 12, C1, Arts Articles.

Pronko, Leonard C. 1982. *Eugene Labiche and Georges Feydeau: Macmillan modern dramatists*. New York: Grove Press.

Rawson, Christopher. 2002. "[Stage Preview . . .]: [Region Edition] City Theatre Premiere Continues Christopher Durang's Edgy Comic Tradition." *Pittsburgh Post-Gazette*, Nov. 10, E-3, Arts & Entertainment.

Rendell, Carolyn B. 1992. "Small Screen on Stage: Media Amok Satirizes TV." *The Harvard Crimson*, April 23.

Rich, Frank. 1981. "Theater: One-Acters by Durang." *New York Times*, Oct. 22, C21.

Rich, Frank. 1982a. "New Angry Playwrights Are Taking Center Stage." *New York Times*, Jan. 3: 2:1.

Rich, Frank. 1982b. "Stage: Nancy Marchand as Sister Mary Ignatius." *New York Times*, Oct. 7: C:20.

Rich, Frank. 1983. "Stage: 'Baby,' New Durang Comedy." *New York Times*, Nov. 9, C21.

Rich, Frank. 1985. "Stage: 'Bette and Boo' By Durang at the Public." *New York Times*, May 17, C3.

Rich, Frank. 1987. "Stage: By Durang, 'Laughing Wild.'" *New York Times*, Nov. 12, C23.

Richards, David. 1988. "Theatre; Durang's Biting 'Baby'; At Round House, a Superb, Potent Comedy." *The Washington Post*, Sep. 14, C1.

Roddick, Nick. 1980. "Only the Stars Survive: Disaster Movies in the Seventies." In *Performance and Politics in Popular Drama*, edited by Louis James David Bradby and Bernard Sharratt. London: Cambridge University Press.

Rooney, David. 2009. "Why Torture Is Wrong, and the People Who Love Them (Review)." *Variety*, 32–3.

Rose, Lloyd. 1994. "Redefining the Broadway Hit; Christopher Durang Targets the Heavyweights—and Doesn't Miss." *The Washington Post*, Dec. 11, g04.

Ruff, Felicia. 2008. "The Laugh Factory: Humor and Horror at the Theatre du Grand Guignol." *Theatre Symposium*, 16. Comedy Tonight!

Ryan, Michael and Douglas Kellner. 1988. *Camera Politica*, Bloomington: Indiana University Press.

Scannell, Paddy. 1996. *Radio, Television & Modern Life*. Oxford: Blackwell.

Schevill, James. 1977. "Notes on the Grotesque: Anderson, Brecht, and Williams." *Twentieth Century Literature* 23 (2): 229–38.

Shayton, Robert Lewis. 1959. "Laugh, Soundman, Laugh." *Saturday Review*, April 18, 44.

Sheward, David. 1996. "Sex and Longing (Review)." *Back Stage East*, Oct. 21: 39.

Sheward, David. 2008. "The Marriage of Bette and Boo." *Back Stage East*, July 17: 11.

Shirley, Don. 1989. "Comic Relief from Christopher Durang in 'Laughing Wild.'" *Los Angeles Times*, Oct. 26, 7.

Shklovsky, Victor. 1965. "Art as Technique." In *Russian Formalist Criticism: Four Essays*, 2nd ed, translated by Lee T. Lemon and Marion J. Reis, 3–24. Lincoln: University of Nebraska Press.

Works Cited

Siegel, Ed. 2001. "A Stage Satire, a Movie Mockumentary, and the Actor They Have in Common Betty and Lisa and Nat Betty: 'Vacation' Mines Big Laughs from Blend of Camp and Modernist Despair." *Boston Globe*, Nov. 2, C.1.

Smith, Dinitia. 2005. "Christopher Durang Explores the Afterlife, Including His Own." *New York Times*, Nov. 26, B9, B15.

Smith, Jacob. 2005. "The Frenzy of the Audible: Pleasure, Authenticity, and Recorded Laughter." *Television & News Media*, 6 (1): 23–47.

Spivak, Robert. 1991. *Christopher Durang: Satire and Beyond*. M. A. Thesis at Concordia University, Montreal, Canada. Held at National Library of Canada, Ottawa.

Stasio, Marilyn. 2005. "Miss Witherspoon." *Variety*, Dec. 5, 59.

Stasio, Marilyn. 2007. "Adrift in Macao." *Variety*, Feb. 19.

Stein, Howard. 1995. "Introduction." In *Christopher Durang: 27 Short Plays*, vii–viii. Hanover, NH: Smith & Kraus.

Sullivan, Dan. 1985. "Stage Review Durang's 'Baby' Has It Out With Parenthood." *Los Angeles Times*, July 1, 1.

Taylor, Ella. 1991. *Prime-time Families: Television Culture in Post War America*. Berkeley, CA: University of California Press.

Troy, Leonard Appling. 2010. "Liturgical Legacies of Arthur Miller: Uses of Religion as Ideological (De)Construction in the Plays of Christopher Durang." *Arthur Miller Journal* 4(1): 1–7.

Tuck, Greg. 2009. "Laughter in the Dark: Irony, Black Comedy and Noir in the Films of David Lynch, the Coen Brothers and Quentin Tarantino." In *Neo-Noir*, edited by Kathrina Glitre, Mark Bould, and Greg Tuck, 152–67. New York: Wallflower Press, Columbia University Press.

Turan, Kenneth. 1977. "Durang; A Film Junkie's Dramatic Revenge; A Film Junkie's Dramatic Exorcism and Theatrical Revenge." *The Washington Post*, May 22, Sunday, Final Edition.

Volkov, Andrei I. 2011. "Dostoevsky Did Say It: A Response to David E. Cortesi (2011)." Available online: http://infidels.org/library/modern/andrei_volkov/dostoevsky.html.

Waters, Harry F. and Nina Archer Biddle. 1994. "Your Show of Shows." *Newsweek*, Jan. 24, 123 (4): 55.

Wilcox, Clyde and Carin Robinson. 2011. *Onward Christian Soldiers? The Religious Right in American Politics*, 4th ed. Boulder, CO: Westview Press.

Wilder, Thornton. 1957. *Three Plays: Our Town, The Skin of Our Teeth, The Matchmaker*. New York: Harper & Row.

Winer, Linda. 1999. "The Summer House from Hell." *Newsday*, March 15: B2–B8.

Winer, Linda. 2012. "Chekhovian Themes, Played for Laughs." *Newsday*, Nov. 13: B6.

Zinman, Toby. 2012. "'Mrs. Cratchit' Spoof Falls Flat." *Philadelphia Inquirer*, Dec. 3, C.4.

CONTRIBUTORS

Robert Combs retired in 2017 after teaching in the English Department at George Washington University for forty-six years. His research interests have included Hart Crane, Wilde, Pinter, Albee, and others, though chiefly the plays of O'Neill. He lives in Baltimore with his partner of many years, Carol Malone, and their beloved lab-shepherd Juno.

David Lindsay-Abaire is an American playwright, lyricist, and screenwriter. Among his many plays are *Fuddy Meers*, *Kimberly Akimbo*, and *Good People*. He received the Pulitzer Prize for Drama in 2007 for his play *Rabbit Hole*, which also earned several Tony Award nominations. He is currently codirector of Juilliard's Lila Acheson Wallace American Playwrights Program.

Jay Malarcher is an associate professor and dramaturg in the School of Theatre and Dance at West Virginia University in Morgantown. His primary research area is comedy, in both theory and practice. His book, *The Classically American Comedy of Larry Gelbart*, stands as an important study of American comedy, the media and arts that carry it, through one of its most important figures. He taught "American Comedy as Cultural Mirror" as a Fulbright Scholar at the University of Zagreb (Croatia) during the 2009–10 school year. Besides his work as a dramaturg and playwright, he is at work on *The Situation of Comedy*, a book-length investigation of the genre.

INDEX

9/11, World Trade Center disaster   87, 169, 174

absurdism   36, 60–1, 72, 86, 95, 106–12. *See also* Camus, Albert; Theatre of Absurd
Adventures of Ozzie and Harriet, The   33, 116
Agnes of God   105, 208
Albee, Edward   11, 47, 189, 190
Allen, Woody   49, 202, 204
Anderson, Sherry   94
Aristophanes   202, 209
Augustine, John   11, 94

Bakhtin, Mikhail   30–1, 87, 214
Barnes, Djuna   29
Beckett, Samuel   23, 78, 107, 111, 204, 215
Berkeley, Busby   40–1, 43, 45
Bicentennial Minutes   36–7
Bin Laden, Osama   176
Black, Lewis   8, 158
black comedy   14, 16, 21, 65, 67, 118, 122, 189, 194, 214
Bobbitt, Lorraine   167
Bogart, Humphrey   41, 44, 57
Book of Job   62
Borzage, Frank   40
Boston Marathon bombing   177
Brando, Marlon   41, 44
Brooks, Mel   202, 204, 208
Brothers Karamazov, The   23–5, 28, 209
Buddhism   87–8, 91
Burnett, Carol   100
Bush, George W.   161, 171–2, 176

Caesar, Sid   202
Cagney, James   41
Camus, Albert   60, 78, 86, 112, 146
caricature   31, 95–100, 112
Casablanca   40–1, 44, 56, 208

Catholicism   20, 65, 68–74, 77, 92, 141, 144, 192. *See also* Durang, Catholicism (personal)
Cat on a Hot Tin Roof   103
censorship   73–4
Chekhov, Anton   1, 23, 25–7, 93, 178–81, 186, 203
Christ, Jesus (as character)   61, 63, 69, 71, 73, 77–8, 84–5, 87, 89, 90–1
Christian Right. *See* Religious Right
Christmas Carol, A   49, 50–1, 55, 56
Constitution, U.S.   83, 85
Coward, Noël   4, 110–11, 119, 204

Dean, James   41, 44
Dickens, Charles   23, 37
disaster films   48, 117, 120–1
Doestoevsky, Fyodor   25
Douglass, Charley   194
Drama of the Gifted Child, The. *See* Miller, Alice
Dukakis, Olympia   141
Durang, Christopher
   Catholicism (personal beliefs)   3–5, 8–9, 14, 59–63, 68–9, 74–5, 145, 190–3, 210, 216–17
   education   3–4
   family   3, 5, 11–13, 67, 215
   Harvard   5–7, 21, 40, 59, 73, 107, 152, 217, 219
   John Augustine, partner   13, 94
   mother's death   9
   Tony Award for Best Play   1, 178
   works
      "Actor's Nightmare, The"   58, 95, 110–12, 198, 205, 207
      Adrift in Macao   56–8
      Baby with the Bathwater   13–14, 17, 20, 23, 131–8, 141, 147
      Banned in Boston   4
      Better Dead than Sorry   125–6, 131

Index

Betty's Summer Vacation 17, 20, 60, 149, 161–8, 189, 192–3, 195, 197, 199, 200
Beyond Therapy 11, 14, 17, 150–5, 186
"Book of Leviticus Show" 109–10
"Business Lunch at the Russian Tea Room" 95, 107–8
Businessman's Holiday 5
"Canker Sores and Other Distractions" 106
Christopher Durang and Dawne 13, 94
Das Lusitania Songspiel 11
Death Comes to Us All, Mary Agnes 97, 121–5
Identity Crisis 17, 22, 125–31, 137
"Desire, Desire, Desire" 103–4
"Diversions" 107
"DMV Tyrant" 100
Durang Durang 13, 95, 100, 104, 112–13
"For Whom the Southern Belle Tolls" 21, 95, 102–3, 204, 208
Greatest Musical Ever Sung, The 7
"Funeral Parlor" 100
"Hardy Boys and the Mystery of Where Babies Come From, The" 101
History of the American Film 9, 11 21, 38–49, 58, 200, 204, 206–7
Idiots Karamazov, The 18, 21–32, 38, 204–5, 209
"John and Mary Doe" 17, 108–9
Laughing Wild 17, 60, 61, 74–9, 86, 92, 149, 215
Marriage of Bette and Boo, The 3, 13–14, 131, 138–47, 210
"Medea" 101, 204
Media Amok 149, 155, 156–62, 168, 186
Miss Witherspoon 14, 60, 61, 86–92, 96, 178, 186
Mrs. Bob Cratchit's Wild Christmas Binge 49–56
"Mrs. Sorken" 95–6, 168
"Naomi in the Living Room" 98–9
Nature and Purpose of the Universe, The 16, 61–8
"Nina in the Morning" 97–8
"Phyllis & Xenobia" 106

Sex and Longing 74, 79–86, 109
Sister Mary Ignatius Explains It All for You 9, 11, 20, 68–74, 79, 95, 111, 144, 190–1, 198, 199, 200, 213, 215
"Stye of the Eye, A" 95, 104–6, 208
Titanic 11, 18, 20, 36, 117–21, 137, 147, 177
Vanya and Sonia and Masha and Spike 1, 22, 177–86, 203–4, 213
Vietnamization of New Jersey, The 11, 18, 32–8, 117
"Wanda's Visit" 18, 95, 99–100
When Dinah Shore Ruled the Earth 8
Why Torture Is Wrong, and the People Who Love Them 2, 17, 96, 168–77, 186–7
Woman Stand-Up 96, 197
Durkheim, Emile 149

Enron Corporation 51, 217
Equus 105
Esterson, A. 127
existentialism 5, 47, 57–8, 60–1, 75, 78, 86, 95, 107, 112, 154–5, 185, 207, 217

family, televised images of 115, 149, 170
farce 1, 8, 21–2, 25, 106, 119, 131, 138, 151, 164, 167–9, 171–5, 213, 216
Father Knows Best 116, 170
Fonda, Jane 170, 205
Freud, Sigmund 24–5, 68, 75, 195

Garnett, Constance 24, 26, 30, 209
Gelbart, Larry 195, 202
"Gift of the Magi, A" 52
Glass Menagerie, The 138
Goffman, Erving 198–9
Grand Guignol Theatre 17, 122, 125, 173
Grapes of Wrath, The 43–4
Griffith, D. W. 42
grotesque 1, 17, 18, 22–3, 30, 31, 65–6, 71, 84, 109, 117, 120, 124–5, 130, 136, 145, 166–7, 214–16
Guare, John 214
Guest, Christopher 208

Harpham, Geoffrey 120
Helmsley, Leona and Harry 55

Index

Henry, O. (William Sydney Porter) 52
Hitchcock, Alfred 57, 208
homosexuality 20, 28, 60, 69, 71, 77, 80, 103, 109–10, 120, 214–15
Hutcheon, Linda 22, 27–8, 49, 50–1, 55, 57, 62, 101, 105, 203–4, 207
Hyde-Pierce, David 185

I Love Lucy 2, 116, 182, 194, 197
Innaurato, Albert 8, 11, 23, 25, 209
Ionesco, Eugene 21, 69, 108, 124, 130, 210, 215
It's a Wonderful Life 50, 54

Jack Benny Show 33
Jarry, Alfred 65
Jazz Singer, The 42
Jesus Christ, as character. *See* Christ, Jesus

Kerr, E. Katherine 11, 75
Kopit, Arthur 16

Laing, R. D. 127
laugh track 164–5, 194
Lay, Kenneth 50–1
Lila Acheson Wallace American Playwrights Program 2
Lindsay-Abaire, David 2
Long Day's Journey into Night 23, 28, 138

Mamet, David 11, 21, 105, 190, 208, 214
Man's Castle, A 40
Maugham, W. Somerset 81
media culture 156
Melnick, Peter 57
Miller, Alice 121, 139
Monk, Debra 75
Moral Majority. *See* Religious Right

narcissism 14, 17, 113, 121–4, 152, 180
National Endowment for the Arts, controversy 74, 81
Nielsen, Kristen 88, 166–7, 175, 184
Nin, Anaïs 23–5, 29–30, 209
Norman, Marsha 2, 190
nostalgia 115, 181

Oliver Twist 53
O'Neill, Eugene 23–5, 27–8, 38, 104, 116, 138, 202

Orton, Joe 21, 119–20, 131

parody 21–8, 31–2, 39, 50–8, 62, 95, 100–5, 111, 121, 202–11, 216, 219
Pennies from Heaven (film) 206
Pielmeier, John 105
Pirandello, Luigi 210
Pitoniak, Anne 157
Plato 49, 200

Rabe, David 32–5, 38, 214
reality 162–3, 167, 193
The Real World (MTV) 162
Reiner, Rob 208
Religious Right 72, 77, 80–5, 92, 109
Rich, Frank 11, 13–14, 71–2, 76, 138

Sally Jesse Raphael (show) 77, 156–7
Sanity, Madness and the Family.
   See Laing, R. D.
satire 7, 20–3, 33, 38, 46–50, 58–60, 65, 72, 85–6, 108–12, 124, 158, 163–5, 177, 181, 193, 200, 202–11, 214–16
Seagull, The 203
Second Ecumenical Council.
   See Vatican II
Shaffer, Peter 105
Shaw, G. B. 56–7, 91, 131, 209, 213
Shepard, Sam 11, 21, 104, 208, 214
Shklovsky, Viktor 189, 191
Simon, Neil 1, 202, 214
Skilling, Jeffrey 50–1
Skin of Our Teeth, The 34–6
Sondheim, Stephen 5, 13, 206, 209
Steinbeck, John 43
Stewart, Jimmy 41
Sticks and Bones 32
Streetcar Named Desire, A 103

tabloid 158, 164
Tale of Two Cities, A 37
television 2, 109, 116, 156
Theatre of the Absurd 72, 110, 145, 215
Titanic, film 118
Tolkien, J. R. R. 90
Twain, Mark 202

Uncle Vanya 23, 25, 178–9, 181

233

Index

Vatican II, Second Ecumenical Vatican Council   70, 191

Wasserstein, Wendy   1, 8, 13, 101, 204
Weaver, Sigourney   8, 47, 80, 126
Wedekind, Frank   80–1
Welles, Orson   44
What the Butler Saw   119, 131
Who's Afraid of Virginia Woolf?   189

Wilder, Thorton   34–6, 74
Williams, Robin   100
Williams, Tennessee   81, 102, 104, 116, 138, 208, 215
women's movement   31

Yale Cabaret   8, 94, 125–6
Yale School of Drama   7, 22, 209
Young, Loretta   41

www.ingramcontent.com/pod-product-compliance
Lightning Source LLC
Chambersburg PA
CBHW050326020526
44117CB00031B/1809